Love and Power:
Parent and Child

Glenn Austin, M.D.

Robert Erdmann Publishing
Rolling Hills Estates, California

Published by Robert Erdmann Publishing
28441 Highridge Road, Suite 101
Rolling Hills Estates, CA 90274
(213) 544-5071

Printed in the United States of America
First Printing

ISBN 0-945 339-01-1 (Hardcover)
ISBN 0-945 339-00-3 (Paperback)

Library of Congress 87-0837322

Does there exist a nobler inspiration than the desire to be free? It is by his freedom that a man knows himself, by his sovereignty over his own life that man measures himself. To violate that freedom, to flout that sovereignty, is to deny man the right to live his life, to take responsibility for himself with dignity.*

ELIE WIESEL

---

*From "What Really Makes Us Feel Free," Parade Magazine Dec. 27, 1987. Reprinted with permission from Parade and Goerge Borchardt, Inc, Copyright 1987.

Recently I mentioned to a friend that rational-authoritative parents raise competent children. At this, she grinned broadly and replied, "That lets me out on both counts!— She was kidding, of course, for she is an excellent parent — both rational and authoritative. You do not have to walk on water to be a good parent. (Not that it wouldn't help!) Nor do we have to be overly solemn about our responsibilities as a parent. Most of us can improve with a little effort and learn now to use our innate parental powers to the best advantage. This can make parenting more fun and more rewarding. For our children, it makes growing up a far more productive and enjoyable task.

G. A.

Contents

DEC   1989

Acknowledgements

During the three years of work on the manuscript, I have asked for and received help from many people. Parents in my practice have shared their problems and accomplishments, their joys and sorrows, and I have had the pleasure of watching their children mature into admirable adults. This book, to a large degree, represents a distillation of their experiences over the years.

My wife has been a constant source of encouragement and support, practical help and penetrating insights. My children reviewed the manuscript and we had fine times discussing their memories of childhood in the Austin clan. I have valued their suggestions and have learned from their experiences with each of my grandchildren.

In addition, this book has benefitted from some very meaningful research in child development. Particularly worthwhile are the findings from the investigations of Diana Baumrind, Ph.D. in the Institute of Human Development at the University of California, Berkeley. Her three decades of objective scientific measurements and observations of a group of parents and their children offer valuable insights into the issues of parenting — and the success rates of various forms of parenting in producing competent children. Her upcoming scientific monographs on parenting have added much to the book. It was a pleasure working with her and with her assistant, Steven Pulos, Ph.D., who generously gave of his valuable time and advice.

I have also enjoyed conversing with Burton White, Ph.D., and examining his remarkably productive investigations. His Harvard-based studies demonstrated ways to increase the power and effectiveness of parents, as well as the power of children, in the first three years of life. His educational techniques as described in his book, *Educating the Infant and Toddler,* have been used with success by the Missouri Public School system. In addition, I owe a debt of gratitude to Dr. Morris Green, M.D., Lesh Professor and Chairman of the Department of Pediatrics at Indiana University for his gentle but insighful help; Berry Brazelton, M.D., Chief of Child Development at the Children's Hospital and Professor of Pediatrics at Harvard Medical School (best known for his books on child-rearing), for critiquing an early manuscript; psychologist Catherine Lewis, Ph.D of the Langely Porter Clinic in San Francisco, a worthy critic of Diana Baumrind's interpretations, for her insights and suggestions; child psychiatrist Stan Fishman, M.D., for his counsel; and adolescent specialist and professor George Commerci, M.D., for his review and encouragement. Many other friends, mothers, pediatricians, old patients and new patients helped by reviewing parts of the manuscript. My office nurse Ann Marie and her husband Bud Tomafsky also gave hard thought and effort to improve the book. My editor, Claudette Wassil-Grimm, enthusiastically immersed herself in the book and contributed significantly.

I should especially like to thank my publisher, Bob Erdmann, for his faith, expertise, and support.

Most of all, I want to thank you, the reader, for your interest in this subject and your devotion to healthy, happy, and productive children. The final product and responsibility is, of course, mine. The final evaluation is yours.

G.A.

The Power and Limits of Knowledge and Love

Love and power, parent and child — these ties bind families, alter the outcomes of children and ultimately shape society. Everyone recognizes that love is essential, rewarding and usually productive. But over the years, I have learned that love alone does not assure good parenting. The job of parenting demands much more.

Some of the most difficult problems parents have with children and that children have with parents revolve around the balance of power within the family. Some parents are paralyzed, unable or unwilling to act. They do not use their natural powers because of anxieties, philosophy or distorted feelings about what constitutes proper parenting. Others who had overpowering parents themselves mimic this behavior with their own children or, instead, rebel against authoritarianism and consciously underuse power as parents. However, a good number of parents rationally and effectively use their power to control and demand good behavior while allowing their children increasing freedom. They know how to discipline and how to go beyond discipline and balance their own power with their child's power needs. Children of these parents usually become more competent than the children of parents who demand either too much or too little.

While the subject of power is volatile, we can learn a lot from it. Parents and children need power and use it whether they consciously admit it or not. And when power is used blindly or is out of balance, children do not do as well as they could. Power gets out of balance rather easily if you are unaware of it or do not admit its existence in your relationship with your children.

In the myriads of books on parenting, few directly meet the concerns of parents about the responsible use of power. Most offer platitudes or summary advice. Everyone seems bent on simplifying parenting, on making it easy. It is not easy. Parenting is complex, hard work, demanding and rewarding. It challenges the best in each of us. In moments of frustration it can bring out the worst in us.

When I first started in pediatrics, it often amazed me to see really bad behavior of children whose parents sounded like strict disciplinarians. The parent often looked stern and told me of all the deserved punishment he or she gave the child while agreeing that the child's behavior was unacceptable. Yet the child continued to misbehave. The parents seemed powerless.

Like many pediatricians in those days, I recognized that we did not have enough scientific knowledge to simply tell parents how to raise their children. I was much better at diagnosing meningitis or strange fevers than telling a parent how to effectively demand that a child mind. But over the years parents continued to talk with me about the behavior problems of their children and we would sit down and explore these problems together — and follow up on them until, usually, we got better results.

We learned that parenting skills improve when we understand rational and authoritative methods of using power. That is the first aim of this book — to help you develop your own rational and authoritative parenting style. The second aim is to build the power of children so they have a better chance of becoming fully competent adults. To achieve these aims, we must look objectively at the various powers and duties of parents. These include:

- support and protection
- reward and punishment
- the control and training of discipline
- the ability to demand, act, teach and stimulate
- the encouragement of responsible personal and social values
- the controlled use of parental anger and love
- the instilling of confidence and competence

We also will examine the growth and development of the power of children. And lastly, when the power of love and discipline do not work, we will look for the reasons and possible solutions.

Raising Competent Children

No one can offer a complete blueprint or solve all your problems. Most of what I learned on the subject of raising children came from families I have counselled. I observed their successes and failures, problems and accomplishments and have synthesized and shared this experience over a period of many years. When I made suggestions, I not only had the feed-back of parents, but have often been fortunate enough to observe the results on their children as they grew. *In the process, it became apparent that children develop into truly competent adults when their parents use their power not only to discipline with love and demand good behavior, but also to nurture the child's power, granting the opportunity for freedom with respect.*

At times parents must cease using most of their power and give the child room to use his own. A child's growth requires space, emotional freedom. In order to develop the independent thinking skills needed to become a competent socially responsible citizen in today's complex society, the child needs some time free from discipline, free from parental power and control and, at times, even free from the leash of parental love. Surprisingly, as we will see, this need starts in the first three years of life.

Balancing power challenges parents. But then parenting always challenges. However, today's parents face new and formidable problems. How can a parent effectively function as a single mother or as a working mother and father with latch key children? Should boys and girls be raised the same, and how can you protect your child against drugs and sexual molestation? How can you stimulate your child to work hard enough and learn enough to become competent and able to meet the challenges of tomorrow? How can you teach your child good values with some assurance that they will be put into practice? Power — the parents' or child's power — is central to the resolution of all these issues.

The Power of Knowledge

Research on parenting methods shows the importance of a proper balance of demand and control with freedom and respect. These supportive findings come from several sources starting with Stanley Cooper-smith's classic measurements of self-esteem in school children. Burton White's impressive Harvard studies about the first three years of life contribute greatly. The University of California's Family Socialization Project, in the Institute of Human Development at the Berkeley campus, has also shown that parents can demand and stimulate competent behavior while respecting and building their children's autonomy. This important study, directed by Diana Baumrind, followed the same group of parents and children for thirty years. Careful and continuous measurements recorded the outcomes of various parenting styles. All of these investigations differ significantly from many other psychological and child development experiments. Rather than being based on animal studies or contrived situations designed to test a theory, they are drawn from objective measurements of real people in normal family life.

The results of these measurements of different kinds of parenting corroborate my long term observations of parents and children. Many of the parents I encountered in my practice were exceptionally skilled and successful. Their rational and authoritative methods of child-rearing resulted in happy, confident children who become competent adults. Baumrind calls this authoritative parenting — I think of it as rational parenting. Here we will call it *rational-authoritative parenting* to clearly distinguish it from authoritarian parents who abuse power.

The Limits of Advice and Knowledge

Knowledge gained from research alone will not automatically make us better parents. Generally we each approach parenting through our individual genetic makeup, personality and life experiences. Often this brings out emotions and reactions based on our inner child of the past (the instinctive imprint or reaction to the way we each were raised) more than our knowledge about parenting. Such emotions can interfere with rational parenting. To become a rational-authoritative parent, to help our children develop to their maximum, we need to temper our instincts with the power of knowledge and understanding. We must first learn to control our inner child of the past — and the emotions it stirs.

We next need to approach outside advice with healthy skepticism. Parents should not regard advice, from anyone, as biblical, as "the word." Experts frequently give conflicting advice and even "good" advice is rarely useful to everyone for a very basic reason: each and every parent is different and each and every child is different. Genetic scientists have determined, on the basis of the amino acid building blocks which make up the genes and chromosomes of humans, that the potential exists for 64 billion unique genetic individuals! The miracle of the dance of the genes in procreation is awe-inspiring. To this individual human variability, add ethnic traditions and customs, wide differences in social needs and personal experiences. It is easy to see why general rules are shaky.

The Power of an Open Mind

Even in general terms, it is hard to get nonchallengeable scientific evidence about raising children. Maybe it is impossible in human relations. But more worthwhile information about child-rearing is available now than in the past — even if we still have a long way to go.

Most of you would not be reading this book if you did not anticipate or plan to prevent problems with your children. Your attitude of curiosity and open mindedness shows that you already understand the power of knowledge. It allows you a chance to take an objective look at the power of love, discipline, teaching and freedom. This helps you to better understand reward and punishment — and, above all, yourself. Probably that last look — at yourself — is the most important and not all that easy.

We need to carefully examine ourselves while we study the research findings and parental successes and failures presented here. The priority will be on extracting usable parenting wisdom with emphasis on how to balance your power with that of your child. Some of the information, research measurements and opinions shared here can assist you in helping your children learn to behave and to use their own power productively.

Finally, be reassured that parents like you who care enough to read books such as this can learn to use your power in the child's best interest. By caring enough to demand productive behavior you can increase your children's power, giving them the opportunity to strive for the self-mastery that leads to self-esteem and competence. This book will provide the techniques and insights. Your individual background, as well as your affection for and knowledge of your particular child, will allow you to personalize your approach and maximize the effect of your constructive use of power.

PART I

Balancing Love, Power and Freedom: The Need

Every social group, no matter what its size, must establish patterns of authority and delegate power, status, and responsibilities to its members.

Stanley Coopersmith
The Antecedents of Self Esteem

I

The Power Balance

Children deserve effective parents who know how to use power. Power enables parents to nurture and support, protect and discipline, control and train, to demand — and to teach good and productive behavior. This prelude prepares the child for the future. Rational-authoritative parents know how to use such powers efficiently. They also use their power to respect their children. The child needs this respect from his parents, along with the experience of freedom, to develop self-esteem and competency. Wisely used, these parental powers nurture the child's power.

The concept of power, however, bothers many parents. A mother wrote me, "I truly dislike the term 'power' used in a relationship which should be based on respect, love and communication." In my experience, however, respect, love and communication, while essential, are frequently not enough. The job of parenting involves far more; it requires power and parental power exists, like it or not.

Power

Power is not just strength, muscles or punishment. Webster's Unabridged Dictionary lists sixteen major synonyms for power. (See Table I.) None mean punishment. They do refer to productive power; the effort exerted for the purpose of achieving good results, the ability to get results! Conversely, the opposite of power is impotence, weakness, inaction, incompetence and a lack of fitness. Yes, children need powerful parents. Whether or not power is laudable depends on how it is used.

Table I

SYNONYMS AND DEFINITIONS OF POWER

Vigor, Force, Strength, Potency
Mastery, Self-management, Assertiveness
Ability, Gift, Talent, Endowment
Effectiveness, Dynamism, Leadership
Competence, Capacity

1. The power to think clearly.

2. *The ability to get results*

We generally appreciate and exercise power, control and freedom more with our feelings than with our intellect. The concept of power in parenting can create vigorous emotional reactions. Perhaps this explains why, in all the plethora of advice given or sold to parents, power and its use are rarely discussed directly. Yet the history of mankind seems to revolve around struggles for power, for control. Family dynamics, tacitly or openly, often revolve around the relative power of family members. Yet the rational role and use of power are usually only obliquely discussed in parenting literature. Each individual has his own loose understanding colored by his genetic disposition and childhood experiences. Considering our strong and frequently different emotions and approach, it is no wonder that the subject is complex and often murky.

Some only think of the power to control as physical with a mind set on punishment. Others concentrate on the power of education, or of politics, or money. Power is force, and as such it can be used constructively or destructively.

The Balance of Power

The primary task of a parent is to produce an independent adult powerful enough to meet the world on his own. This is what nurturing your child is all about. Parents must strive to develop enough competence and good values to make their children welcome members of society. It would be nice if a formula existed to consistently achieve this result. The formula would have to show the ideal balance of parent/child power and control versus freedom and responsibility. Such a formula would change during the various stages of growth and development. Illustration 1 shows a crude symbolic graph of the growth of the child's power and the withdrawal of the parent's power.

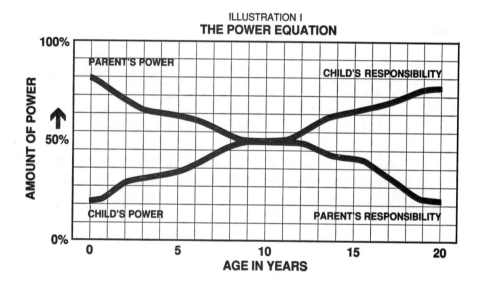

ILLUSTRATION I
THE POWER EQUATION

The Growth of Power

Nurturing a child from birth includes preparing him for the eventual freedom from parental power. Early in life the child learns about parental power and control while receiving parental love and respect. This creates security, offers a model to imitate and helps build the baby's self-esteem. With a secure base, the child's own developing power fuels his ability to become a socially welcome and effective adult. Power gives the young confidence, creativity, control — tools to exercise a developing brain. Just as food nourishes the body, power nourishes the personality and intellect. But while born with a need for power and independence, the child still requires parental control, a teaching apprenticeship to guide him in using his own unique gifts. His power must be rationed as well as encouraged. He must be trained in the skills and attitude needed for the future. He must be controlled to protect him from danger. Nurturing parents learn how to discipline while they encourage the development of the child's power in appropriate amounts at appropriate times in the child's life. This delicate balance of power shifts as time goes on. Finally his life becomes his own, and his own responsibility. Yet there are few guidelines except for personal experience, folk wisdom and instinct. For instance, take the case of Orsel:

> We who love our children can share the frustration of Mrs. Torres, a Buddhist mother from Spain whose child, 2-year-old Orsel Hita Torres, sat on a throne brought from a Buddhist temple in the Himalayas. A team of high lamas searched the world for him and identified Orsel as the reincarnation of the recently deceased Lama Yeshe, a revered spiritual leader of Tibetan Buddhists. Mrs. Torres, too, recognizes her son as the reincarnated Lama Yeshe. But, she asks, "Orsel is my son like my other children, but he is also my guru. When he is bad, how do I spank my master?"*

The specifics of Orsel's case are unique, but a generic principle emerges. A young California mother in my practice put it succinctly, "Every mother's child is her guru!"

The question now arises, "How can I use power on my child? How can I discipline my guru?" Ready or not, parents have power and use it on their children. Some "gurus" must be disciplined. They occasionally require punishment to ensure control. But what sort of discipline should be used. And for that matter, what is discipline?

---

*Mark Kaufman, "The Littlest Lamb," The Philadelphia Inquirer, March 18, 1987. Reprinted with permission.

The Power of Discipline

Dictionaries list a whole host of definitions of discipline. Many professionals dealing with children prefer to think of discipline as teaching so they can de-emphasize punishment. However, teaching is not listed as a definition of discipline in most dictionaries. Nor do most people think first of teaching when "discipline problems" occur. They first think of control, training and punishment. Yet discipline is listed as a synonym for teaching, as having "nearly the same meaning." Vague terms such as this stand in the way of clear meaning and can create poor communication between author and reader.

To avoid confusion, discipline here means control and training with insistence upon obedience. As we will see, discipline often implies punishment (if that is required to get control) to train a child — to teach. Punishment is sometimes required to demonstrate parental authority. Parental authority is vital and parents must be in charge. Because we teach and guide as we use discipline, it is as necessary as parental love. Yes, we do teach with discipline. We also teach as we reward. We teach as we use power of any sort.

Table II

DEFINITIONS OF DISCIPLINE

Training — Control
Order — Rules — Obedience
Punishment — Chastisement
A field of study

Using the power of discipline well and being a good parent does not always occur naturally. Parents usually depend upon their own parents as role models. Most have the same attitudes toward their children that they feel their parents had toward them. But problems inevitably occur in child-rearing and these problems can create doubt. Most of the parental doubts and fears I hear concern, underneath it all, the amount of power a parent has and should use. When doubts occur, some parents increase the amount and severity of their discipline. Others reject their own parents' ways and use different methods to raise their children. Some vacillate, powerless, caught between instinct and the advice of experts as well as good and bad examples, and their own emotional reactions. Uncertainty and vacillation represent insecurity in the parent and create an insecure child. Both parents and children have a deep and abiding need for security as well as freedom and autonomy. So does society. A workable balance of power between freedom and control is required.

Power and Society

Society has a lot at stake in the way that parents use their power, for as the twig is bent the tree grows. Young adults, products of genetics and parenting themselves, must understand the use and limits of power in our civilization. Though often debated, a social pecking order of control does exist. Many accept the ranking of God, Country, Family and the Individual as fundamental to our security. Much of our social effort revolves around defining how we relate to each other. The issue of power and domination are key here. We establish rules and laws, define crime and punishment, and attempt to agree on the amount and type of power which society and individuals are permitted to use. Such limits are essential, for uncurbed individual human wants can create a lust for power without limit. This leads to dictators such as Hitler and to twisted religious messiahs like the infamous Jimmy Jones of the Guyana massacre. Uncurbed power can also lead to large or small tyrants lording over an individual family. Uncurbed power can be fearsome. Yet without the use of power and control, there is anarchy.

In society we are, to a degree, all dependent upon one another and we share a common body of values. Parents have a duty to pass on socially laudable values. Much of this process is automatic — your childen place great stock in how you act, in what you are. However, many parents do not know how to get their children to accept their values. Parents do have this power and ability. Your children will mimic you if nothing else. But there are many other examples to mimic in our complex society.

Parents can live up to their values yet still fail to pass them on. Their children mimic others. Why? Some parents overuse their power and create rebellion which leads to rejection of parental values. This rejection spills over into society at large, often creating adults who mindlessly fight authority. Others — the so-called permissive parents — do not use enough power to control their children. This approach often creates incompetent children who become incompetent adults, who end up feeling that life has generally given them a "bad deal." Also, many parents who believe they do discipline their children do not really control them. But whether the parent is authoritarian, permissive or simply ineffective and uninformed, either excess control or lack of control leads to problems for the child and for society. Some children do not discover that there are inviolate rules until they are caught breaking the law. Society must have laws to protect us from each other. It establishes rules of acceptable conduct and makes certain of our compliance. Similar rules are required within a family as the child conforms and learns the value of accepting some control. The lessons are much harder on the child or young adult when they require the power of law enforcement to make the point.

Self-Control

Aside from the social imperative, children need control for other more personal reasons. Allowed to grow up undisciplined and unguided, they can waste their potential and make serious mistakes. Some never experienced enough control from their parents to learn self-control and thus are unable to fully develop their potential talents. The unpruned fruit tree produces an insignificant crop. A properly disciplined (pruned) tree produces better fruit. Like the gardener who learns that fertilizer alone is not enough, so a parent also learns that love alone is not enough. If children are to develop their capabilities fully, then we as parents have to wisely use our power to demand high goals, teach, guide, and (occasionally) even forcefully control. If we do not use the power to discipline, to train and control, the child often becomes insecure and uncertain. Dr. Bonnie E. Robertson of the University of Toronto Faculty of Medicine, in discussing preschoolers writes, "The lack of parental discipline is perceived as emotional withdrawal. Parents should provide their children with constant structure, routines, and discipline."

Often children without such limits keep searching for limits, thus creating stress for both their parents and society in the process. Setting limits for children requires the use of parental powers. From both social and personal standpoints, the power balance is critical.

Too Little Power

Some parents seem to avoid using their innate power. The reasons are varied. A few rebel against the demanding and complicated task of being a parent with the responsibility to control their child. They may be just a little lazy or perhaps lack the self-esteem which would allow them to feel competent enough to do the job. Some mistakenly believe that it does not take much work or time to raise a child. Others had such poor role models and teaching by their own parents that they never learned that they have parenting power. Nor have they seen how it can be used to control and teach children. Some rebel against themselves — against their work, against society, or against their spouse. Often part of their reaction covertly or openly urges the child to rebel. Other permissive parents were raised by harsh authoritarian parents and have emotionally rebelled against the concept of overpowering parents. Philosophical rationalizations that "I won't raise my child that way!" follow rebellion.

Some permissive or oversubmissive parents are so anxious to keep the child's love that they cannot bear a scowl from the child. This may be out of love for a desperately wanted child. They feel so rewarded by having the child that, in turn, they give the child everything he desires, warranted or not. Another type of permissiveness occurs in mothers who are preconditioned to "love too much." They become servants to their children. Psychiatrist Hugh Missildine, in his fascinating book *Your Inner Child of the Past*, feels that such women will do almost anything to avoid scenes of disagreement and describes two types of backgrounds which result in such "overmothering."

> . . . those who were reared by very demanding parents who permitted them no rights as individuals and trained them to serve their frequent parental demands. In motherhood such women automatically serve their child with no thought of themselves. Submitting to the child's immature whims is the only way they know of responding to any demanding person within the family.
>
> Others have so consistently and persistently belittled their own feelings that they believe they have no rights. They place their children's whims above any needs of their own. While they may see the need to limit the children's impulsiveness,

they cannot respect their own rights sufficiently to stand firm in the face of the children's tempestuous demands.

Aside from difficulties in raising children, such parents may also have significant problems with their mates. They tend to fall in love with difficult people. Robin Norwood, a marriage, family and child therapist explores some of these problems in her popular book, *Women Who Love Too Much*. Such problems frequently, again, go back to childhood and she notes parental sources of such emotional crippling.

> If our parents related to us in hostile, critical, cruel, manipulative, overbearing, overdependent or otherwise inappropriate ways, that is what will feel "right" to us when we meet someone who expresses, perhaps very subtly, undertones of the same attitudes and behaviors.

Thus a high price is often paid by adults who were raised by either authoritarian or permissive parents.

Too Much Power

Most of us tend to mimic our parents when we raise our own children. Many of us were raised by parents who overused their power or displayed it in a harsh, authoritarian manner. Those parents had probably mimicked their own authoritarian parents — your child's great grandparents. Psychiatrist Missildine says that the most common pathogenic parental attitude in America is overcoercion.

> Few of us escaped the influence of parental overcoercion. Indeed, most of us grew up in households in which there was a steady stream of directions, new directions, revised directions, commands and reminders, all delivered in anxious, irritated or threatening tones: "It's late. Get up this minute! . . . Don't forget to brush your teeth . . . Hurry! Your breakfast is getting cold . . . You'll be late for school. Don't forget your mittens . . . and your overshoes."

This type of parent constantly tries to overpower the child with an endless stream of directives which suppress the child's initiative and cripple his ability to pursue his own interests. The child is taught to rely excessively on outside direction. It leads to dawdling, daydreaming, forgetting, procrastination and other subtle forms of resistance.

The way we were raised has major effects upon our individual parenting styles. A few parents, abused as children, find themselves abusing their own children. Others react to their past insecure childhood and to the problems they suffered from the excess freedom they experienced. They then vow not to be permissive with their own children. A wild, ultraliberal teenager frequently becomes a stern conservative taskmaster when she grows up and has children of her own. The same mistake will not be made again! The pendulum swings one way or the other. Throughout this presentation on the use or abuse of power, you will see more and more reasons why you need the knowledge to rationally use, yet limit, your power. Do not always depend on love or on "gut level" instincts that come from your inner child of the past.

The Power of Love

All of these various types of parents try to raise their kids properly. They love their children whether they succeed or not. And that love is worthwhile — power and control aren't everything. Pediatrician Robert Chamberlin observed that "considerably more important to the child's development is the amount and quality of 'positive contact' received by the child. This term refers to the amount of praise, reassurance, affection, companionship, and intellectual stimulation that occurs between parent and child."

Pioneer psychologist Coopersmith found that 96.8% of mothers of children with high self-esteem thought mother and child should do things together, so the children can feel closer to Mom and can talk more easily. Nothing replaces affection and closeness and time. Nonetheless, your knowledge about the need to use the power of discipline and the understanding of your child's need for the power of freedom and autonomy will make it easier to meet the challenges of parenting.

Parents should certainly not feel embarrassed about a lack of knowledge when using power and control in child rearing. Competent psychologists still disagree. Diana Baumrind's careful objective investigations indicate that firm demanding control by warm, caring parents produces competent and socially responsible children. At the same time,

Catherine Lewis, Ph.D., of the University of California Medical School's Department of Psychiatry in San Francisco, thinks that emphasis should be on the child's response to the warmth and care shown by rational-authoritative parents more than on the parents' demands and control. We all underscore the need for parental love, respect and involvement. One way of demonstrating this is by demanding good behavior from your child. In later chapters, it will become apparent that Baumrind's emphasis on parental power and firmness, or "demandingness" as she calls it, is gaining a lot of support from other research.

Parents react to the child's declaration of independence in a variety of ways.

Alma S. Friedman and
David Belais Friedman, M.D.
"Parenting: A Developmental Process"
Pediatric Annals

II

Meeting the Power Needs of Your Child

Children need to learn to use their innate power and to practice with it as they grow. They especially need to have some feeling of control over their lives. *New York Times* writer, Daniel Goleman says, "The feeling of being in control, of having a say over what happens in one's life, has far reaching consequences for physical and mental health, for achievement at school and work, and even for sex."

Goleman quoted a study in which elderly men and women in convalescent homes were given a chance to increase the sense of control of their lives. This made them happier, increased their alertness and — perhaps more dramatically — lowered their mortality rate by 50%. The increased control was of simple things like allowing residents to decide what they would have for meals and how the furniture in their rooms should be arranged. The same needs exist for children. They, too, want respect and the power to control their own lives, at least a little bit. Everyone needs some elbow room, some sense of power, even if just over oneself. But how do we treat our children?

Parents are bigger, usually smarter and certainly more experienced than their children. Granted, your child may outsmart you or outrun you once in awhile, but overall, you still have the upper hand. You use your power in many ways. You teach and suppress, encourage and criticize, reward and punish, and offer love or rejection. But children have power too, even babies whose cries and smiles control parents. And their conscious need for power increases as the child grows. This manifests it-self as the crawler/toddler develops. She experiences powers such as walking and soon learns the power of that pervasive and magically potent word "No!" She learns that she has the power to refuse to give up the right to make deep-rooted very personal decisions about eating and going to the toilet. For preschoolers, the use of power increases. They learn to cooperate or resist, to charm or to anger parents, to proudly develop new skills or to withdraw in defiance. Older children manifest power in learning or rebel-ling, socializing or withdrawing, deciding to lead or to follow. A critical balance must be maintained between parent and child if we hope to have a harmonious and stimulating home and use power constructively rather than destructively. Constructive use of power rewards both child and parent.

Many rewards flow from parenting. The instinctive love, joy and pride of having one's own child comes first. The sense of possession warms the heart and builds self-esteem. Even here, the issue of power and control becomes apparent. It is amusing and instructive to hear a mother say to her toddler, "We learned how to go to the potty today!" Mothers, especially, identify closely — after all, the infant was an integral part of mother, growing inside her until birth — so, "he is me is we" can be ex-pected. The feeling is rewarding. Other positives exist. Parenting chal-lenges us as one of the most important and necessary roles of mankind. It assures the future of the human race. Vital mothering and fathering careers deserve a lot more respect than current American society allots.

Toddlers need respect too, but they are at the bottom of the totem pole within the family. Everyone in their world does everything better than the toddler. Yet if they exert great ingenuity and effort and manage, for example, to open the front door or get into a high cupboard, the giants in their world descend on them with alarm, with scowls, scoldings, "no's" and even spankings. It can become a very frustrating world. Few adults would put up with being treated the way we treat children.

What happens if children have no power, no choice? They, too, like the elderly can wither and withdraw. Or some may rebel and fight. Power is essential to the ego and ego is essential to a well-balanced person. This truism, ingrained in the American character, explains the genesis and growth of our country. The colonists refused to accept the power of a dis-tant King George who would not listen, nor would they give in to the power of his local Redcoats. From the Boston Tea Party on, the watch word has been "Don't tread on me" or you will regret it. Our power as American citizens is represented in our rights. We declared for liberty and justice in 1776. We can do no less for our children now.

Author John Steinbeck, who had a perceptive sense of humanity, writes in his book *The Log From the Sea of Cortes*,

> Adults, in their dealing with children are insane. And the children know it, too. Adults lay down rules they would not think of following, speak truths they do not believe, and yet they expect children to obey the rules, believe the truths, and admire and respect their parents for their nonsense. Children must be very wise and secret to tolerate adults at all.

Power and Learning

Positive power in the hands of children in the first three years of life increases their ability to learn and even increases their IQ. The important work of Harvard psychologist Burton White who measured the results of different types of parenting on children's learning and intelligence quotients has been confirmed by further research. A child in the first three years, who can explore his environment and has the power to get the help of the giants in his world when he wants it, increases his IQ around 15 points. The mother of a child with the higher IQ typically allowed freedom and some self-control. She frequently respected the child's wishes and responded to them. She was also willing to let the toddler use his power to initiate, to explore and at times manipulate her. She instinctively recognized that the baby needed to experience "doing his own thing." In contrast, the control children in this study had less freedom to follow Mother around. The typical mother in the control group kept a very neat house, kept the child out of trouble in a playpen, and forced the child to listen to her read or to play with her on mother's terms.

As adults it is difficult to put ourselves in our toddler's shoes. To them we must seem to be on a real power-trip. We pick them up, lay them down, scold, and say "no" and grab them away from attractive things — we are on their backs most of the time. So when you can allow your toddler to make you mind some times, let him do it! Turn-about is fair play. Do not engage in any unnecessary power struggles with your child — there are enough necessary things you must control without that!

Giving Children too Much Power

Children sometimes need to be able to manipulate the adults in their world. But what if they are allowed too much power? What if they get too much control over their parents? That can lead to problems for the parents now and for the children later. Jane and Teresa demonstrated what sometimes occurs when the children have excessive power.

> Easy going and likeable Joe, let his wife, Isobel, a frail and rather anxious-looking woman, manage the children. Their two good-looking daughters aged 11 and 15, did moderately well in school but did not have many friends. Isobel had allowed the girls to become tyrants. "Mother, are you going to help me with this home work or just keep talking on the telephone!" snapped 11-year-old Jane. Isobel apologized to her friend and said, "I have to go help Jane with her math. I will call you tomorrow!" Teresa then scolded her mother for not having ironed her dress properly. "Look mother," she complained, "I am going to a dance tonight. You don't expect me to go in a dress like that do you!" Isobel said, "I'm sorry honey. Let me do it over as soon as I finish helping Jane."

The girls' permissive overindulging mother had not prepared them for the give and take needed for their future. Both later "became bored" in college and dropped out. Because of their arrogant demands, they each married and divorced twice. Neither could keep a job long because they each felt abused, as if they were being asked to do too much. Adults raised by oversubmissive parents may have a tendency for temper outbursts and impulsiveness, and they feel unloved if people do not give in to them. Such children are unprepared for the real world.

To prepare children for the real world requires that the parents exert their power by having firm limits, insist that the child always do her best, and demand obedience while respecting the child by giving her the freedom to respond.

Research seems to indicate that children raised by demanding parents have higher self-esteem than those who are raised by less demanding parents. Many children react as if firm parental control expresses parental concern and respect, confirming the child's importance. Even children of overbearing parents usually seem to like their parents. But do not confuse demands for good behavior with punishment. Parents of children with high self-esteem do not punish as harshly or spank as often as parents of children with low self-esteem. One can limit and control without harshness or frequent punishment. Then why do many parents find it necessary to spank their children repeatedly? Some children just seem to ask for spankings.

Searching for Power

Children are pragmatists. They want power and will act in ways which give them the best results as they see it. We, as adults, may recognize that a child's actions can be destructive or self-defeating in the long run — but young children (and most of us partially mature adults) tend to look at the here and the now. A child who desires to be center stage will even court a spanking if that is what it takes to get there. Some will pay a heavy price to get attention. A practical lesson can be drawn from this. *If you find yourself repeatedly spanking your child then recognize that you may be rewarding the child by your action and the attention it brings.* It may seem odd to you to consider a spanking as a reward, but children do ask for it for a variety of reasons. Some court punishment to relieve guilt feelings. Frequently this follows the child's anger toward the parent, often over losing a power-struggle.

For most children punishment just means that Mother or Father mean business. *Parents who follow through and act more than they talk and holler, convince children that they really mean what they say.* The action need not be physical punishment. Often it need not be punishment of any kind. Preferably, it may allow the child the ability to earn or to lose a reward. Reward or punishment usually works if the parent exerts power, following clear instructions with reason and then action — in the here and now. Tomorrow is another day for young children — an eon away. Unfortunately some children do not respond easily to either rewards or punishment. They seem to value their own power and independence above all. They want to always win, regardless of the cost. We need to teach them better ways to obtain power. This may involve teaching them that they do not always win — they do not always get their way.

Power Through Adversity

The emphasis on power through winning, of always being the best, presents American children and their parents with significant problems. First, not everybody can win in competition or life. If you have to win to have self-esteem, then the majority can have little self-esteem. Using power to make certain that the child always experiences success, may not be entirely wise for another reason. Children who always achieve, who are always at the top of their class or their team, may turn out be incompetent when they face real adversity. Sooner or later competence includes the ability to deal with failure. And some overachieving youngsters find it impossible to deal with loosing. Some, unrealistically, even feel that they can never fail — and when they do, they become depressed — even suicidal. So winning and being first does not always demonstrate the ultimate in competence. A Stanford University dean told an admitting freshman class that when they entered Stanford 90% of them had a grade point average of 4.0, or straight A. When they graduated from Stanford, only 10% would have a 4.0 G.P.A. Competence includes the need to help your child develop the power to deal with failure, to cope with rough times, to not always be in the top 10%.

If a person feels good enough about himself, he will be less likely to fall apart if he loses. One way a parent can build this feeling is to demonstrate that the child is loved and respected as an individual, win, lose, or draw. Parental love should really be unconditional. You should love the child for what he is, not just for what he does or what he accomplishes. This may mean that you do not always encourage or allow the child to make too big a deal about winning. It also means that you show respect for the child as an individual, perfect or not. One way to teach this is by admiring models who are able to lose gracefully and with dignity.

The Power of Demand

Children should not have the power to ignore legitimate parental demands. Baumrind's findings indicate that rational-authoritative parents demand a lot from their children. These demands should start early and include the demand that children generally show respect for their elders — including the parents. After all, if elders do not require and receive respect why should a child want to grow up and become an adult? Parents should not put up with sassing and open defiance. At the same time, parents should respect the child enough that they will listen to the child's side. Parents should also demand that the child try hard in school, study enough, be socially responsible and earn his privileges. Children should have and complete family chores. Simply giving privileges is not enough. There really is no free lunch in life. So if the chores are not finished, the reward is withdrawn. If the child refuses to do the chores, then punishment is substituted for reward. Parents must use their power to demand proper behavior if children are to become competent and develop their own power. But parents must understand what acceptable behavior is, at the different stages of a child's growth, and learn when to demand and when to ignore.

Children's Power Needs and Techniques

Parental demands do not always produce desired results. Some children demand too! We often speak of a strong-willed person or of having the willpower to accomplish a task. The strong-willed person usually has enough power and determination to achieve his goals. At times those may not be the parent's goals. Some of this starts early. Babies frequently announce their genetic personality to the world at birth. Some appear demanding and mad, others cool and relaxed. But even relaxed infants have the power to punish by crying or to reward by smiling. Pediatrician J. Michael Cupoli of the University of South Florida says, "It is amazing to see the energy and control a 28-lb baby unleashes on a family. This child can conquer a family of four, no matter how much of a fight you put up. When parents have trouble with getting the baby to eat, sleep or stop crying, they need to understand that most parents have these dilemmas."

Most babies get what they need by charm. Yet little babies can be really stubborn. Then some parents who were punished a lot in their own childhood, may find themselves frustrated and angry. It can become a power-struggle between baby and parent. In rare instances, this reaction can become rage and parents have seriously brain-damaged their babies by shaking them, not realizing that the tender brain can be easily and permanently damaged by sudden jarring motion. For parents who get in a rage, it is better to handle the baby's stubbornness by laying the baby in the crib and walking out of the room until the anger has passed. Such a power compromise becomes an exercise in power over oneself.

Toddlers fight for their rights and their self-esteem. Parents frequently find that it is easier to stop a child from doing something than it is to get him to do something. The child's power needs are such that he may go hungry rather than eat to satisfy a parent who tries to force him to eat, who tries to overpower him. *Eating, sleeping and crying should be personal choices, even at this age. Do you as an adult let others force you to eat when you are not hungry? Can sleep be forced on you when you are not sleepy? Even toddlers require some power and choice about their personal basic needs.* That does not mean you cannot put them in bed and force the "opportunity" to sleep. Nor does it mean he should get all of the junk food he wants. But it may be better to let him experience a little hunger rather than trying to force him to eat something he does not like. How often do you order and eat something that you do not like?

In the toddler stage, the child usually responds with passive aggression. "You can't make me do it!" his actions proclaim. This major trap in discipline teaches the child that the parent does not always have the power to force him to cooperate. So he learns to win by refusing to act. There are, of course, other ways for the child to win.

Running the World

Children instinctively try to exert power, to see if they can run the world. This phenomena has been the theme of the Dennis the Menace comic strip, one of my favorites, for years. Yet a group of concerned parents monitoring comics put this strip in its top-ten list of objectionable strips. The creator of Dennis, Hank Ketchum, responded, "Isn't that a pity. Dennis is an All-American kid. He's like all five year olds. They try to subvert authority from the word go. Kids are always testing adults."

Probably adults more than kids appreciate Ketchum's strip. We all remember the feeling of trying to assert our own power when we were little. Most of us accept the child's need to try, and have enough of a sense of humor to enjoy the childish efforts to run the world. Ketchum teaches adults the silliness of declaring war on kids for acting like kids.

We might learn even more about children by comparing Dennis to Asian children. These children currently outshine the Dennis's of America in school and in business — with higher grades and greater achievements.

In general Chinese, Japanese and Vietnamese parents tell me that they are very strict with their children when it come to enforcing respectful treatment of adults, attention to studies, and achievement in the world. Their children are instilled with the need to prepare themselves to get a good job. Yet many of these children seem to me to have their parents "wrapped around their finger." They often have the power to get their way on little things. In any case, such children usually seem as happy as the Caucasian Dennis's of our world. Perhaps it represents a different use and balance of power within the family. I do not know. Maybe Asians demand more. Demanding parents do seem to produce more competent kids. But one way or another children need and will exert power, whether it is Mary Chin demonstrating her superiority in school or Dennis bugging his neighbor.

Empowering our Children

The importance of letting children rationally share in the use of power was underscored by Dr. Robert Aldrich at the International Congress of Pediatrics in 1986. He recommends that children should have the opportunity to be involved with societal decisions that affect their future and advises,

> Every city should have a grass-roots organization involved with city government that . . . has children in it, something that reflects what children think . . . when children have a voice in regards to the environment surrounding them, they feel they can affect their future; they're not powerless. They can work to improve the quality of life.

As an outgrowth of this concept, the Mayor of Seattle established a Kid's Board. The kids select their own board members. The Seattle City Council consults with the Kid's Board on items that might affect the kids, even the city budget. Looking to the future, Seattle decided, "If you want to develop civic leaders, you have to grow your own."

Dr. Aldrich spoke of children's need to have a voice in social planning for the future. Within families too, each child needs a sense of power over herself, a sense of some control over her future. After all, it's their world too!

Each family should involve children in the decision-making process. Parents can remain firmly in charge yet still allow the child a voice in family affairs. Obviously, the amount and type of power the child can handle varies with age. The power equation shown on page 11 represents a symbolic graphic equation of the relative amounts of power a child and her parents might have at any given age. If you assume that a newborn's cry and smile have 20% of the power balance and the parents 80%, then the gradual power shift leaves the young adult with 80%, and the parents with the pocketbook.

To prepare a child to function effectively in the adult world, parents should encourage the child to practice using power. The confident parent can allow the child a lot of independent choice and decision-making without sacrificing discipline. Discipline alone is not enough. The rational-authoritative parent learns that parents must go beyond discipline. The parent achieves this by granting freedom and offering respect. How much freedom depends on the parent's knowledge of the particular child's development, capabilities and needs. Parental demands can stimulate the child to develop his abilities. The resulting sense of accomplishment increases his self-esteem and helps him become a self-assured adult.

From a theoretical perspective — the use of reasoning accompanied by power assertion should be more effective with young children than reasoning alone; with young children, a display of power captures their attention and clarifies in their minds that compliance is required, whereas the use of a reason without a display of power often signifies to the child that the parent is indecisive about requiring compliance.

Diana Baumrind, Ph.D.
Institute of Human Development
University of California, Berkeley

III

Parents' Power

The Clinical Results

Research psychologist Baumrind divided parents into five types. The outcome of this sophisticated thirty-year objective study will be presented in the next chapter. To make these styles of parenting real for us, it helps to look at real people — not just at figures or descriptions. The composites of cases presented in this and other chapters are based on my clinical experience as a practicing pediatrician.

I was attracted to the research done by The Institute of Human Development because it substantiates the experience of parents and children I have seen over the years. Baumrind willingly shared her unpublished research monograph with me because she too recognized the similarity between her own findings and the cases I described to her from my own thirty years of practice. My clinical experience and Baumrind's psychological research draw strikingly similar conclusions.

Outcomes From Authoritarian Parenting

Authoritarian parents allow their children little power. They often raise their children in the same way they were raised. Little respect was offered; discipline was harsh. The child was not allowed to stand up for herself, was not allowed the autonomy or freedom necessary for full development.

Joan, age 14, was brought to the pediatrician for counseling because she was sullen, failing in school and depressed. The parents were quite nice to the pediatrician although somewhat overbearing. They were worried and anxious. They had "done everything to straighten her up" but things had gone from bad to worse. The doctor talked with Joan alone and found her both depressed and hostile. After a while, though, she opened up a little, recognizing that he was really trying to help her. When asked why she was doing poorly in school, when she obviously was intelligent, she shrugged her shoulders and said she did not care. When asked how she got along with her parents, Joan shrugged her shoulders again, raised one arm mechanically, and said bitterly, "To them I am just a puppet." Then she parodied with the other arm coming up as if pulled by a string. Her well-meaning parents tried to run every aspect of her life. She was allowed no choices for "Father and Mother knew best!" As a result, she withdrew and became depressed.

One could argue that Joan's parents were not overtly harsh and, therefore, not authoritarian. In fact, they were quite overpowering and gave Joan very little freedom to be herself, to make her own mistakes or to learn and practice self-control. She withdrew into sullen depression. *Parents should seriously listen to their children and respect their need for independence whenever they can.* Some children's desires are unrealistic. Yet, often many of their desires can be accommodated. They can be given more power to run their own lives.

Passive Resistance And Active Solutions

Boyd, age 4, took a different tact. His mother, an intelligent, stern and rather angry-appearing perfectionist came to the doctor with the complaint that Boyd would not mind, would not dress himself, and had her completely frustrated. She, too, had "tried everything" including scolding, spanking, and isolating all without results. Boyd simply would not dress himself. Oh, he would start when she scolded him, "Boyd, if you aren't dressed in five minutes, I am going to be mad!" She would go back in five minutes and find Boyd with one leg in his pants sitting on the floor playing with a car. "Boyd, I told you to get dressed! Now if you don't get dressed, I'm going to spank you!" Boyd said, "I will, I will." Five minutes later Boyd was still playing on the floor although he did have the other leg in his pants but they were not buttoned and his nightshirt was still on. In anger and desperation, Mother would spank him and then roughly dress him because she was late for an appointment. "I simply had to go!" she explained.

Boyd rebelled, in the form of passive aggression, delivering a silent but clear message: "You can't make me mind." Boyd would say "yes" but would cooperate only to the most minimum degree. Spanking had not helped, yelling and scolding had not helped. Mother was at her wits' end but Boyd had a twinkle in his eye. His "authoritarian" mother found that she could lead a horse to water — but she could not make it drink. Many children rebel to demonstrate their power to an authoritarian parent by becoming passively aggressive. They find that the overbearing parent does not always have the power to force them to cooperate. Oh, they will not go out and get into trouble which they know will lead to punishment; instead, they will retreat into silent stubbornness.

Boyd's mother can take a two-pronged approach in getting cooperation. First, she should reward Boyd when he has partially dressed himself by remarking to a friend in Boyd's hearing, "Boyd is really beginning to grow up. Why today he almost finished dressing himself." On the other hand, when Boyd wants to go next door to play, she can say, "Boyd, I'd like to be able to let you go but you are still too young. Why you do not know how to finish dressing yourself. When you are able to dress yourself completely, then I will be able to let you go next door to play. Meanwhile why don't you see if you can put this puzzle together?" *What Boyd needs to learn is that he puts his clothes on for himself, not for his mother.* Unwise use of parental power frequently creates rebellion. It does not offer the child respect or teach the child that something can be gained by acting grown-up. It does not teach the child that he has the freedom to improve his skills, to make up his own mind and learn to live with the results of his decision.

Rebellion by Withdrawal

Rebellion takes many forms. Some rebel by retreat. In Lacy's case, she retreated into her own magic world.

> Lacy, age 5, took a different route to deal with her demanding parents. She had found that a lot better world existed in her imagination. She refused to give up the fully developed fantasy world to which she had retreated since she was three. She would obey her folks, although they sometimes had to shake her to get her attention. But when the chore or minor crisis was over, Lacy would immediately revert back to talking to her imaginary friends. In that world, she had the power to make her friends and her imaginary relatives do what she wanted. It was a much better world than her real powerless world where she was forced to submit to stern discipline. For although she was "loved" and hugged by her parents, she was not allowed the freedom to make any of her own choices. However, they could not penetrate the fortress of her make-believe world — there she was Queen!

Rebellion by Fighting

Other children would rather fight than retreat. They rebel openly and can act quite tough. Rejecting parents sometimes beat and abuse these children. Yet some still fight.

> James, age 9, had yet another way of dealing with his authoritarian parents. He was hostile and vindictive. Even though his mother had washed out his mouth for sassing her

and his father had whipped him with a strap, James would mind only under direct threat. He would sneak out of his window when sent to his room, cut school and sass the teacher. He glowered at the doctor during his physical examination and Mother explained that he did not like adults. But his mother then implied that he was going to be all right because she and his father were going "to make certain he behaves."

It is not easy to deal with a hostile child. James's folks needed a new approach. Nearly everything they did he viewed with suspicion. He regarded his parents as enemies. An approach which sometimes works takes advantage of new milestones in the child's life as a logical time to change.

When James graduates from the fourth grade, or has his tenth birthday, give him a party. Along with the gifts, give him new respect and enough of a reward for being big and responsible that mature behavior will pay off. This requires a marked attitude change on the parents' part. *Such parents must reduce their emotional reactions and let James's problem be his own and let James's rewards be the result of his personal efforts, not his parent's coercion. Children need to learn to control their own life and understand that their own personal decisions, not parental love or meanness, result in reward or punishment.*

The Guilt-Ridden Child

While the above reactions are bad enough, I am bothered more by the child who fights back, "gets his licks in," and then feels terribly guilty and fearful.

Little Cory's rigid mother was cool and collected and did not think that there was any problem when she brought her 4-year-old boy in for his annual check-up. When asked how discipline was going, she said that she had to spank Cory almost every day. He would get mad and holler back at her and say he hated her. However, she reassured the doctor, "That's all right. Later he comes to me and hugs me and says he loves me."

She understood and accepted Cory's rebellion because she always "won" and made him mind anyway. She did not understand that Cory's tantrums and anger at her were more frightening to Cory than to Mom. He recognized that his power to chastise her, by making her mad, had a price. If he could get that mad at her, he reasoned, then she must be really mad at him. Her coolness kept him in suspense. Did she really love him? If he could plan to run away maybe she could plan to throw him out! So in a panic, Cory made amends. He would hug and love her to make certain that she still loved him and would not abandon him. *Parents should recognize after a "blow up" the child may be insecure and seeks reassurance that he is still loved. This implies that the child feels the parent has threatened to abandon him — using the power of anger, a withdrawal of love and an implied withdrawal of support to punish.*

Adult Children of Authoritarian Parents

What is the long-term result in families where children are not allowed power as they grow and develop? Authoritarian parental dictatorships can seriously inhibit the development of children.

Diane's mother described herself as "the top sergeant." She did not punish her children physically very much, but she insisted that they "toe the line." She did love her children and demonstrated this by hugs and kisses interspersed by a continual litany of commands and demands. Diane reacted by becoming somewhat withdrawn. She was friendly but uncertain with people. In junior college, she did poorly and had problems getting to class on time and completing her assignments. Later, she was "absent minded" enough so that she had trouble keeping jobs.

Then she began neglecting her personal appearance, would forget to take baths and went to work sloppily dressed. Jobs became harder to get for her and she began spending more and more time living with her top-sergeant mother out of necessity. Her only real interest was art, but because she had assumed a debt which she could not pay, her mother made her sell all of her art equipment "to teach her a lesson." With little to look forward to, Diane became depressed and would often stay in bed the entire day in spite of her mother's scolding.

Diane's brother, Ned, reacted to his top-sergeant mother angrily. He quit high school before graduation and established an independent life for himself as a mechanic. When he married and had his own child, he found himself unable to discipline her. As a result, the little girl began acting like a top sergeant herself — bossy and bratty.

As we see, the excessive use of power by Diane and Ned's mother caused different problems with each child. In Diane's case, it led to submission, insecurity and ineffectiveness. In Ned's, to rebellion. Then, when Ned's child arrived, he overreacted to his own upbringing. He became permissive, refused to use his power to parent and teach, and left his child with excess power, thus creating a little tyrant — a small top sergeant.

How Much Power?

In spite of these examples of adverse reactions, Baumrind's team found that the children of authoritarian parents seem better off than the children of permissive parents. When they measured the results of permissive parenting on the children, they found less competence, self-assurance and friendliness. Although children need to develop power over themselves, while doing so they require limits, guidelines, and discipline. Children of permissive parents may seem self-assured on the surface, but they often fear that their behavior will create problems for them. Limits seem vague. Thus, the results of permissive parenting seem poor. Yet psychologists disagree about the ideal level of parental power.

Researchers who study social control experimentally argue that if parents use too much power to force children to mind, in the future the children will be less likely to adopt the forced behavior. Baumrind, however, carefully measured parenting styles and their long-term results on children. It appears that powerful firm parents who give a lot but demand a lot from their children, have the best results. Likewise, psychologist Stanley Coopersmith, who used teacher ratings, school records, questionnaires and interviews with parents and children in his investigations, found higher self-esteem in children whose parents exerted powerful controls, reasoned with the child and emphasized high goals and good behavior. Hence, in both Coopersmith's and Baumrind's studies, the less the demand and control by parents the lower the competence and self-esteem of the child.

Permissive Parenting

Noncontrolling, permissive parents allow immature children more power than do rational-authoritative parents. What makes a permissive parent? In my experience, all parents want to do well. I simply have not encountered the few lazy ones who just do not care. A good number become permissive as an outgrowth of their rebellion against their own authoritarian parents. A few may be permissive due to frustration, anger and guilt over their inability to understand their children. Lewis feels that permissive parents are just disorganized. Others, raised successfully by their own permissive parents, naturally follow the same principles of child-rearing. Whatever the reason, it appears that generally *permissively raised children are given too much power. Such children come to expect to always be first in line or center stage. These may be the children who grow up and become politicians. They are not always easy to live with.*

The Lonely God

The out-of-balance permissive power equation leads to consequences such as the "child-god" or the "little-princess" syndromes, in which parents literally worship the child who can do no wrong. Later the child may become disenchanted with a world which refuses to pay it homage. This may result in low self-esteem and ineffectiveness in life. Permissiveness can rebound against the child as we will see in Gregory's case.

The other mothers in the park did not like 24-month-old Gregory. They scowled at Gregory's mother as one or another would rush to get their toddler away from Gregory's aggressive clutches. Gregory threw sand, hit and pushed his would-be playmates down. Most of them would leave when he came up to them and run to their mothers. Gregory, of course, was rather pleased with his sense of power, although he did not have any friends. Finally one mother, angry because Gregory made her little 15-month-old girl cry, sharply asked Gregory's mother, "Why don't you make him stop?" Gregory's mother, with a superior, cold expression on her face, replied, "Gregory does not have a father, so I have to let him act up. It isn't right to limit him." Soon Gregory and his mother had the play area to themselves.

Because of his mother's permissiveness, Gregory not only did not have a father, he also had no friends. This did not help his self-esteem. Mother's guilt and and anger interfered with rational discipline. Gregory should have been told that he would not be allowed to play with other children until he stopped being mean. When he misbehaved, he should have been immediately taken away from the playground after a brief, calm explanation. Later, when he has settled down, Gregory could be asked to apologize. Then Mother can promise to give him a chance to behave better the next time they come to the the park.

Although some parents purportedly "do not believe in permissiveness," they may inadvertently create unfriendly children.

Cynthia was a bright, alert 6-year-old who usually charmed adults she met for the first time. She was outgoing and a bit bossy and challenging, yet cute; however, Mother said she had social problems in school, could not make friends and was often unhappy. She did get along with most adults, respecting their power or, at least, their perceived power. Overall, however, she was out-of-control and unhappy much of the time. Cynthia's teacher reported that the child had no friends in her class as she was bossy and mean. The teacher had witnessed, by chance, an episode in the neighborhood bakery where Cynthia was whining to her mother that she wanted a cake. Mother told her, "No." Cynthia, thereupon, crawled behind the counter, grabbed a cake and took a bite. Mother sighed and told the upset baker that she would pay for the cake.

Cynthia was depressed and unhappy because, she said, "The kids are mean to me!" In spite of her innate ability to charm most adults who saw her on a casual basis when she was not having a tantrum or acting out, she had no friends or playmates and little self-esteem. Her power-trip did not get results except with Mother, who permitted her to do whatever she wanted, even though Mother occasionally got mad and hollered and scolded to "relieve my feelings."

This permissive mother believed she disciplined her child because she got angry and depressed at her child's bad behavior and "told her off!" Cynthia's teacher managed to control her in the classroom, but did not have much regard for either Cynthia or her mother. Thus Cynthia's mother's permissive child-rearing created for Cynthia a world which rejected her. *For the child's sake, if for no other, parents must control them to keep them from outrageous, self-defeating behavior.*

Overindulging

Permissiveness is not limited to mothers. Fathers, too, can be permissive.

Steve, age 7, was at a picnic and could not get any of the other children to play with him. He ran around yelling nonsense things to catch their attention but that did not work. So he jumped up on an adjacent picnic table and ran over the food to the shock and anger of the family sitting there. When the lady at the table said, "You get off here, now!" Steve's father came over and told the lady in an icy tone, "Mind your own business!" The astonished family was so taken aback that they just looked in amazement as father took Steve and left.

Steve's father loved him deeply, showered him with gifts and tried, always, to make Steve happy. As a result, Steve did not understand why other children would not play with him, would not do what he wanted. His father had grown up in a poor family and had felt deprived of many things his parents could not afford. He had worked hard, became affluent, and had given Steven everything. Such parental actions create the "shirtsleeves to shirtsleeves" sociologic phenomenon so typical of American society. The immigrant arrives broke and in shirtsleeves, peddles apples to get a start, works hard and becomes wealthy. He then gives his child everything. The child, who has never had to work for anything, nor learned to use his own powers, squanders his inheritance. His own child then starts over with nothing, in shirtsleeves. The child who is given everything frequently grows up to be bored and aimless — a drifting complainer. Affluent Americans have not always made good parents. Most Americans are rich by the standards of the rest of the world. So if you are a "rich American," keep this in mind!

Other parents overindulge their children because of guilt, not because of wealth or early deprivation. This is common among working parents who cannot give the children enough attention and time and so try to compensate with presents. Divorced parents also have this problem. They often compete with each other to be the "good guy" and win the child's affection with presents and entertainment. The child should develop his own powers, earn his own money and meet his own needs. It is even all right to let him be bored. That may stimulate him to begin to learn how to use his powers to figure out how to do things on his own. Otherwise he is robbed of the right to try, to succeed or fail on his own. The permissiveness of guilt tends to destroy the work ethic and produce incompetent children who grow up to become nonproductive, dissatisfied adults.

Adult Children of Permissive Parents

The children of parents who do not discipline, limit, and teach, grow up uncertain of themselves and of their role and place in the world. Their actions and attitudes often lead to rejections by society. Some drop out and rebel, while a few with good brains become the ineffective graduate cynics we occasionally meet. Perhaps the most bothersome result is the attraction of some of these children to power-hungry cults when they become young adults. Those who command and use power usually offer security. Often these power groups operate under the label of a religion, and cults of all sorts spring up whose basic similarity is that the applicant who accepts the control of the leader becomes a secure member of a closed and "superior" society.

More often the results of permissive child-rearing are less dramatic than the preceding examples. But many permissively raised children adjust poorly. When a mother never leaves a child with a baby sitter, when the child is her "life" and she obeys him — he has problems. He will later expect the world to mind him and will be upset and angry when it will not. Another unhappy outcome of permissive parenting is childish impulsiveness which has never been rationally controlled. As adults, these individuals may over-spend, over-eat, over-promise. Often they detest doing their share of work in a relationship. Frequently, they have no initiative and seem to expect the world to take care of them — like Mother did when they were bored. Expressing boredom resulted in Mother entertaining him. He even expects people to understand his needs when he does not state them. His dependency, his being spoiled, leads him to expect the world to solve his problems for him. The world doesn't!

Children of rational or even authoritarian parents seem more content and self-assured. Baumrind's measures have shown children of permissive parents to be the least competent and poorly adjusted. Society can ill afford to have children raised to become incompetent or socially maladjusted adults. Nor can society afford to have children grow up with low self-esteem, a feeling of worthlessness and powerlessness. As noted earlier, Coopersmith's study demonstrated good correlation between high self-esteem and powerful demanding and controlling parents who respected their children. These parents reasoned with their offspring and listened to them before using force or punishment.

Traditional Parenting

Traditional fathers provide and dominate, while traditional mothers nurture and serve. The differences between the sexes is not limited to the plumbing! Most of us recognize that boys are generally more innately aggressive and risk-taking, while girls are more sensitive and aware of others feelings. This leads easily to the adult male provider and the female wife-mother. However, the major changes in American society have partially altered this traditional concept. To meet the challenges of tomorrow's environment, both boys and girls should develop optimal competence — should become powerful on their own. Does traditional parenting work well enough to accomplish this? I believe that overall, traditional parenting works well if one excludes those mothers or fathers who think of themselves as traditional but are really authoritarian, permissive, or uncertain.

Not all traditional parents function as a team. When the differences between a traditional mother and father are marked enough that Father comes close to being authoritarian and Mother close to being permissive, significant differences occur between the way these mothers and fathers discipline their children. This was strikingly demonstrated when Melissa was brought to the office by her mother. When Melissa commanded, her mother jumped and tried her best to meet Melissa's demands. Mother rarely seemed to discipline.

> Melissa, age 3, had had some routine immunization shots last time she visited her pediatrician and she was not happy to be back with a cold, fever and earache. In fact, Melissa wanted out. When the nurse put her in an examination room, she threw a tantrum and screamed to her mother that she was not going to stay in that room. Mother asked the nurse if they could use another room so Melissa was moved — only to scream that she did not want to be there either. Mother took her to the waiting room again. Melissa was finally seen, sobbing and angry, and given medication for her ear infection.
>
> On the return visit, Melissa was with her father. She started to scream that she did not want to be there and he said in a very firm no-nonsense voice, "That's enough, Melissa. You are going to stay here and be examined whether you like it or not! I am not your mother!" Melissa immediately quieted down and was happy and cooperative through the examination and said a friendly good-by to her doctor.

Melissa responded very differently to her permissive, unassertive mother and her firm assertive father. She understood that her father would not put up with her misbehavior. She turned on the charm to handle him. Children understand and adapt to power. In most cases they feel more secure and less anxious when they sense the power and strength of a parent. Melissa's family has the potential to become like rational-authoritative families when Mother becomes firm and demands better behavior.

Would things have been better for Melissa had her mother used more of her innate power? An effort should probably be made to increase the assertiveness of many girls, most of whom will become mothers as well as workers. A similar effort should probably be made to increase the social responsibility of most boys. Usually boys are naturally assertive unless squashed by authoritarian parents. Others, however, are not assertive. They have a different temperament and need help to develop their self-confidence and self-esteem. Also, some girls are too assertive and not as nurturing as future citizen mothers and spouses should be.

Rational-Authoritative Parents

Of Baumrind's group of parents, only 15% were the ideal rational-authoritative parents. In my experience, a much higher percent of parents are both rational and authoritative. Admittedly, most of the families I see are in the office. I may have missed problems because I often had a somewhat limited view of the dynamics of non-complaining families whose children developed into competent adults. Yet many of these ideal parents had shared with me the problems they had had with their children — probably see if I approved of their methods. I did approve.

Rational-authoritative parents demand that their children behave admirably. The resulting admiration by the parent becomes a powerful tool, a powerful reward to the child. Usually, these parents have taught their child early in life that the parent is in charge. They demonstrated to the child their considerable power to reward or punish, depending upon how the child responded to situations. So they did not need to punish very often.

Andy, age four, received a small friendly bulldog, Gypsy, for his birthday. He was delighted with his new pet and eagerly promised to accept the responsibility to feed Gypsy every day before his own dinner. After a few days, though, Andy forgot and ignored Gypsy's whining. Mother fed Gypsy but that evening she did not put a plate on the table for Andy. When he complained, rather shocked, she explained that she had forgotten Andy's plate. "You know Andy, just like you forgot to feed Gypsy. I'll put a plate on for you now, but let's both not forget from now on!"

A few weeks later Mother noticed that Andy was sometimes mean to Gypsy. He had put Gypsy into a gunny sack and tied the opening. Mother asked him why he was so cruel, but got no answer. She told him firmly that he had to stop being mean or she would give Gypsy away to an older child who would treat her better. Andy really liked his dog but he enjoyed his childish game and the sense of power it gave him. After Mother's warning, he was better for a few days but then started the same game, putting a complaining Gypsy in the sack, tying the opening and dragging her around. So Mother gave Gypsy away and calmly told Andy that he was too much of a baby to take care of a pet. "When you grow up some more," she told him, "and can be more responsible and take good care of a pet, then you can have one."

Andy was probably too young and certainly too immature and ir-responsible to have a pet. Some children may be able to handle a pet prop-erly at that age. But the key lies in their demonstration of responsibility to show they are capable. If they do not accept the responsibility, then the re-ward of having a pet is withdrawn. Andy's parent did not scold or punish him by spanking. Rather she used her authority to take the reward away. This rational behavior demonstrates that the parent is in charge, demands good behavior and gives the child a chance to demonstrate responsibility and explain his actions. When he fails, then the parent acts decisively.

Later in life, when Andy was the usual self-centered 15-year-old, he still respected his parents. They both worked and Andy, from habit instilled since early childhood, had taken over many of the routine chores in the house. His grades were good and it appeared that he would go to a good university. But between chores and school he often felt limited in the time he had for fun. So he was unhappy when his mother told him that she had volunteered to have him spend a Saturday helping an elderly retired neighbor, Mr. Jones, put in a cement walk along his house. For no pay. The neighbor was on social security and could not afford to have the job done. His bad back and age made him unable to load and push the wheelbarrow full of ce-ment.

Andy was sturdy and able. But he objected and said he was not going to help. He had plans. Saturday was goof-off time. His mother flatly told him that he was going to help. She reminded him of the past kindness of Mr. Jones to Andy and clearly described Mr. Jones's need. She pointed out that everyone has a duty to help those less fortunate. She demanded that he help and was both unyielding and obviously annoyed at Andy's attitude.

Concerned that he would lose respect to say nothing of privileges, a somewhat upset Andy gave in. As a side benefit he learned quite a bit about cement laying. And after a hard day's work with resulting blisters and sore muscles, the walkway was finished. Mr. Jones was appreciative. Andy found that he felt proud of his work and the respect he had earned.

Again the lesson is that rational-authoritative parents demand and act. The proof of the pudding is in the eating, not the recipe. They demand good behavior and they do not threaten action without meaning it. They assess situations fairly, then logically explain their stance and give the child an opportunity to explain his side. The child learns to respect the parent's word and the parent's power. This model of rational and authoritative use of power makes a lasting impression on children. Zelda still remembers.

Zelda, age 13, was not studying very much at home since she had entered junior high. So far she had good grades and was generally a fine student, so Mother and Father did not do much more than question her occasionally about why she had so little homework. She had a new friend, Cynthia, who had a horse; so she eagerly spent as much time as she could with Cynthia and her horse. Horses were in! The parents thought that spending time with horses was a healthy occupation. But Zelda's mother noticed that Cynthia did not visit Zelda often and something about her attitude bothered Mother. She told Zelda that she wondered about Cynthia. "Is she a nice girl?" Mother asked, "Didn't I smell cigarettes on her breath yesterday?"

"Oh, Mother!" Zelda replied, "You just do not know her. She is really nice. And so what if she smokes? She doesn't do it much. And, anyway, she's a horsewoman!"

Mother then checked with a friend who knew Cynthia's family and the friend told her that "horsewoman" Cynthia was into marijuana and had been in trouble with the police for shoplifting. To add fat to the fire, when Mother called Zelda's teacher she was told that Zelda was not turning in her homework. She had dropped to below a B average. The final straw occurred about the same time when a stranger called and said that Zelda had ridden his horse without permission. It seemed that Cynthia "borrowed" the horse for Zelda. Mother immediately declared Cynthia off-limits for Zelda. She was to have nothing to do with her. Also, Zelda had to spend three hours a night studying, at least until her grades came up to a B average. When that occurred, she would be allowed occasional rides at Buck Norde's Stable — but not with Cynthia.

Zelda did not argue too much. She was ashamed of Cynthia's pot smoking and the fact that she had tried a joint, although she did not like it. She was also upset when Cynthia let her ride the neighbor's horse — only to find it was without permission. She suffered the consequences of misjudging Cynthia and being carried away into doing things she knew her folks would not approve of — that she knew were wrong. She was, underneath it, relieved that her folks would not let her associate with Cynthia anymore.

The Rejecting-Neglecting Parent

Rejecting-neglecting parents do not bring their children to pediatricians often. When they do, they are unlikely to reveal their attitude. Yet a mother, told of my book, wrote to me: "Crazy as it may seem, there may actually be rejecting-neglecting parents who will read your book because they are interested in being better parents than their abusive parents were. I have seen college-educated rejecting-neglecting parents."

She then recalled her own alcoholic parents who were both authoritarian and harsh. She recalled the traumas she suffered. She had vowed not to be like her parents. "But that left me knowing what not to do . . . not what to do. I had vowed not to spank because spanking is a form of hitting and I had not always made it to the closet to hide from my father when he was drunk and on a rampage, so I remember what being hit was like. I had vowed to talk with my children . . . to reason with them.

"But when I became a parent, I was confronted with millions of daily decisions (and although I have only one child, he is hyperactive, so I mean *millions*). Many situations came up when I knew not what to do — I was paralyzed."

As a result, when her son was about four years old, he started swearing at her. She tried to ignore this behavior but he continued. She felt abused and angry and felt like "hurling the back of my hand at his mouth." Like anyone else, she reacted emotionally with feelings of rejection for the child who was rejecting her. However, soon after, she learned the value of action when she observed her neighbor sending her daughter to her room the minute she sassed her mother. She then cured her son's swearing by sending him to his room! She had been permissive because of her lingering childhood reaction to her parents. This had led to her son being so out-of-control that she had feelings of maternal rejection. The pendulum swings and our inner child of the past often becomes the driving force for better or worse. That there are better ways can be seen by looking at solid research results.

*A pediatrician takes a big risk by insisting that changes
in child rearing are essential to the child's well-being.*

Alvin Rosenfeld, M.D. and
Dorothy Levine, M.D.
Pediatrics in Review

IV

Parents' Power

The Research Results

Everyone has opinions about parenting. Many devote their lives to a study of parenting. As a result, their valuable observations and penetrating insights provide us with a reservoir of accumulated wisdom. Most of the observations cited here contain a great degree of truth and some may be entirely true. But rarely are they proved scientifically. In fact, much of what is presented as science represents only an attempt to be scientific. The search for truth, for facts and understanding has never been easy. Most people, for example, do not realize that within five years after publication, 50% of papers in the medical literature prove to contain erroneous material. This is because the study of the human body is intensely complex. There are, theoretically at least, 64 billion different genetic individuals possible — each a very complicated being. It is no wonder that scientific studies are difficult! We still grope for knowledge.

Understanding the Significance of Research

The human brain and emotions still remain a challenging scientific frontier. Early philosophers attempted to understand human behavior by example and by description. We can still appreciate the innate facts and truths in many ancient discourses, in ancient stories and plays. Humans do fascinate. One can, perhaps, put early explorers of psychiatry, like Freud, in the same group. They observed, studied, recorded and attempted to understand. Then they, or those who followed, invariably tried to develop theories which would simplify our understanding of people and their behavior. Some of what they discovered and described remains of great value. For example, Missildine's understanding, reflected in his book, *Your Inner Child of the Past*, may not be strictly scientific, yet it has the ring of truth — the essence of understanding people.

Much literature, often under the name of science, does not have the ring of truth. Even scientific studies of animal behavior, which are essentially valid, have been misused by some researchers to propose unwarranted understanding of human behavior. Many of the pronouncements of animal researchers were thoroughly debunked by Arthur Koestler, while he was working at the Center for Advanced Study in the Behavioral Sciences in Stanford, California. In his fascinating book, *The Ghost in the Machine*, he writes, "In the course of the last century, science has become so dizzy with its own successes that it has forgotten to ask the pertinent questions..." All this implies that we should be skeptical of the works of science, as true scientists are skeptical even of their own works. Yet, parents face questions about how to best raise their children now. Can we get help from scientific research?

Researcher Burton White accumulated seventeen years of research before publishing his book, *The First Three Years of Life*. In reviewing the manuscript for this book, he commented: "[You have] quotes from novelists, media writers, psychologists and scientists and researchers of all kinds ... I find myself [asking] how valid is that statement likely to be ... how good was the research?" I too have asked myself these key questions throughout my own professional career, both as a parent and as a pediatrician. We need the best advice we can get, and we need it now — for our children are growing and developing now. Although not entirely scientific, the opinions and research I cite will hopefully cast some light and offer different views on the issue of power in child-rearing.

Both Burton White's work about the first three years of life and Diana Baumrind's three decades of careful research in measurements of parenting styles and their outcomes on the children lend support to this book. They strengthen some of my views about the use of power. After reviewing my clinical observations and conclusions, Baumrind (whose work represents a new era in the scientific investigation of parenting) wrote, "I believe that you have translated the kernel of what it means to be an authoritative parent into a practical strategy of use to middle-class parents to whom this book is clearly directed."

The current era of productive scientific measurement of parenting styles and results began with University of California Psychologist Stanley Coopersmith's interviews and questionnaires of parents, teachers and their children. From these he was able to measure the self-esteem of the children and compare it to the type of parenting, thus drawing some conclusions about power:

> The family necessarily and invariably presents us with an unusual distribution of power.... We would expect that those persons who are delegated power and who are treated in a respectful manner would regard themselves as more significant than people who are unrecognized and powerless ... Parents have the strength and power to enforce their demands and they establish the limits and framework within which their children function.

Yet, Coopersmith found, on the basis of statistical measurements, that "The parents of children with high self-esteem are more likely to establish and enforce strict rules than are the parents of children with less esteem." At the same time, he notes that the essential features of a democratic home are ". . . clearly established policies which permit individual discussion, disagreement and deviation by individuals [within established limits] without punishment or coercion." This encourages self-confident, competitive and assertive children who are creative and persistent. Sounds good, doesn't it?

On the other hand, Coopersmith discovered that overpowering, dominating parents (the authoritarian type) produced a different sort of child. By obeying their parents, these offspring were rewarded with acceptance and security in the family. Clear limits and obedience are valuable, but when authoritarian parents did not allow their children the power and freedom to begin to spread their wings, to dissent or disagree or present their own opinions, Coopersmith observed, ". . . these children abandon all hope of self-respect." Many became either shy and withdrawn or belligerently refused to grant consideration to others. Yet parents who were permissive, hesitant, vacillating, noncontrolling, or non-demanding had still fewer children with high self-esteem. Overall, comparing the results of parental control, Coopersmith found that highly to moderately controlled children had higher self-esteem than children who were less controlled.

Table III

THE EFFECT OF THE EXTENT OF PARENTAL CONTROL ON THE SUBJECTIVE SELF-ESTEEM OF CHILDREN*

Degree of Control	Low Self-Esteem	Medium Self-Esteem	High Self-Esteem
High to Moderate Control	16.7%	41.2%	45.4%
Limited Control	83.3%	58.8%	54.5%

*From Coopersmith, Stanley *The Antecedents of Self-Esteem* New York, W.H. Freeman and Company, 1967.

On the basis of one-time measurements and scientific correlations, three types of parenting styles can be described: authoritarian, authoritative and permissive. All are basically defined by the balance and use of power between parent and child. The results of Coopersmith's measurements indicate that parents should be firm, controlling and demanding; at the same time, affectionate, accepting and involved with their children. They should especially allow the child the freedom to try to develop his own power. By offering respect for the child, they build his self-esteem.

To see what finally happened over the full period of growth and development, researcher Diana Baumrind established The Family Socialization Project within The Institute of Human Development at the University of California at Berkeley. She recruited a group of families and carefully recorded the parents' styles and their children's outcomes over a period of three decades. Her team used neutral observation and interviews to measure parental control and "demandingness" and measured the competence, confidence and social responsibility of the children. This study, still in progress, offers one of the first scientifically valid measures of the long-term effects of parenting style. Still to come out of the data are the effects on IQ. Hopefully, we can look forward to further investigation of how the children of these different types of parents will raise their own children. Baumrind's monograph on Familial Antecedents of Social Competence will be of great value. Her research is funded by the William T. Grant Foundation. She is also the recipient of a Research Scientist Award from the National Institute of Mental Health and has been supported by grants from the National Institute of Child Health and Development and by the National Science Foundation.

In this University of California study, the parents were initially grouped into three categories: authoritarian, authoritative, and permissive. Here, as noted before, I call the middle group rational-authoritative, to clearly distinguish it from overpowering authoritarian parents. Further study resulted in the expansion and redefinition of parenting types into five groups, now including traditional and rejecting-neglecting parents.

Each of these groups of parents differed in the amount and type of control and attention they gave to their children, in their attitudes toward the children, and in their use of power. This expansion of the types of parenting recognized by psychologists offers some basic lessons. First, the phenomenal variability of humans makes it difficult to pigeonhole people. Second, the overall knowledge about parenting continues to grow. Third, while we do not have final answers or magic solutions, scientific investigations about parenting increase our understanding. The rejecting-neglecting parent and the traditional parent are discussed later. Here, in terms of understanding the use of power, we will confine ourselves to examining the first three basic parenting styles — authoritarian, rational-authoritative, and permissive:

1. *Authoritarian* parents are harsh in their demands, strict and punitive and often angry; they overpower and over-control their children and give them little freedom or respect.

2. *Rational-Authoritative* parents use the power of demand but punish less harshly. While insisting on obedience with clear limits, they respect the child's feelings and listen to the child's side — beginning the process of helping the child develop enough power and self-respect to stand up for himself. They offer freedom for the child to develop.

3. *Permissive* parents essentially let the child have the power to run himself. They set few limits, tend to vacillate and do not demand good behavior.

Let us look at a fairly typical situation facing parents and see how each of the three types of parents might react.

It was Wednesday night. Jim, age 11, wiggled excitedly as he came into the living room where his parents were relaxing after dinner. He had just received a phone call from his friend Mark. "Mom and Dad, can I go to see *Star Wars III* Friday night with Mark? His folks will take us and I can go with them. Can I? Huh?"

Rational-Authoritative Parents

Mom and Dad exchanged looks and Dad said, "First, what about this note from Mrs. Jones that you brought home from school today? She says that you didn't turn in your history homework again? How come?"

Jim hung his head and said, "Oh, I forgot it. Anyway I hadn't quite finished it. But I can do it tonight!"

Mom replied, "But this is the second time that you have been late turning in your homework. I don't know how you can expect to go to the movie when you don't really act like a responsible fifth grader. What are you going to do to make up for turning your homework in late?"

Jim gulped and said, "Well, Mrs. Jones told us we could do some op, opt, er, optimal work if we wanted to get better grades. Can't I do that and still go to see *Star Wars?*" Mother smiled and said, "You mean optional, o-p-t-i-o-n-a-l work don't you?" Jim responded, "Yea!"

Mom and Dad looked at each other and Dad nodded. Mom said firmly, "If you can finish the assignment tonight that you were supposed to turn in and get it in tomorrow, and finish the extra optional assignment tomorrow evening and turn it in Friday, you can go. But you show both of those assignments to me before you take them to school. If you turn any more assignments in late there will be no more movies in the future until you learn to finish your homework on time! Understood?"

Authoritarian Parents

Mom and Dad both glared at Jim and Mom scolded, "How do you expect to go to the movies when you aren't turning in your homework on time?"

Dad slapped his hand hard on the table and with his cheeks flushed hollered, "Get in your room and finish that assignment! Don't come around whining that you want to go to the movies when you're bad. I've a mind to spank you now! Go!"

Permissive Parents

Mom smiled and said, "Of course, honey!" Dad looked up from his paper and asked, "But what about that late homework, Jane?"

Mother said, "Oh, heavens, he is only young once. Let him go!"

Dad nodded in agreement and went back to his newspaper. Jim raced back to the telephone.

The Results

The long-term results of these three types of parenting were measured by the outcomes on the children — the degree of competence, friendliness, social adjustment and self-confidence they each exhibited. The winning vote goes to the parents who used, but shared, power with their children — the rational-authoritative parent. The authoritarian, power-trip parents were runners-up. Their children were not as competent, confident or adjusted. Evidently their lack of experience in using power, in developing self-control and their resulting rebellion slowed down development. The worst results occurred in children raised by permissive parents.

Before we accept fully the results of such objective research, we must recognize the weakness of statistics in relation to individual parents and children. For example, psychologist Coopersmith measured self-esteem in children and then asked their mothers if their children should have a part in making family plans. Of mothers who allowed children a say in making family plans, 77.4% had children with high self-esteem. On the other hand, 22.6% of mothers who did not allow children a say in family plans had children with high self-esteem. Statistically it would seem better to allow children the power experience of helping in family plans; yet even if this did not happen, 22.6% of the children still had high self-esteem. Obviously such measurements are of some value, but there are too many other factors, known and unknown, which play a role. *People are different — and children are people.*

How you and your particular child react to situations such as those described by Coopersmith or Baumrind remains to be seen. It pays to be a little skeptical when deciding what style of parenting you are going to use and how you will meet the power needs of your children. Researcher Catherine Lewis agrees, for example, that mothers of sons with high self-esteem have more control than other types of mothers but she argues, that "they do not, however, necessarily exercise control more frequently." My experience leads me to believe that these parents conditioned their children to obey early in their lives and, therefore, rarely had to use overt control. We can learn about balancing power from both statistics and the debates. But first let us take a look at the characteristics of the competent child so we know clearly just what outcome we would be working toward.

Characteristics of Competent Children

In order to appreciate how results of parenting styles were judged, we need to have a clear idea of the characteristics of children considered ideal in the study. A detailed description of competent children was developed by the University of California Family Socialization and Developmental Competence Project. Baumrind asked the opinions of many experienced psychologists. Their consensus of the 21 most important characteristics are listed in order inTable IV.

Overall, this list is a good one; however, one key characteristic of competence has been left out. A child should be able to deal positively with adversity. Many children who have always won find it impossible to lose gracefully or without becoming quite depressed. In addition, one characteristic feature which the study advanced seems "off the mark." They believe it important for the child to express negative feelings openly and directly. Granted, this recognizes the need to ventilate and offers a way to measure a child's self-confidence; but it does not recognize the diplomatic need to control negativism nor the need to respect the feelings of others. Competent children must learn how to diplomatically disagree and constructively criticize in order to achieve the best short and long-term results. The child must feel powerful enough to persist and self-confident enough to resist running other people down to achieve a goal. Social skills which enable productive relationships with others should become a major concern in his life.

Table IV

THE MOST CHARACTERISTIC FEATURES OF THE OPTIMALLY COMPETENT CHILD

Has a sense of identity
Socially confident with adults
Interacts smoothly with other children
Comfortable and secure with adults
Willing to pursue tasks alone
Accepts responsibility for wrongdoing
Trustworthy
Will question adult authority
Persistent
Peer leader
Optimistic
Sees adults realistically
Challenges herself/himself intellectually
Altruistic
Internally motivated to get good grades and to learn
Argues with other children to get her/his point across
Confident of her/his intellectual abilities
Respects the work of other children
Challenges herself/himself physically
Problem oriented
Expresses negative feelings openly and directly

The Competence of Various Parenting Types

In this same study, it was found that 85% of children raised by rational-authoritative parents were optimally competent, while only about 50% of those raised by traditional parents were similarly competent. The overall breakdown of parenting types and competence is shown in Table V.

		Table V						
PARENT TYPE	**COMPETENCE OF CHILDREN**							
	fully competent		*partially competent*		*incompetent*		*numbers*	
	boys	girls	boys	girls	boys	girls	boys	girls
Rational-Authoritative	83%	86%	17%	14%	00%	00%	6	7
Traditional	43%	50%	57%	33%	00%	17%	14	6
Authoritarian	18%	42%	55%	58%	27%	00%	11	12
Permissive	20%	00%	60%	71%	20%	29%	5	7
Rejecting-Neglecting	00%	00%	33%	63%	67%	27%	9	8
Total							45	40

Girls and Boys Respond Differently

Both boys and girls of rational-authoritative parents turned out to be fully or partially competent. None were incompetent. However, major differences occurred between boys and girls raised by other types of parents. Traditional parents ranked second in the percentage of fully competent children. However, traditionals can be better understood if we first examine the results of authoritarian, permissive and rejecting-neglecting parents.

Authoritarian parents, more than others, overpower their children. However, they evidently overpower their boys more than their girls, possibly because they perceive that the boys are more impulsive and risk-taking than girls. Probably because such parents "squash" their boys and offer them little respect, 27% of the boys were judged incompetent; only 18% were fully competent. Baumrind's researchers noted that authoritarian parents allowed their girls to express opinions more than boys. Perhaps as a result of this respect, more of their girls were competent than boys. This seems a clear indication that children should be both seen and heard by their parents — allowed to state their own opinions and present their side of an issue.

Another factor which may explain why more of the authoritarian group of boys were incompetent could be maternal warmth. Preadolescent boys appear more sensitive than do girls to this lack of mothering warmth denied them by an authoritarian parent. Apparently, if boys do not get the warmth and support they need, they become anxious and lose self-esteem. Girls seem emotionally tougher. Child psychiatrist Dr. Joseph L. Woolston notes:

> Studies of children's reactions to many different types of traumatic experiences have emphasized the importance of gender of the child: girls are more resilient and are less symptomatic to the acute effects of trauma than are boys. The explanation for this greater strength of girls is much debated but poorly explained.

Suppressing open rebellion, as authoritarian parents do, leads to subtle rebellion. Often it occurs later, when the child becomes a young adult and can finally rebel against parental values. This can be seen as a rejection of success, which might be felt as giving in to the parents. One type is the adult dawdler and day-dreamer who still fights the overpowering parental demands of his youth. On the other hand, some achieving adult women evidently have authoritarian mothers who give approval only if the child succeeds and respond with hostility and rejection if the child displeases them. One wonders about the emotional price paid for such achievement.

Permissively-raised boys and girls react quite differently to the lack of demand and control by their parents. Possibly the innate aggressiveness of some boys gives them the self-confidence and self-respect needed for competency — 20% were fully competent. These boys did receive maternal warmth, and many were able to cope and develop well. However, for a good portion of both boys and girls, parental love alone was not enough and they became incompetent. Permissive parents do not use enough power of demand or control to stimulate adequate development of their children. Love alone will not compensate. And some permissive parents I have seen appear to be quite close to being neglecting parents.

Rejecting-neglecting parents probably reject their boys more than their girls. Anyway more of their boys were incompetent than their girls. Some rejecting-neglecting parents I have seen are in a sense authoritarian, harsh and punitive when they do give attention. This would affect their boys more than their girls if most girls are, in fact, stronger emotionally than boys.

Traditional Parenting

Typical traditional parents are sex-typed in the "Father knows best" and "Mother loves most" mode. Traditional fathers are dominant and demanding, but not as responsive as rational-authoritative fathers. Traditional mothers demand less and nurture more. They parent as a team, generally with good results. Many competent children and few incompetent children come from traditional families. Statistically their girls have higher than average scores for social assertiveness; however fewer of them are as balanced with a sense of social responsibility as are girls of rational-authoritative parents. Some of the traditionally-raised girls were incompetent, while traditionally-raised boys scored close to the sons of the rational-authoritative group in social responsibility and half of them were optimally competent. But we must ask: Can we increase the odds for producing optimally competent children?

While stereotypical parents do exist, undoubtedly variations occur among traditional parents. In traditional families where Father is a bit authoritarian and Mother tends to be permissive, the effect on both sexes seems to be poor. I suspect that the more authoritarian traditional father does not allow his son the freedom needed to develop much self-confidence, and some permissive traditional mothers may be too weak a role model for their daughters. On the other hand, stronger traditional mothers offer more powerful models, and thus encourage competence in their daughters. (Only 17% of traditionally-raised girls were incompetent.) However, boys do not benefit as much from a strong authoritarian mother because as they reach adolescence, boys have a natural need to differentiate themselves from women and to separate from Mother.

Will competence develop fully if father functions mostly as the major provider and disciplinarian? Or if Mother functions mostly as the prime source of support? In my experience, the common form of balance and teamwork in the traditional family — where the father is reasonably dominant and the mother reasonably nurturing — usually creates competent children. But in traditional families where Mother and Father do not function as a team and instead disagree about the use of power and the type of discipline, fewer optimum results occur. These families will be considered further in the chapters titled "When Discipline Doesn't Work."

Balancing Demand and Response

Rational-authoritative parents produce more fully-competent children. The key principle of rational parenting is a good balance between parental demands and parental responsiveness. Authoritarian parents demand too much and respond too little. Permissive parents demand too little and respond too much. The art of parenting involves using the right amount of power in both demand and response, tailored to the individual needs and temperament of the child.

Some traditional and permissive women do need to learn to demand more of their children, and some traditional and authoritarian men need to respond more. All need to avoid overpowering the child by inflexible demands which can squash the child or by overindulgence or by overinvolvement in the child's life which can smother him. They must give the child enough time and attention, freedom, values and goals. They need to go beyond the discipline of demand and control. Parents should nurture the child's power by respectfully listening to him and at times acceding to his rational arguments — admitting he is right or at least close to right often enough to encourage him to stand up for himself and his beliefs.

When women develop their confidence and exert their power over the children almost as much as the father, and Father becomes involved with the children almost as much as Mother, the family moves into the top statistical range of parent effectiveness. Both parents demand good behavior, yet are warm and responsive; in other words, rational and authoritative in their behavior toward their children. They control and respect while offering freedom within limits. In the Baumrind study both the boys and girls of such parents turned out to be highly competent, self-assured, academically successful and socially responsible. This type of parenting reduces impulsiveness and over-aggression in boys, while increasing their social responsibility. It also reduces the excessive need of some girls to please everybody, no matter what the cost, and builds their assertiveness and self-confidence. Which side of the statistics will your child be on? Although Baumrind's investigations are about as objective as you can get, parenting is still an individual art, not a science. However, out of all of this, we can offer specific suggestions for parenting techniques that can increase your child's self-esteem and competence. (See Table VI.)

Rational parents want their children to be well-balanced. They encourage the development of or compensation for those aspects of character, either biological or social, which may be relatively weak because of temperament, talent or sex predelection. They also emphasize the growth of the child's innate strengths. Thus some girls may need to learn to be more socially assertive and to recognize that it is not always necessary to please at any cost. While others may need to develop a greater personal social conscience and nurturing qualities. Some boys may need to learn better control of their impulsiveness and aggressiveness — and increase their sense of personal responsibility to both family and society. Others need to be toughened up in order to deal with the world outside the home.

You can use the power of rational-authoritative parenting to help achieve these aims and produce more competent children. It is not a matter of "liberating" women or "reforming" men, but of helping each individual of both sexes develop his or her talents and abilities to the maximum so they can ultimately become better parents themselves. To accomplish this requires the power of knowledge and an understanding of how to use specific parental skills in imparting values and rewarding or punishing children. None of this comes easily in the face of today's tough challenges.

Table VI

TO BUILD YOUR CHILD'S POWER

1. *Demand good behavior, high values, hard work and development of talents.* Confront your child when you have to.

2. *Listen to your child respectfully, even enthusiastically, whether you agree or disagree.* This increases his sense of self-importance and gives him experience in presenting his views.

3. *Encourage him to present his views about rewards and punishment.* When you understand his side of the story, your rewards and punishments tend to be more just. This also teaches the child to stand up for himself and look at and analyze his behavior. In addition, allowing him to win an argument through good reasoning skills increases his respect for logic and fairness and builds his self-confidence.

4. *Let his problems be his — do not make them yours.* Do not allow yourself to become angry or upset as you discipline. Intercede only when it is necessary to force him to accept the consequences of his own actions. This forces him to look at his own actions and their results instead of focusing on your emotions. Further, it reduces his natural tendency to blame others when he is wrong and increases his confidence in himself when he is right.

5. *Give him choices whenever possible so he gains experience in choosing.* This allows him to learn the power inherent in choosing and the consequences of choices. He loses from bad choices and wins from good choices. This helps him understand that he is responsible for his own actions.

6. *Allow him to occasionally manipulate you.* This gives him experience in the use of power and reduces fear of adults. It validates his importance and equalizes the balance of power between parent and child, reducing his need to rebel.

7. *Refuse to be manipulated on important values.* Use your authority as a parent to control your child when it is required. Demonstrate your own power of self-control by rationally and authoritatively assessing, planning and acting on problems. This offers your child a model of power to emulate and emphasizes your values.

8. *Keep a positive attitude toward your child and offer a positive image of him now and in the future.* Your children tend to respect your opinion and believe what you say. If you believe in them, they are more likely to believe in themselves.

> "My grandmother used to say
> What you think of me
> I'll think of me
> And what I think of me
> I'll be"*

9. *Avoid angry criticism which damages self-esteem.* Avoiding anger in criticism reduces the child's need to rebel and leaves the child's self-confidence and power intact.

10. *Punish as little as possible and impress on him that when you do punish it is because he made the wrong choice.* When the punishment is over, start over fresh. Calmly explain to him what was wrong about his bad choice and warmly tell him that he has learned from this and will make better choices in the future.

11. *Praise him, respect him.* This may be the best of rewards.

12. *Give him the freedom to try things on his own as much as possible.* Let mistakes be accepted as normal, as learning experiences. Encourage him to try again and offer alternative ways which might help him succeed. Teach him how to deal with adversity in a healthy way.

13. *Involve him in decisions about himself and the family* — whether it is about education, vacation, planning, or other family events. As he matures, allow him to become more and more a part of the planning process. This gives him experience in planning, while demonstrating respect for his opinions.

14. *Spend enough time with him that he realizes you value him.* This encourages him to value himself and increases his power to stand up for himself with the rest of the world.

---

* Billy Thomas and Tom Novak, *Who Stole Mrs. Wick's Self-Esteem.* The National Commitee for Prevention of Child Abuse.

Because the social fabric in which families are embedded has been unravelling over the last 40 years, there has been a correspondingly increased need for family structure, engagement and discipline.

Diana Baumrind
Familial Antecedents of Social Competence in Middle Childhood

---

V

Today's Tough Challenges

Parents want to raise their children to become powerful and content, happy and responsible. Historically this meant raising "Junior" to be strong and competitive and "Sis" to be giving and social. The traditional male was the breadwinner and protector, the female the homemaker and mother. The result: a prototype macho father and sweet mother. However, people in real life were rarely like the historical prototype. On the surface, the traditional nuclear family often had a more dominant demanding father and a more nuturing socially conscious mother; but more frequently the decisions were mutual and mother had her say — usually her way, her impact, and her respect. On the other hand, the American male was king until he left the workplace by the millions during World War II. Then Rosie the riveter soon proved that females could be as competent in the workplace as in the homeplace. Now society, in its ponderous way, acknowledges women's liberation and tries to equalize the treatment of boys and girls.

Does this mean that boys and girls should be raised the same? Does women's liberation and the movement for equality between the sexes mean that feminist parents should attempt to raise what research psychologists term "gender-aschematic children?" Apparently, this means nonsexist, opposite of the expected. Would such girls grow up to be gender-aschematic mothers? What would that mean to the profession of mothering — and to their children? The concept of "gender-aschematic children" does not please psychologist Diana Baumrind, who has a hunch that if, indeed, any such children could be generated, they would not be optimally competent. Sexual self-concept is the key to how children and adolescents organize their central values, attitudes and activities — the key to what they are. On the other hand, exaggerated sex type behaviors such as the macho, overdomineering male and the quiet, unassuming mother do not seem effective in current American society.

Baumrind recommends that child-rearing practices should prevent girls from becoming unassertive and oversocialized; that is, too shy, supersensitive to others' feelings and too eager to please. Boys should be prevented from becoming destructively aggressive and undersocialized — that is, overassertive and overdomineering in peer groups, insensitive to other peoples' needs and uninterested in long-term friendships. At the same time, we should be very careful not to lose the nuturing qualities of girls or the confident assertiveness of boys. Although social change has occurred, women still bear and nurture the babies and men still function mostly as bread winners. If we can strengthen the possibly weak but needed qualities in both sexes, perhaps we can increase each child's power and effectiveness. Studies indicate that the types of power most parents have traditionally used with their boys and girls differ, and that this has an effect on the competence of children of both sexes. But the profound changes which have occurred demand that we take a hard look at tradition. What can parents do to help their children cope best with this, our "brave new world?"

Sex Roles In Modern Society

Traditions of many sorts have been largely abandoned. For example, massive changes have occurred in child-care during the 1970's and 1980's. More than half of all mothers work outside of the home. Single and divorced parents have markedly increased. The problems of day care, of latch key children, of reduced extended families, and those introduced by conflicts between outside careers and mothering careers have markedly raised the guilt and worry level of parents. There is increased need to find ways to parent better with less time. It may help to recognize that historically there have been somewhat similar problems. Pioneer women and farm women in America may have been home, but they worked as hard as the men and few had much time to spend coddling their children. However, they did demand that their children help with the chores and the farmwork. They were there to serve as a model and source of security. In the military, wives have forever acted as single parents a good portion of the time. The children survive, and most do well.

The Mother's Perspective

There has not been as much public debate about this profound change in family function as one would expect. The lack of commentary probably reflects the frustrations felt by so many who can see no simple solutions. In an article on Mother's Day by an editor of the popular *People Magazine,* a survey was reported in which 50% of working women said they felt cheated — that they were missing out on the best years of their kids' lives. At the same time, the great majority of stay-at-home mothers enjoy their children and are satisfied enough with their role that they would "do it over again" given the choice. Most working mothers have limited choice. In the article, women were asked if women were quitting their jobs to become full-time mothers. They reported,

> That is happening but only among women who can afford it. Most women work because they have to — they don't have a choice. What this trend does show is that we are gaining some perspective on the changes that have taken place during the past twenty years, when there has been a great intellectual and economic push for women to work. We're beginning to get a sense of the good things that were left behind.

So we have dedicated at-home mothers and dedicated mothers and fathers in the work force. All must deal with similar age-old challenges of raising children, plus relatively new problems and new demands. Drug and sexual abuse represent two major traps for today's children. At the same time, educational and future job challenges demand increased competence. The need for effective parenting has increased for both mothers who make a career outside of home and leave the children a large part of the day and for mothers who make a career at home, raising children. Parenting power and knowledge become invaluable. It takes a lot of power to give children enough protection, nurturing, education, demand and control, stimulation, confidence, competence, values, and time.

Parents should secure the most stable child-care situation possible. Ideally, one or the other parent, relative, or, at the least, a single stable day care mother should be with the child for the first three years of life. Frequent changes of caretakers tend to create insecurity, especially in children six to twelve months old. Whoever is with the child should heed the work of Dr. Burton White and make certain not only that the crawler/toddler has a safe world to explore and reasonable limits, but also receives enthusiastic respect from the "giants" in her world. Specific suggestions will be offered in Chapter XII, but one basic cannot be ignored — time. At the very least, mothers and fathers must devote at least a couple of hours nearly every day to model for, play with, teach, stimulate and enjoy their toddler.

Father's Expanding Role

As part of the team, fathers can meet some of the child's needs. Some may feel doubt and discomfort about their parenting abilities. It is not always easy for a man to admit that he may be afraid to take care of his baby, but in studies by Cowan and Cowan, where a group of new parents shared their experiences, their leader reported that "a father might reveal his initial feeling of terror until he was able to calm his screaming newborn when left alone with her for the first time. Much rueful laughter would follow, accompanied by comments of 'you too!' from others in the group."

The positive results of fathering make the effort worthwhile. Children raised by rational-authoritative parents, where the father demonstrates as much interest in the kids as the mother, will more likely turn out to be quite competent. Fathers who spend the necessary time and energy have that inescapable sense of pride and power which lets them brag, "That's my boy!"

Good fathering should begin at birth, but it's never too late. If the children are old enough, Dad can take them to work for an hour or so once in a while, or take them to the park; they can help Dad weed the garden or "help" him shop. Even simply taking the children out for a walk while Mom gets dinner, gives Dad an opportunity to listen to the children, play with them, and share their lives. Dr. Berry Brazelton writes for fathers in his book, *Working and Caring:*

... if you try it, you may like it. There's no substitute for seeing your child's early development with your own eyes and no greater sense of satisfaction than knowing you helped play an active role in it. Mothers have known this for millennia; now it's your turn. Enjoy!

Working Parents

If you are a working parent or a single parent, do not let your guilt feelings distort what time you have with your child. Do not overindulge just to make yourself feel better. Rather look at your child carefully and decide what strengths you need to improve. Use your power — challenge her, guide her, discipline her. Demonstrate love that way — not just by giving gifts or always trying to have "fun" to make up for the time you are away. Of course, you should take her to the park to play — but insist on improving her civilized behavior at the same time!

Most school age children have no problems with both their parents working, especially if they have a trustworthy someone to turn to after school. Latchkey children can do well if they are safe and if they are taught proper behavior and values. Kent State University Professor John Guidubaldi reported that: "Elementary-age children of working mothers scored better on IQ tests, were rated higher by teachers for academic achievement and were more adaptive and self-sufficient than children of stay-at-home mothers."

However, there are no studies of latchkey children which give the whole picture, and sweeping generalizations should not be made. Judge your own child's reactions and growth individually. The statistics don't matter. The jury is still out. A conference of experts on latch-key children has produced a booklet, "When School is Out and Nobody is Home."* There were intense emotional reactions on the part of some of the participants in the conference who do not like the idea of millions of school-age children fending for themselves. Others sympathized with the stresses of working parents and the dilemmas they face.

---

*The booklet, *When School is Out and Nobody is Home* by Coolsen, Seligson and Garbarino can be obtained from the National Committee for Prevention of Child Abuse, 332 South Michigan Avenue, Suite 950, Chicago, IL 60604-4357 for $4.50.

Children Can Grow From Self-Care

Some latchkey children, especially low-income city children, face risks. On the other hand, the older suburban child in a safe environment may benefit. Coolsen reports that being on one's own after school can be a positive rather than a negative influence, an opportunity rather than a risk. Challenge, in a positive "You are big enough and smart enough to take care of yourself" atmosphere, can be growth-inducing.

Self-care gives the child experience in the personal use of power. It helps strengthen the critical foundation skills needed by adolescents. But the need for parental monitoring continues. Close emotional attachment, even with adolescents, encourages their identity, their worth and their self-confidence. Routinely ask about the child's day and listen to and observe the child. It is a duty and pleasure which parents can impose on themselves and enjoy whether working outside the home or not.

Most children will thrive on the opportunity of self-care, others will just manage to cope or will be at risk; still others will be harmed. A study of Midwestern children found that less directly supervised children were more susceptible to peer pressure. Also, children raised by authoritarian or permissive parents succumbed to peer pressure more than children raised by rational-authoritative parents. This supports the findings that parents who use their power and authority rationally in raising their children — parents who ask children for their opinions, watch their activities closely, demand good behavior and maintain firm control while allowing adequate freedom — produce more competent children.

The same type of parenting has a positive effect on the grades of high school children. Stanford University Professor S.M. Dornbusch studied San Francisco Bay area high school students and found that the children of both authoritarian and permissive parents had poorer grades than the children of rational-authoritative parents. Inconsistent parenting (usually trials of authoritarianism mixed with other types of parenting) produced children with the lowest grades. It is important to note that more single mothers and single fathers were permissive than married parents, and their children had lower grades. This challenges single parents to look carefully at their methods of parenting.

Increased Peer Pressure

Children in the adolescent period are especially susceptible to peer pressure and at risk for experimenting with drugs and sex. Parental absence, physically or psychologically, increases these risks. Presidential advisor and pediatrician Donald Ian Macdonald of the Federal Alcohol, Drug Abuse and Mental Health Administration says that youngsters at high risk of alcohol abuse include those where there is "excessive permissiveness, or, conversely, very severe discipline and little parental praise...a lack of strong bonds to family, school, church, and other conventional social institutions, producing a sense of no direction."

When parents are absent or unattentive, children frequently turn to peers or other adults for support and love. To earn that support and love they may adopt the attitudes and values of those around them in order to ingratiate themselves. This makes it especially important to parent in a manner which will help your child develop good values and the power to say "No" to peer pressure or to adults with values different from yours. That "No" is the magic word which can help him avoid drugs, premature sex, crime and troubles of many sorts. This means you need to help your child develop her own powers, to be assertive about her values. Children without the power of self-confidence are vulnerable. For instance, adolescent specialists have found that young girls who become pregnant usually had a low self-image. Judith S. Musick, Ph.D., executive director of the Ounce of Prevention Fund of the Illinois Department of Children and Family Services, reports in a recent study that "some girls don't know how to say 'no' to their boyfriends because they never learned to say 'no' to the significant men in their lives."

The Danger of Sexual Abuse

Sexual abuse can be imposed by peers, siblings or adults. A series of news articles using court records and transcripts about sex abuse reported the case of 41-year-old Charles who estimated that he had molested sixty children. He stated, "I find these kids from unhappy homes. And I have a way of becoming friends with kids immediately. I'll listen to them when they want to talk, all the things their parents won't do . . . I like having sex when I want it, being in complete control of the situation."

Several lessons can be learned from Charles. First, he listens to the children — makes them believe that he respects and likes them. Second, children who feel important enough to be listened to by an adult are more likely to do things for that adult. Third, child sex abusers want children they can control. This usually means powerless children with low self-esteem who are unassertive and lack confidence in themselves and their values.

In order to resist sexual advances, children must understand their values and feel powerful enough on their own to hold to them. This means children need the practice of standing up for themselves, even when being confronted by their parents. They must be sufficiently respected for their parents to listen to their opinions. They also require specific education from parents they respect and trust about the taboos required to hold together our basically hedonistic society. Children benefit from close supervision and require parental time and attention.

Children must develop self-confidence, assertiveness and competencies to be able to resist unwise temptations or escape dangerous situations. Parents can help build these characteristics in their children by rational-authoritative parenting.

Rational-Authoritative Parenting

It appears that we can best meet today's tough challenges by becoming firm rational-authoritative parents. Such parenting has been shown to be statistically associated with children who develop high self-esteem. This self-esteem includes a sense of "can do!" a sense of power, security and respect engendered by firm parenting. Set clear limits and demand good behavior. Rational parents also make a point of listening carefully to the child's side of the story when those limits are transgressed. They follow through and *act;* they don't just talk and scold.

Rational parents are in charge without question, yet will allow the child to win an argument if he has a good case. The self-confidence of this type of parent encourages creativity in the child as well as the willingness to explore new situations and the confidence needed to say "no" to temptation. Young adults need such characteristics to tackle the problems of our world in an effective way. Some of this comes from the child's respect of his parent's power and the desire to be like the respected/loved parent. Much of it comes from the experience of using power as a child.

Go beyond discipline and give your child the opportunity and freedom to be himself, to succeed or fail on his own. Give him enough elbow room to develop his own unique powers. Granted, all this is not easy, but if you are not a perfect parent don't let it "get you down." Perfect parents often make it difficult for children. The child's self-esteem may suffer from his inability to live up to the perfect model. Maybe this explains why some children raised by "impossible," incapable or absent parents grow up to be such successful people, while other children raised by "perfect" parents — psychologists, ministers, doctors, and so on, turn out to have relatively poor self-esteem and become social failures. On the other hand, rational-authoritative parents need not be perfect. By allowing the child to interract and offer opinions, the burden of making the best decision does not sit solely on the parent's shoulders. Together, the parent and child have a system of checks and balances that is superior to any one person's judgment — no matter how perfect that one person may be.

Guidelines for Parents

Whatever your parental style or situation, important lessons can be learned from various successful and unsuccessful parenting experiences, professional observations and research. The guidelines for parents in Table VII may help you improve your parenting skills. Obviously it is easier to lay down dictums than to actually follow such advice. The remainder of this book will explain how parents can use such guidelines to establish rational-authoritative control and support both for themselves and for their children.

Table VII

GUIDELINES FOR PARENTS

1. Each parent brings into his or her role their inner child of the past which may or may not make it easy to become a rational parent. It helps to look dispassionately at your past and learn to control your emotional reactions so you can function authoritatively (as a team with your spouse or as a single parent) and meet the needs of each of your children.

2. Successful parents flexibly balance parental power requirements and the need to control with the individual childs' need for power and freedom. Each child's personality and abilities differ and these differences should be respected.

3. Parents have both the power and the duty to give to and expect of their children. This power to support, protect and encourage your child should be balanced with your power to control, demand and teach.

4. The distribution of power must shift from parent to child as the child matures. Allow your child to develop and experience his own power. He needs elbow room. He needs to learn to say "no" — even to his parents.

5. Each child has a unique personality and an individual melange of strengths and weaknesses, of potentials and of problems. An on-going assessment of how the child is developing helps parents guide the child to use his strengths and cope with his areas of weakness.

6. Parents have the innate power to rationally control themselves and their children. To use this power properly you need an understanding about your own strengths and weaknesses, as well as knowledge about how to raise your child.

7. Much of the advice you get, even from the "experts," will be contradictory. Parenting is an art. As psychologist Steven Pulos so aptly put it to me, "The opinions and findings of the various experts are like the paints on a pallette — yours to use along with your own experiences to produce the best results you can for you and your particular child."

8. Your goals for your child should be high while realistically reflecting his abilities and taking into account the demands of his environment. Believe in him so he will believe in himself.

9. Your child's self-esteem requires that you respect his own desires, temperament and personality while you demand that he try to succeed academically, socially and ethically.

10. Parents should insist that children do their share at home and learn to work with and contribute to the family and society.

11. Explain the reasons for the ethics and principles you live by and value, and encourage your child to adopt them as his own.

12. When disciplining your child explain the reasons for your actions without apology.

13. Teach your child the realities and limits of life in your society while you offer hope that he will develop the power to constructively expand these limits.

14. Give your child security by the consistency of your love, your interest in him, your rules and limitations, your faith in his future, and your self-control.

15. Use fair rational-authoritative discipline which allows your child to make as many of his own choices as possible, and let him experience the logical consequences.

16. Teach your child to deal with adversity by allowing him to succeed or fail on his own. Teach him that it is rewarding to attempt high goals whether he succeeds or not.

17. Demonstrate, by your own behavior, the rewards of helping others and improving oneself. Emphasize our responsibility to others.

18. Help your child to understand diversity and, when possible, to show respect and tolerance for others.

19. Respond to your child's good behavior with love and respect. Respond to your child's bad behavior by withdrawal of privileges and demands for better behavior.

20. Learn to control both your love and your anger so you neither overindulge nor overpower your child.

21. Admit to your child that parents are not perfect and that you are open to his well-reasoned opinions about his life.

22. Use your powers to reward and punish your child carefully and in a balanced way.

23. Try to understand your child's feelings, abilities, strengths and weaknesses and take pride in both your parenting efforts and his development.

Moral internalization is the learning process by which children come to adhere to society's rules even when they are free of external surveillance or the expectations of rewards or punishments from socializing agents.

David G. Perry and
Louise C. Perry
Social Learning, Causal Attribution and
Moral Internalization

VI

The Power of Values and Self-Control

"Give me your children and I will have your world" was the underlying message of Hitler when he formed the Hitler Youth Corps in Nazi Germany. Impressionable children assimilate values which they then adopt as their own. In the ethnic melting pot of democracy in the United States, conflicting values are the norm. Our ability to resolve these conflicts, to accept a common social platform, enables our civilization to exist, prosper and progress. While we may not have a Hitler, many other forces compete for the attention and future of our children. The power inherent in the media seems immense and sometimes excessively negative and misguided. Cults, drugs, and hedonism entice our children. Somehow in the face of all this competition, parents, bless them, still generally manage to give their children meaningful values.

Most parents want their children to share their personal values and convictions. But if the family structure is not strong and protective enough, the children can be lost on a kaleidoscope of shifting sands of change. Parents also need assurance about the values of other individuals who take care of children: teachers and principals in the schools, and the organizations to which we entrust our children, be it the Boy Scouts, Bluebirds, Little League or high school bands.

When a child grows up in a stable small town with an accepted common religious and ethnic basis, adolescent rebellion seldom occurs. The young people securely tread a defined path. Some families move out of urban areas so their children will grow up in a predictable, manageable and emotionally healthier environment — often with good results. However, job imperatives prevent most of us from moving. This challenges families, whether they be single parents or the traditional nuclear couple, to ensure that their children understand solid values and learn the self-control necessary to live up to their values. The child must learn how to confidently and rationally deal with the morass of conflicting ideas in our society.

Ethical Influences

Involving the family in a religion is one traditional and often effective method of handling the value question. We have a large choice in America. Whether or not you are religious, it might be well to make certain that your child goes to the church or synagogue of your choice long enough to determine if he finds it acceptable. Of course, you need to approve of the values and guidance offered him. At the very least, it gives your child a needed experience and exposure to an important facet of society. Historically our social values have been largely based on the Judeo-Christian ethic. This is now being increasingly modified by the influence of other religions brought in by fresh waves of immigrants.

If you choose to avoid religious exposure for your children, then consider "nonreligious" organizations such as the Girl Scouts or Boy Scouts of America. They offer basic ethical guidelines to help protect a child's values during transition from family to the world. However, the major value system which will affect your child is yours — if you live up to your values in everyday life. It can be confidently said that the way you act, the way you are, has the most powerful affect of all on your child.

The Parent as Primary Value-Giver

From the biblical injunction of "Spare the Rod and Spoil the Child" to the advice of modern humanist philosophers, parents are told how to use or not use their power to teach children values. But before you use your power, you need to decide what values to teach. Then, whatever your values, you need more than simple acceptance by your child. Children need to put cherished values into practice now and when they become adults.

If parents force a child to behave in a certain way, what occurs when the parents are gone? Some interesting research in the fields of child development, educational psychology and animal studies has been done on this subject. Researchers express differing views but the psychology team of Perry and Perry offers this advice:

> "Effective socialization begins by imparting to the child a clear understanding of proper and improper behavior and by requiring the child to conform behaviorally to these standards. Almost certainly this will frequently entail external control."

If the child accepts external control, willingly or unwillingly, repetitive behavior seems to become accepted as normal. The child has "internalized" the value, accepting it as the correct way to believe and act. Part of the difficulty faced by parents in attempting to inculcate values involves how much control they should exert and how to use the right amount of reward or punishment. Psychologist Coopersmith found that 80% of the mothers of children with high self-esteem felt that reward was more effective than punishment, while 52% of mothers of children with low self-esteem thought punishment more effective. Aside from the punishment aspect, we are creatures of habit. A child habitually permitted to disobey becomes convinced that disobedience is normal.

Most psychologists agree that the child who receives only mild punishment will more likely internalize a value than a child who receives severe punishment. Also, too much parental control interferes with the child's developing self-control. Parental attempts to overpower the child represent a lack of respect for the child. Overuse of power in place of reason encourages resistance. *The more powerful the reward or punishment used to induce a child to do something, the greater the resistance.* If overpowered, the child is likely to believe that what he is being asked to do is either boring or unpleasant. In other words, really "hard sells" may be counterproductive. This does not necessarily mean that the child feels the value is unworthy. Rather, the child resents parental manipulation and lack of respect, so that he no longer examines the value on its own merit.

Psychologist Lepper studied second grade children who initially resisted the temptation to play with a forbidden toy under the threat of either mild or severe punishment. Later tested for honesty, mildly threatened children cheated less than did severely threatened children. In essence, the power to teach children moral behavior must be carefully rationed and not overused.

Modeling Teaches Values

Further research shows that providing the child with a model for a certain value produces better long-term behavior. Two groups of children were given pennies for completing a certain task. Researchers showed one group a model demonstration of the "good" child who would give back the pennies if he did not complete the task. The other group was simply instructed to give the pennies back if they did not complete the task. The freedom and power to judge, to decide to be "good" like the model child evidently had more of a long-term effect than did the direct instruction to put the pennies back. Direct instruction is an exercise of adult power, not the child's power to choose.

Consensus is another mechanism which can be used to get children to mind. If "everybody does it" the child will more likely do it. Researchers punished children for touching a forbidden toy by scolding and told one group, "All the other kids didn't touch the toy." They said nothing to the second group about the "other kids." Most of the first group (those told that the other children acted "good") behaved better later. This illustrates a form of reasoning and consensus motivation.

In another experiment, researchers would catch children not obeying instructions and confront, criticize and upset them. Then they would tell one group, "You are upset because you feel that what you did was wrong" and the second group, "You are upset because you were caught." Later, when there was little likelihood of being caught for the same disobedience, the children in the first group disobeyed less than the children in the second group. Children tend to live up to an adult's expectations. A parent may increase the potential for future good behavior by saying, "You did that because you are that kind of person; you care about people."

Interestingly enough, children tend to forget that their behavior was induced by someone else. Instead they feel that they responded to their own power of reason rather than to the direct teaching power of the parent. You can get a lot done if you do not mind who gets the credit.

Reasoning Gives the Child Power

Investigators also found that when adults accompanied their punishment for misbehavior with verbal explanations as to why the behavior was bad, later those children misbehaved less than did children who were punished without an explanation. Reasoning reduces the child's perception that the parent's use of power was the issue, and makes a power struggle with the parent less likely. It reduces the need to fight in an attempt to retain self-respect. But for reasoning to be effective it helps to have the child settled down and in a listening mood. Understandably one may not listen well when upset or distracted. Also, harsh, scornful or sanctimonious scolding tends to "turn off" the child and he rejects the words of wisdom because of the adult attitude. Keep in mind that one man's reasoning is another's soapbox!

At the same time other researchers observed that,

> Reasoning is unlikely to be effective unless parents teach their children that they "mean business" when reasoning with them. Research confirms that parents who are the most effective "reasoners" are those who back up their words with action and firm enforcement — even physical punishment, if necessary.

This was not meant to imply that reasoning should always be accompanied by a demonstration of parental power — especially if the child understands from past experience that the parent has and will use power if reasoning does not work. Reasoning works best when the parent is decisive, clear and consistent with instructions, yet not too "pushy." It may often be best to let the child decide whether he will mind or take the consequences. Then, if need be, parents must enforce the consequences of not minding.

Exercising Direct Control

While the techniques cited above can help parents instill values into their children, more direct use of power also gets results. Both Coopersmith's and Baumrind's work demonstrate that powerful firm control, with clear limits, produces more moral children. For example, the most "altruistic" preschoolers were the ones who had been scolded by their mothers when they did not help others. The message was, "You have no choice but to help others. It is very important that you do help others. I will not tolerate your not helping others!" Here the mother clearly punishes by scolding, thereby implying that she has power to punish even more if the child does not obey.

Observation and research indicate that parents can teach their children values and behavior which will be internalized. Such values would guide the child whether or not the parent or policeman is watching. It starts when little children are naughty within earshot of their mothers. Convinced that no one is watching, that no one knows — they are still caught, and punished. Apparently, this persuades small children that parents have the remarkable power to always know when they misbehave, so the child is then motivated to control himself.*

Be Powerful and Consistent

All of the techniques to enforce proper behavior and instill positive values require unwavering, consistent, and often subtle use of parental power. So if you really want your child to behave in a certain way, then mean what you say and always follow through with either reward or punishment. Act! Otherwise, your words will lose much of their power. By forcing your child to behave, while providing a clear explanation of why he must behave, you will convince him to accept your power and believe your word. Evidence demonstrates that forceful insistence on good behavior promotes good behavior.

---

*It takes time to learn to lie. University of Southern California researchers noted that children under the age of nine years give themselves away with nonverbal signs: voices rising in pitch, increasing blinking, dilation of pupils, moving of legs and feet, many "ah's," pauses between words, and many "you know's".

Most children respond best when they are convinced that the parent is not just on a power trip to show who is boss, but rather is simply trying to get the child to behave in her own best interest. This requires that the power used by the parent must be balanced with respect and affection for the child. Baumrind noted that harmonious parents, "recognized differences based upon knowledge and personality, and tried to create an environment in which all family members could operate from the same vantage point, one in which the recognized differences in power did not put the child at a disadvantage."

Table VIII

HOW TO HELP YOUR CHILD DEVELOP A SENSE OF RESPONSIBILITY

1. *Offer a good example* by helping others, completing tasks, living your good values, being honest and trustworthy, following good leaders, leading good followers.

2. *Expose him to others who behave admirably and responsibly.*

3. *Demand good behavior.* Establish and consistently enforce rules of good behavior. Contract with him and give rewards for good behavior, but withhold rewards for bad behavior. When necessary, use punishment to force proper behavior.

4. *Control your child's behavior and insist on responsible behavior* by consistently punishing irresponsible behavior and rewarding responsible behavior.

5. *Establish repetitive habits of good behavior by consistent rational control and firmness.* This gives him experience in acting properly which tends to become ingrained, assuring future habitual good behavior.

6. *Offer the child a positive image of herself.* Tell her that she is a responsible and trustworthy person and point out the innate reward of respect she will receive by behaving accordingly.

7. *Insist that he help with necessary family chores without any more pay than the rest of the family receives for similar services.* This shows respect for him and allows him a sense of belonging.

8. *Let him share in the planning and outcome of family decisions.* Start with minor choices when he is young and as he matures increase his voice in major decisions.

9. *Encourage him to complete his tasks* by giving the contracted reward for his services *only* when the task is completed.

Catherine Lewis has challenged Baumrind's interpretation of the data on rational-authoritative parents. She notes that such parents tend to." . . . withdraw demands after being convinced by the child's argument. . . ." and argues that this may be more important than the parental tendency to clearly demarcate and firmly enforce rules. Baumrind, on the other hand, believes that the great self-confidence of rational-authoritative parents requires them to issue few maxims. They recognize the complexity of social interaction and use their intelligence to deal flexibly with their children. In the process, they grant power and respect to the child without surrendering any of their own power.

In my view, children raised by rational-authoritative parents mind because they know that their parents are powerful enough to demand obedience. Therefore, the children do not challenge them as often. This leads to a good social conscience by direct teaching and respect for the parent's power. Smart parents do not have to punish very much because they have convinced the child in the past that the parent will punish if necessary. Yet such parents respect the child enough to listen to the child's reasoning. The parent does not lose if the child wins — indeed, the child's winning demonstrates parental sagacity.

PART II

Power and Love:
The Tools

Parents need to understand clearly the differences between hurting and retaliation, and teaching through discipline and punishment; they need to examine how to resist exerting either power or authority for its own sake, rather than as a tool for the edification and education of the child.

Forman, Kerachbaum, Hetzneke, and Dunn
"Socialization, Discipline and Punishment"
Nelson Textbook of Pediatrics

VII

The Power of Reward and Punishment

In raising children, when it comes to choosing between the carrot and the stick, I prefer the carrot. Honey does catch more flies than vinegar. Being a parent allows you the pleasure of rewarding your child, one of the happier duties in life. Rewards make people of any age happy. Especially rewards that have been earned. Just having a child may be reward enough for many parents, and having parents who love them can be reward enough for many children. But it takes more than love to prepare your child for life. Adequate preparation requires motivation, hard work and, at times, unpleasant duties for the child — like washing behind the ears, going to school, and learning that society demands even more.

Reward and punishment motivate. But not always. Rewards do not always work. So before we look at the various types of rewards, let us first see if we can figure out why rewards sometimes fail to motivate children to behave in the way we desire.

Rewards Can Fail

First, the reward must fit the particular child. Rewards which appeal to an adult or to one child may be insignificant to another.

The 10-year-old boys nervously flexed their muscles as they stood on the starting blocks waiting to compete in the free-style race at the community pool. Jake smiled at Sean, poised next to him, and hoped he could at least keep close to him in the race. Sean was the best swimmer in the club for that age group. Jake badly wanted to have Sean for a friend and to win his admiration.

The boys settled down into position and dove at the sound of the starter's gun. Jake desperately tried to stretch his arms out fully, as the coach had shown him, so he could keep close to Sean. As he struggled he became aware of his mother running alongside the pool screaming at him, "Jake, try harder! If you win, I'll give you twenty-dollars. Try harder!" Jake was mortified. The other parents, sitting back from the pool edge, were at first astounded and then a little angry. Sean heard Jake's mother and angrily pushed harder to win the race. Poor Jake not only did not win, he would have lost if he had won.

The incident about Jake is real, even if his name is not. Had he won, his mother would have been the victor. Jake would have been bribed to reward his mother. Jake lost what he really wanted, the friendship of his hero Sean. When we think of rewards, it pays to put ourselves in the shoes of the child or youth we want to reward and try to understand his desires.

Sometimes even appropriate rewards do not work. A good reward can fail because the parent uses it for the wrong reason, such as trying to force good behavior. Rewards used to overpower the child, or to please the parent, frequently do not work. Parents may be startled at the confusion over who really gets the reward, but children are more perceptive. If the parent wants to pay them to act in a certain way, and they do, then the parent wins. Does the child win? It probably depends upon his pre-existing attitude which, in turn, often depends upon whether his parents respect him enough to allow him to make some of his own choices. In a harmonious family where the child both loves and respects the parent, the child may behave in an approved way to please the parent. In a squabbling family the child may perversely act just the opposite to thwart the parent. When "winning for Mother" becomes the issue, the child may feel he loses in a power struggle if she wins. Then the reward will not compensate him for his loss.

Worthwhile rewards may also create problems. Some children feel guilty and unworthy of a reward. For children with low self-esteem, a reward may imply demands which they do not feel capable of meeting. Too much attention feels uncomfortable. As a result, some children who receive praise withdraw. If the child does respond, he may feel manipulated by the power of praise.

Reward vs. Bribery

Rewards are easily confused with bribery. Even a well-meant reward may appear to be a power attempt to buy "good" behavior. Jake's mother wanted him to win far more than Jake himself did, and in her anxiety she offered him an inappropriate reward. Many parents do not realize that when they say, "You are a good girl!" they are really saying, "You are good for me!" Direct praise often contains the hidden message, "I want you to be good. You had *better* be good. Or else!"

It is not wrong to tell a child she is good, but the child needs to be good for herself. Most children want to please Mom and Dad and appreciate praise, but if the child realizes her actions may reward the parent more than herself, she may feel resentful or used. Because children are often volatile and negative, she may not want to reward the parent. By refusing to reward the parent by being "good," she can demonstrate both her displeasure and her power. Thus direct praise, perceived as an implied power demand, may lead to a power struggle rather than the desired behavior.

Power of Praise and Respect

Praise can be divided into two types: praise for you as a person or praise for what you produce. Both have value but most of us would rather be praised for what we are. Would you rather be thought of as a good worker or a wonderful person? Would a wife prefer a husband to praise her housekeeping or smile at her and comment on what good company she is? Children, too, want to be appreciated for themselves.

It is fine to praise grades; however, it may be more effective to say to Father in Mary's presence, "Remember when Mary was talking with Mrs. Jones the other day? Afterwards Mrs. Jones told me that she couldn't get over how fast Mary has grown and how sophisticated she has become.

She said that she bets Mary is a super student. So naturally I told her she was right!" Parental praise strengthens the child's feeling of being loved and important. It helps build the self-esteem that is so important in motivation. Such praise can be used effectively even with the unproductive child. It helps build a base of self-esteem that ultimately leads to production.

I once asked a contented straight-A high school student why he wanted to be a straight-A student. He replied, "I want to please my folks." In a harmonious family a child may be more than willing to please his parents with good behavior. Likewise, parents are pleased by their child's successes, and should show it. In the above case, the boy's folks had made it clear that his success pleased them because it was good for the boy himself. Mutual respect and a rational power balance is the key.

Do not spoil your praise by trying to use it as a method of buying good behavior. Instead, motivate your child by indirectly demonstrating that you respect her. For example, when talking on the telephone with grandmother, mention some of your child's positive virtues. Do it "by chance" in the child's hearing. You might say, "Mary's teacher told me that Mary is one of the best liked children in her class — and one of the best students!" Or, "It really helped today when Mary cleaned up the kitchen. I was so busy working on our taxes that I couldn't get to it." Sooner or later Mary's ears will pick up at her name and the conversation will capture her attention. When she hears objective, truly non-demanding praise, it becomes praise without strings.

Praise indicates admiration and respect. We all desire the reward of respect and need it to feed our self-esteem and build our confidence. Respect honors our worth or our power — a potent reward to bestow on our children, certainly one of the most valuable. It helps the belief-in-self which powers the mobilization of all of one's energy, drive and talents.

Love as Reward

The child's reaction to parental love, as with praise, can sometimes confound parents. Love can reward, but it may be misunderstood by either the giver or the recipient. Love is certainly a powerful feeling which keeps the world going around. And love bonds parent and child. However, unless it is mutual or helps the loved one in some way, love may not be the reward many imagine. In fact, to be loved by someone you do not like can be a rather unpleasant experience. It becomes a demand rather than a reward.

Some parents love their children so much that they smother them and deny them the freedom to develop other rewarding relationships — or other loves. Jealous love can almost become a form of punishment. We should recognize clearly that the feeling of love in the lover rewards the lover. Certainly it can reward the loved one — if the loved one wants the love. "To bask in your love is paradise." However, reciprocal love doesn't always exist — even in parent/child relationships. Power without love can be a form of tyranny in child-raising, and love which does not recognize the needs of the child can be another form of tyranny. Pure parental love is unconditional, not just to be given in response to good behavior or in return for your child's love.

If you love only in response to the child's "good" behavior, then you love what the child produces, the way she acts — not the child. It seems rather crass to use the gift of love to get the person to produce something you want. Perhaps this feeling explains the traditional social abhorrence of prostitution. Buying "love" is bribery.

Appropriate Rewards

Rewards should be not only sincere, but also appropriate. Too small a reward can create hurt and resentment. An undeserved or excessive reward can make some people uncomfortable. An appropriate reward used as honest pay induces positive future behavior in children (and adults). A reward seen as a tool to manipulate behavior will be less valued. The reward should be deserved. It should indicate respect.

Table IX

TYPES OF REWARDS

A. Security and Love
B. Respect and Power
C. Privileges and Freedom
D. Tangible items, including money

Rewards obviously need to be tailored to the age of the child. In the first years, parents usually react instinctively and give the baby the needed support, attention and time. They respect and attend to Baby's powerful cry and smile. Her first word produces applause, evidence of parental pleasure and pride. The reward of getting positive attention for a word tunes the baby to the power of speech. On the other hand, I often see parental pleasure, pride and applause in response to a burp — and wonder what on earth the baby thinks about that!

In addition to respecting your child's individual personality, you will later respect the child's growing signs of maturity. These include her efforts at developing her talents, and her attempts to live up to laudable values. Naturally, our expectations for behavior change with the age of the child. We praise a burp from a five-month-old and criticize a belch from a five-year-old who is older, stronger and more in control of his bodily functions. But regardless of age, we help our children develop more effectively when we respect them and appreciate their developing powers.

Privileges as Reward

Granting privileges for mature behavior can be quite effective. Privileges that can be given or withdrawn might include freedom, job opportunities, decision-making power, use of the family car or telephone, and so on. The type of privilege depends on the child's age. For a three-year-old, the privilege of playing in the front yard when he isn't in diapers has great significance and for a seven-year-old, staying up a half-hour later at night when he keeps his room clean indicates respect. The twelve-year-old might appreciate being included in family conferences when he has demonstrated the maturity to do well in school.

How the parents grant a privilege may be of more importance than the privilege itself. Privileges used as a reward for pleasing the parents are not as valuable as privileges granted because the child has clearly earned them by demonstrating mature behavior. Rewards should not depend upon the current mood of the parent but should be given dependably and consistently when the child carries out his part of a task. In other words, the rewards should be earned by the child, not just granted when the parent happens to feel good.

Privileges can extend to earning money and owning material possessions. This variety of reward works best when it is not used to manipulate the child or to buy good behavior. While most children must be forced into certain behavior patterns at times, try to avoid making a reward seem like a bribe or parental power play designed to force good behavior. Instead, let the child have the opportunity to earn a privilege as the reward for good behavior.

I have always been uncomfortable with using money as a reward. Good behavior should generally result in the rewards of respect and power, of freedom and privileges, and of security and love rather than money. Yet, admittedly most adult effort seems to go into earning money. Money allows one the power to do many things, to buy many items, and to increase security. Children should be given the opportunity to earn money, but money and material items are best earned by some sort of productive work.

Recognition as Reward

For young children you can give tokens or mark "brownie" points on charts, leading to a reward. The concept of giving special recognition, of giving medals, is as old as mankind yet many of us do not use this effective reward mechanism for our kids. Recognition can be given in many innovative ways. But however you do it, recognition and attention should be given on a day-to-day basis. We all need this feedback from the people around us to encourage us to "keep up the good work."

As adults most of us measure our rewards partly by the amount of money we are paid for a service. Naturally we have other rewards which help motivate. Some are rewarded simply by the relief of guilt when they have completed a task responsibly. A mature reward is the feeling that we have, in good conscience, done the very best we could. But we still have to deal with the concept of adult tokens usually given as rewards for services and goods; the primary one being money. Money represents an I.O.U., a token of appreciation, or the ultimate recognition for a job completed. Inevitably, we use money — consciously or not — to reward or motivate our children. So as we use it, let us keep in mind that the bottom line of rewards for children is teaching. One of the basics we need to teach is how to use money well — earning, handling, and spending money responsibly is an essential part of growing up. The sense of power a child gains from this knowledge is a reward in itself. Rational-authoritative parents do not just give a child money to make him feel good. Instead, when the child wants money, they use this desire to teach him some basic lessons.

> Doug, age 12, had inherited his older brother's bike, but he badly wanted a new three-speed model. He asked his parents for a new bike. Instead of giving him a bike or promising one, they said that if he would earn money outside of the home, they would put up one dollar for every two dollars he saved.
>
> "You are getting old enough to help around the house without an allowance now, Doug," his father said. "If you want to earn money, why don't you see if you can get some jobs mowing the neighbors' lawns? You are doing a good job on our lawn so you are able to offer good service. Of course, since you're on your way to growing up, it's time you set up two savings accounts. Put 25% of what you earn into an account that won't be touched until you go to college. We will both have to sign to get the money out. It will earn a lot of interest and will be a big help to you later.
>
> You are also old enough to begin taking care of some of your own needs. Put another 25% of your earnings into a second savings account and use it for clothes you want and need. Then, keep the remaining 50% in your drawer and when you have two-thirds of the money needed for your three-speed bike, I will put up the other third. Maybe you had better talk to the clerk at the bike store and find out how much the bike you want will cost, and how much the tax will be, so you can tell me when you have enough."

Doug got several neighbors to let him mow their lawns. It was hard work pushing the hand-mower, but he kept it up. He began to appreciate the value of money and the reward of work. But, like most people, he wondered if there were not easier ways to earn money. He started looking for other sources of funds.

> Doug's mother read a magazine article about do-it-yourself "squirrel" doorstops. She showed the article to Doug and remarked on how easy it would be to make them out of old in-

nertubes, a brick and some cotton. Doug asked, "How much do you think these would cost in a store?"

"Oh, probably five or ten dollars," Mother said. Doug thought it over and enthusiastically began, with Mother's help, to make the doorstops. He managed to sell fourteen of them door-to-door before Mother said she couldn't spend any more time on this project. But by then Doug had collected $140.00 on the doorstops and had made $35. mowing lawns. He put $43. into his college fund and spent $39. for a jacket he liked. The remaining $93. in his drawer was enough to cover two-thirds of the cost of the three-speed bike, and Dad contributed the final third as he had promised. When Doug purchased the bike, his reward was not all tangible — he had also gained a great sense of pride, accomplishment, and responsibility, as well as developing entrepreneurial skills. But the best reward was the respect of his parents, neighbors, and friends.

To gain what you desire for or from your child, rewards work better than punishment. Begin with rewards, explaining why you insist on certain behavior or certain accomplishments. In this way you will not have to punish as much.

Punishment and Power

The necessity of punishment engenders much debate, and many hard feelings. The varied types and degrees of punishment can create vastly different outcomes. The authoritarian parent often punishes harshly, while the permissive parent usually does not punish at all. Practically every professional involved with children objects to harsh punishment, and psychiatrists treating mixed-up adults testify to the problems created by harsh punishment in childhood. But they also point to problems created by permissive, overindulging parents. Is there a middle ground? Can we reconcile love and punishment?

Most parents punish because they have to; otherwise they have no way of controlling most children. They punish because they love the child and must teach him to obey. Obedience allows the parent to protect the child and teach him how to live in society. Punishment under these circumstances is done in the child's best interest. As such, punishment should not damage self-esteem because healthy emotional growth is essential to motivation and the development of one's character and talents.

If we expect our children to become competent, adjusted adults, then we may benefit from the wisdom of a line in a church hymn: "And we'll guard each man's dignity and save each man's pride." Children have pride and the need to develop dignity too! Thus when we do have to punish we should keep in mind this long-term goal and avoid compounding the punishment by scorning, scolding or denigrating the child.

All discipline is not good discipline; all punishment is not effective punishment. Effective discipline or punishment requires parental self-control. As a start, no one should be punished unless one has broken the law; one should not be punished simply because the policeman has had a bad day. As adults we insist on laws that clearly show our responsibilities and rights, as well as the consequences for breaking a law. Even when punished for breaking the law, people usually try to retain pride and dignity. They accept the fact that they made an unwise choice and understand that they have to live with the consequences.

Likewise, punishment should be given only for those "crimes" where the child had a choice and a clear idea of the consequences beforehand. Then when punishment is completed, the parent should follow through with the power of love. Through punishment the debt is paid; let the child start fresh. Give him a hug and buttress his self-esteem with positive attention.

The attitude of the punisher overshadows the significance of the kind of punishment. For example, a study showed that 63% of affectionate mothers judged physical punishment to be effective, but only 43% of unaffectionate mothers judged their physical punishment effective. Evidently many children of unaffectionate mothers interpreted the spanking as simply more evidence of the mother's dislike.

Is punishment really effective in controlling children? Can it help their development or, as some contend, is it the root cause of much of society's problems? These questions bother society. Corporal punishment is now outlawed in most schools and recommendations against corporal punishment by parents abound (even though 87% of parents spank their children). Those who see the terrible results of child abuse try to protect children by laws and education. However, physical abuse rarely occurs in my practice but punishment is common.

Early psychologists thought punishment essential and inescapable. James Baker, author of *Elementary Psychology*, published in 1891, wrote: "It is not enough to let the child grow without restraint as a spontaneous product of nature — he might yield to some undesirable hereditary tendency or develop the nature of an untrained savage."

Psychology professor Victor B. Cline of the University of Utah writes in his book *How to Make Your Child a Winner:*

> A major disaster occurred in a large number of American families, starting in the 1950's. Called by many names — most frequently "permissiveness" — and "family democracy" — it was a noble experiment, based on the mistaken notion that young children are basically wise and good and perfectly able to determine their own destinies.... But the result was a generation of children who tended to be ungrateful, demanding, directionless, self-indulgent with alcohol, sex and drugs — and who later found difficulty staying married.

Pragmatic research psychologists using controlled observations of what actually happens to children raised in different ways, agree that harsh or excessive punishment inhibits the development of conscience, or moral values. But in Baumrind's studies of preschool children, moderate punitive discipline was not correlated with unsocialized or rebellious behavior. These studies seem to indicate that parents must use punishment to raise children who will be competent and moral adults.

Successful Parents Use Punishment

The Harvard studies of Burton White revealed that most successful parents did use punishment to control their children in the first three years of life. Firm limits were set. In an extension of White's work, the State of Missouri Department of Elementary and Secondary Education established a program to help new parents raise their children during the first three years of life. This New Parents as Teachers (N.P.A.T.) Project sent teachers to the homes of new parents to teach them improved techniques of child-rearing. The results confirmed White's findings. Children raised by parents who controlled, but balanced their control by allowing the child freedom to develop his own powers and talents, had a higher learning capacity and IQ than children of parents not given this education.

In the N.P.A.T. Project, respect, freedom and power were used as rewards to induce "good" behavior. But how about punishment? The advice given to parents in the project was to convince their children that they "mean business." Just how the parent should convince the child that the parent has the power to control and will use it, the project syllabus did not directly say. (Public agencies probably cannot legally advise spanking.) However, they did quote Burton White, who insists that parents must use a "loving but firm hand." He states that overindulgence creates the most difficulty and says, in effect, that even if you spank your child regularly they will still love you. His research teams observed that two-thirds of the effective families spanked their children. We will discuss spanking in more detail in subsequent chapters.

"There is a universality of punishment," write psychologists Gary C. Walters and Joan E. Grusec. They point out that there has been a lack of serious, systematic study of punishment because "the subject is unaesthetic and unattractive." However, they gathered enough material from their research to complete a book on the subject entitled *Punishment*. They observe that the research "leads us to an inescapable conclusion: punishment will always be a necessary tool of behavioral change."

Rewards alone do not seem to succeed for most, and children must learn to control lying, cheating, stealing, aggression and other impulses. Parents must prepare their children for group living — they must use their powers to civilize their progeny. Although it probably takes about 100 years to truly civilize a person, if a young person is not well on his way to civilized behavior when he or she leaves home, the law and the police will have to finish the job. It seems more humane for parents to teach this lesson to their children.

Internalization of Conscience

Psychological researchers do not recommend the big stick of external force as the best way to civilize people, but most believe that the use of power is essential. Society, by maintaining an army, navy, coast guard and police force, evidently supports a philosophy of external force to make us all mind. But in an ideal society, each citizen would be sufficiently self-motivated to respect the rights of others and police would be unneeded.

Psychologists call the mechanism to achieve such an exalted state "internalization." It means that parents should attempt to help their children build a conscience which guides them to correct behavior even when the police are not around. Guilt can produce internalization of good social values. Freud believed that socialized children adopt or internalize standards *and will punish themselves if they break those standards.*

Whatever the punishment, all workers in the field of child rearing agree that clear, consistent, parental explanation of values encourages the child's acceptance of these values. If the child receives the impression that the values are his own and the punishment only an incident brought on by his temporarily forgetfulness, he will often internalize the values. In this way, values can be imparted and a conscience developed without much guilt.

In my experience, the "contract" technique works better than direct punishment for both teaching a child to behave and building a good conscience. Under the contract system, children earn a reward for a particular type of mature behavior. The reward depends on the child's acceptance of a responsibility. If the child does not do his part, then the parent simply withdraws the reward. The child has broken the contract. He then understands that he has the power to accept the responsibility and earn the reward, or ignore the responsibility and lose the reward. If losing the reward is punishment, then he has punished himself.

Many techniques have been designed to get a child to cooperate without punishing. Some simply substitute the words "aversive situations" for the word punishment. One such technique uses the satiation principle, insisting that a child continue an undesirable behavior even when he tires of it. For example, the youngster who is fascinated with starting fires is forced to light matches until he begs to quit. Sometimes this works. Another rewards alternative behavior. Here the parent entices the misbehaving child into more interesting activities. For example, getting him off the street corner and onto the soccer field.

The negative reinforcement principle rewards the child by stopping the "aversive sitation" (punishment) as soon as he changes his behavior. For example, rather than say, "Stay in your room for an hour," or "Stay in your room until I come and get you!" say instead, "You will have to stay in your room until you can come out and behave better!" These suggestions still utilize punishment in one form or another. Other techniques can punish even more, although they are sometimes advanced as methods of avoiding physical punishment.

Punishment is an integral, unavoidable part of nature. We have pain endings in our nerves and pain perception in our emotions. Without the ability to feel and respond to pain, we would be in trouble. The consistently punitive, but neutral and nonhostile, law of gravity teaches a toddler not to fall. If we can learn from the attitude of Mother Nature, parental punishment will help more than harm. The results seem to depend upon the balance of power and respect between parent and child.

Punishment is effective when the child has some sense that he has done wrong, he has respect for the punisher, and the punishment follows logically from what he has done, i.e., the punishment fits the crime.

Alan H. Lieman, Ph.D. and
Victor Strasburger, M.D.
"Sex, Drugs, Rock'N' Roll"
Understanding Common Teenage Behavior

VIII

Harnessing the Power of Punishment

Whether you want to punish your child or not, you will. Even if you never lay a hand on your child, never scowl or utter a harsh word, never isolate him or take away rewards and privileges, you do punish. If in no other way, you punish the child with guilt. A child who loves his parent — the source of nurturing love and security — will feel guilty if he disappointed the parent by not helping with work when he was needed, or if he broke the rules.

Of all the types of discipline, guilt is probably the most powerful — and quite possibly the most damaging. It lasts longer than any other type of punishment and, therefore, deserves the most attention. Psychiatrists and psychologists recognize guilt as one of the most powerful socializing agents. Children respond to this powerful controlling force by minding in the present and hopefully developing a conscience so they will mind in the future. However, I believe that guilt should be avoided as a behavorial tool for control when possible, even though it often works.

Psychiatrist Otto Fenichel writes,

The warning function of conscience expresses the ego's tendency to avoid the pains of intense guilt feelings. . . . In "conscience" the fear is internalized, and the danger threatens from within. Fear lest something terrible occurs. The fear of loss [of well-being, protection, security] may be characterized as loss of self-esteem.

We probably need some guilt and we certainly do need conscience. Parental guilt feelings keep a few parents from simply abandoning their children. And even completely permissive parents probably put as large a guilt load on their children as do harsh authoritarian parents. Guilt creates a feeling of anxiety, a feeling that parents will disapprove of the child or even abandon him. It can be so powerful that it can cripple a person in many ways. The example of Mrs. Joseph demonstrates the complexity of guilt, and how it can be passed down generation to generation.

Mrs. Joseph's two preschoolers were out of control. They sassed her, refused to mind, and, in fact, demanded that their mother mind them. They constantly tested the limits of acceptable behavior. Mrs. Joseph would pleasantly try to do whatever she could to keep them happy. But underneath it all she was aggravated and angry. The children seemed unhappy with her much of the time. The pediatrician sensed that the children felt guilty about the way they treated Mother, even at that young age. He asked Mrs. Joseph why she did not make her children obey, as they were obviously out of her control and she was uncomfortable and harrassed by their actions and attitude.

"They are so stubborn," complained Mrs. Joseph, "that I can't make them mind. If I try, I feel so guilty, so bad. I want to give them things to make them happy. I'm not a good mother, so I have to give them things."

Later Mrs. Joseph recalled that she was raised by a mother who overpowered her and made her feel small, worthless and guilty. So when she had her own children, she felt powerless and unable to control them. Guilt, left over from her own childhood, crippled her. In a different way, she was placing guilt upon her own children without realizing it.

Negative Power Trips

Sometimes harsh punishment and overpowering parents make guilt feelings worse. Child psychiatrist Leo Kanner writes,

> Those children who are brought to clinics with major complaints of aggressiveness are the less fortunate offspring of people whose coerciveness and nagging hostility has created and maintained in the child a protracted state of frustration, rebellion, and guilt.

Some parents use guilt consciously. "You make me feel bad!" they will tell the child. Psychologist Thomas Gordon, in his book *Parent Effectiveness Training*, advises that if your child kicks you in the shin, you should say: "Ouch, that really hurt me. I don't like to be kicked." Gordon depends upon the punishment of guilt to motivate the child to stop abusing the parent. But even if this works, it doesn't prepare the child to rationally deal with the rest of the world. Outside of the home if you kick someone on the shin, you will most likely have to pay.

Guilt frequently creates resentment if not discomfort, so using guilt, to say nothing of relieving it, may not be an ideal motivation even when it works. Most of us will go around "Robin's barn" to avoid meeting someone who makes us feel guilty, and we usually become angry at people who make us feel bad. Children act this way too. Even toward parents. I suspect that this direct use of guilt hurts more than a spanking because the punishment and power inherent in guilt results in a loss of love and security.

Children require security, the feeling that they are safe and loved. Whether security should ever be used as a reward, or whether a parent should threaten to remove security as a form of punishment is highly questionable. Security, like love, should be unconditional.

Guilt and Conscience

Conscience grows out of parental warnings. Temptation stirs our conscience, and behaving contrary to our conscience creates guilt feelings. Guilt grows from parental disapproval or the fear of loss of parental love. Some people have been so sensitized that they react, or overreact, to the warnings of conscience as if they were already guilty. Guilt can create both diverse and deep problems. Freud repeatedly noted that one of the most difficult tasks in psychoanalysis is that of helping a severe, unconscious sense of guilt. The problems which can arise from guilt feelings are legion. For example Fenichel writes that guilt creates neurotic depression,

> Adults behave as they once behaved toward a threatening parent whose affection and forgiveness is needed . . . [They] develop a need for absolution [forgiveness]. The need for punishment is a special form of the need for absolution. The pain of punishment is accepted or even provoked in the hope that after the punishment the greater pain of guilt feelings will cease.

Perhaps this explains why a reasonably intelligent criminal who has just been released from jail will rob a liquor store at noon next door to the police station. Many criminals act as if they want to be caught. Likewise, many children deliberately misbehave so they will be punished by the parents they love. Usually this follows childish anger at the parent, which the child assumes will hurt the parent. This may explain why some children of permissive parents continue to act up, seemingly asking to be punished to relieve their guilt about misbehavior or excessive demands. Angry, authoritarian parents also create feelings of guilt — with an added threat of abandonment. The child may feel so guilty and anxious that he literally courts punishment. After a spanking, a child will often be relaxed and happy. He paid the penalty. "I hurt you and you hurt me, so now we are even!"

Table X

THE FIVE TYPES OF PUNISHMENT

Guilt
Withdrawl of Love by Scolding or Anger
Physical Punishment — Spanking
Isolation — Jail
Reduction of Privileges or Respect

Scolding as Punishment

Parents commonly scold to punish — a dramatic demonstration of parental displeasure that threatens the withdrawal of love. "But I never stop loving my child!" protest most parents. Yet listen to what the tone of scolding really says. A harsh, "You stop that!" sounds more like "I hate you" in feeling. And children respond to the tone of speech more than to the words. So do we. We reject a phony "I love you" out of hand and usually with a sense of anger at the attempted manipulation.

Frequently after a scolding, a child will come to the parent and say, "I love you Daddy!" She is checking to see if the security of home base still exists. The child lets Dad know that she loves him, hoping to confirm that Dad still loves her in return, that parental security still exists and that she will not be abandoned. After all, children depend on parents to supply love, security, food, and shelter. What crime can a child commit that would justify threatening the withdrawal of basic needs? Does spilling a glass of milk warrant feelings of guilt and unworthiness which can last for years or decades — which may seriously damage a child's self-esteem? There must be better ways to use parental power to control, to punish, and to teach. If you must scold, you can avoid some of these feelings of rejection by picking your child up after scolding and giving him a loving hug.

Some parents may react to the downgrading of scolding with alarm. "Avoid scolding? Impossible!" Yet do we scold other adults? Not very often. For adults will not tolerate scoldings, deserved or undeserved. Scolding sounds accusatory, angry, hostile. Children are usually powerless to prevent such verbal assults. But underneath it all they react as we do, with anger, hostility and loss of self-esteem.

Scolding has always been objected to when people have had the power to object. We can learn from history. Museums in England display iron face-masks which were put on scolds to punish them for their shrewishness. In early New England, some ingenious citizens developed a way to cool off scolds. A chair was mounted on the end of a long pole which was put on a swivel; the chair with the scold tied in it would swing around over a pond so she could be dipped into the water, presumably until the scold agreed to forswear her sharp tongue.

Parents would not lose any significant parenting power if they stopped scolding. Less anxiety and fear result from a calm approach to a child's behavior. Effective criticisms objectively describe misbehavior and its potential conseqences, coupled with a clear description of a better course of action for the child. We need to call attention to the effects of misbehavior more than to the parent's unhappiness. Usually a child's misbehavior does the parent no serious harm. Teach your child that such behavior hurts him, not that it simply upsets you.

Natural Consequences

It took two nurses to hold 7-year-old Oscar while the doctor gave him a novocaine shot in the cut on his chin so the wound could be cleaned and sutured. Oscar's parents had told him not to ride his bike on the jumping-ramp which some older boys had built, mimicking the motorcycle stunt men they had seen on television.

Oscar's parents wisely did not scold him. He was hurt enough. Dad told him it was too bad that he had hurt himself and calmly offered the opinion that Oscar had learned from the accident that there were rules which were made to protect him. His bike's crumpled front wheel would have to stay that way until Oscar earned enough money to have it fixed.

Rational-authoritative parents use a neutral discipline — something like the law of gravity. When the consequences are the result of the child's attempt to defy gravity, the results, naturally, speak for themselves. If the parents define firm, clear limits which the child disobeys, punishment of some sort must follow. When necessary, the parent naturally enforces the consequences. The form of punishment is less important than the parental attitude and predetermined action which follows disobedience.

Erosion of Self-Esteem

Scolding, even without spanking, can be a severe punishment. One parent, who reported she was raised by a scolding mother who "whipped me with words," said to me, "I wish she had spanked me instead. It would have been easier and kinder. I still resent her for that!" The old saying, "Sticks and stones can break my bones, but words will never hurt me," does not hold true for parents' words. Scolding can easily become child abuse. Ridicule, labeling as "bad," and personality attacks such as, "You are lazy!" may be more harmful than sticks and stones, for the child's self-image reflects his parent's words and actions. Such words damage the self-esteem severely.

Verbal Abuse Hurts Too...

and the pain can last a lifetime.

For more information on children and the importance of self-esteem contact us,

The Mental Health Association in Michigan
15920 W. 12 Mile Rd.
Southfield, Michigan 48076
(313) 557-6777

A United Way Agency

Spanking as Punishment

Some argue against "superfluous" control and the punishment of spanking which they believe can inhibit moral development. Catherine Lewis, of the prestigious Langely Porter Clinic in San Francisco, wrote to me: "All parents know how to hit — it is the lowest common denominator. And we don't need professionals to encourage us to use punishment on children. What parents need, I think, is help setting up positive experiences in which their children can learn the joys of helping and contributing positively to others."

Children instinctively hit and learn that this gives them power. They do not have to be taught. Hitting by parents should be condemned, but rational-authoritative controlled spanking strikes me as another issue. Dr. Lewis offers an excellent alternative, and I recommend it. Some children never need to be spanked. They accept the parent's good will and good sense and will respond contentedly to a simple, soft "No!" Other children are fighters who violently resist parental power, who test the limits repeatedly. A few will not be cowed by spankings or even by beatings. We will discuss these children in the chapter "When Discipline Fails." But most children can be controlled and will respond to a demonstration of parental power if they prove difficult to control.

The Power of Spanking

Personally, I think that rational spanking is preferable to the damage that scolding can do. Most parents spank and most children do, on occasions, need a spank. I believe that hostility, fear and anger on the part of the spanked child represent a reaction to the parent's anger more than to the physical punishment. Angry parents punish their children three ways: spanking, withdrawal of parental love, *and* guilt. That is heavy punishment indeed. If you do spank, don't spank when angry.

A father once said to me, "I will never spank my child. When you spank, you go over the line and it means war!" If he really felt that he could not control his ability to punish rationally by spanking and would "go to war," then he certainly should not spank.

Spanking alone punishes enough. Be a good diplomat, act before war — prevent the need. Discipline, even spanking, should be done because you love the child. And a rational spanking sometimes benefits the child. As pro-football star Ronnie Lott said: "Some of the best lessons I've had grew out of bad experiences — such as my mother giving me a spanking. I learned from it, and I haven't forgotten."

Spanking does not necessarily put you in charge; yet if used in a way which demonstrates that the child brings it on himself, the natural consequence of misbehavior, it often works.

> Fred, age 3, had a stubborn streak. So did his mother. She had decided to never spank her children or force them to stay in their bedroom. But when Fred was tired, he became a "bear." He followed her around whining and fussing, but refusing to be comforted when she picked him up to try to soothe him. When put in bed, he climbed right out and continued his fussing. Mother's permissive orientation, however, had limits. She finally decided to follow her pediatrician's advice and take charge.
>
> "You're tired, honey, and it's time for a nap. Go to your room and get in bed," Mother told Fred. He responded with an angry, defiant, "I won't!" Mother calmly replied, "Well, Fred, if you won't go in by yourself then I may have to spank you. Why don't you go and get in bed so I won't have to spank? Take a little rest. I'll tuck you in."
>
> Fred stubbornly whined and followed Mother into the kitchen instead. So Mother took a wooden spoon from the drawer, pulled up Fred's pant-leg and quietly gave him a couple of sharp, stinging spanks on the calf of his leg. He cried and Mother put the spoon back, took his hand, and gently led him to his bedroom. She tucked him in, gave him a kiss, and said, "It's too bad I had to spank you. You take a rest now and when you get up and aren't so tired, let's go to the park and I'll push you on the swing."

Mother ceased being permissive and became a rational and authoritative parent. She made firm and clear rules, demanded that he follow the rules, and when he didn't, he was quite naturally punished. Her discipline was like the law of gravity — consistent and neutral. Fred soon realized that his mother was in charge, that she meant what she said. He found that the punishment which she predicted did indeed follow; so the consequences made it worth his while to recognize her power and accept her discipline and control.

Abuse by Spanking

On the other hand, anger with physical punishment can lead to child abuse. Psychologist Catherine Lewis objects to heavy use of parental power, especially hitting. She objects to professionals, (including myself), Burton White, James Dobson and others, who recommend spanking. She argues: "Obviously children need to know about rules, consequences, and so forth. But there is increasing laboratory evidence that what punishment does is allow the child to experience his/her own affective arousal at the time of misconduct as fear of punishment, rather than guilt."

Parents who lose their temper and hit their children in anger risk seriously hurting them. Some of the terrible examples of child abuse which occur, resulting in deformity or death, make any form of such physical punishment abhorrent. Corporal punishment is said to cause rebellion and counter-anger as well as perpetuate the cycle of child abuse. As a result, spanking in any form has been condemned by many and most states now have laws prohibiting spanking in public schools.

Admittedly, spanking does model the use of power and possibly aggression. Some argue that spanking causes hostility, anger, or neurotic behavior in the child. Others believe that it violates children's rights, interrupts the learning process, and fails to stop bad behavior. Typically, the child's first impulse is to escape, the second to fight back, and the third to withdraw inwardly.

In Defense of Spanking

There may well be some substance to all of these negative criticisms; however, psychologist Joan Grusec writes: "Child development studies of punishment have consisted largely of theory-based hypothesis-testing . . ."

She thus implies that the criticisms of spanking are based more on rationalizations than on fact. Results of various forms of child rearing seem to support the practicality of properly administered spanking. Professor Victor Cline writes:

I've seen in parents a paralysis of will, an uncertainty about what to do when their children become abusive, destructive and manipulative. I've repeatedly seen parents function as servants and children as masters. I've seen gentle, loving parents goaded to the point of physically assaulting their children ... The notion that exercising parental power is bad developed out of early psychoanalytic theory ... however, most of these hypotheses have been rejected as unscientific ... If spanking is done appropriately, I see no harm in it.

Even those who decry spanking occasionally admit that it may be the lesser of several evils. Alvin Rosenfeld, M.D. and Dorothy Levine, M.D. comment:

Although [we] and the American Academy of Pediatrics find the use of physical force, such as spanking, in child rearing distasteful, many parents who are fixed in their ways rely on this time-tested technique. Deprived of it, they can become less involved with their child, even neglectful, because they are frustrated and believe they have no alternative. This is often more detrimental to the growing child than an occasional spanking.

When we come to more specific age-oriented advice on ways to raise children, we will investigate the importance of teaching the child at an early age that the parent has both the right and the power to spank. It can be clearly demonstrated that if the parent will consistently spank without anger when the child refuses to obey, parents will rarely have to spank. This shows that the parent is in charge. However, if the parent spanks a lot, or hits or spanks in anger, then punishment is not succeeding and it is time for a reevaluation of disciplinary techniques.

Certainly the less a child has to be spanked, the better, but some form of discipline must be used. "A major task," writes Walters and Grusec, "that parents have is to prepare their offspring for group living — to socialize them. Should the parents fail in the task of socialization, it is left to the group as a whole or its representatives to accomplish."

Because many parents fear they might be condemned for spanking, there are a lot of out-of-control kids. For most parents and children, the results of refusal or inability to spank are relatively mild. Usually the punishment escalates to the next step — the withdrawal of love and security by the parent via the mechanism of scolding and anger, leaving a heritage of guilt. Other children are literally made outcasts when they are expelled from school; others learn of the force of the law and the power of society only when they are caught by the police and punished by the courts.

Socializing requires that the child receive love and respect for himself and be taught the rewards and the obligation — the noblesse oblige — of responsibility for the rest of the world. However, many find that positive experiences or the joy of helping others as proposed by Lewis does not always work. The child must first be under control. Power usually has to be used to keep the child from hurting himself or others. The writings of some psychologists seem to ignore this salient point. Without it there would be anarchy. The question is: who is in charge? If you can be in charge without spanking and, I hope, without the use of guilt or withdrawal of love (scolding), great. But if you cannot, consider the consequences. Especially the consequences of anger.

When you are in the right, you can afford to hold your temper.
When you are in the wrong, you can't afford to lose it.

Bernard Metzer

IX

Angry Parents — Angry Children

Parenting is usually fun, but to one degree or another parents often find themselves angry with their children, with themselves, their spouse or their parenting role. And anger has consequences. How you deal with your anger will have a major effect upon your child and your family — on your life. For example, as we have seen, it appears that an affectionate parent can get satisfactory results from spanking far more often than can a non-affectionate, usually angry, parent. Aside from that, adults are powerful enough to damage children physically and psychologically when driven by anger; so we need to learn to avoid anger as much as possible and learn how to handle our angry feelings in the least damaging fashion to ourselves and to our children.

Controlling Anger

Controlling an instinctive feeling such as anger is not easy. Much of the effort of growing up involves learning how to control our childish feelings and actions. Much of our adult maturity depends upon keeping these feelings under control. Such achievement requires considerable effort. Giving in to our instincts takes less work. Perhaps this is why we enjoy little children who can be expected to be "up front," honest and to "let it all hang out!" Temper tantrums, thumb sucking and fears occur routinely in the second and third years of life. But children need to mature. The name of the game in growing up is learning how to control, sublimate or avoid some of these non-productive, childish feelings and actions.

Persistent immaturity creates problems. We rarely respect adults who have temper tantrums, chew their knuckles or have uncontrolled fears. Yet, we use the common excuse that we, as adults, should express our anger so we will not become "neurotic." It is certainly true that holding in a lot of anger can become stressful. On the other hand, unnecessary or uncontrolled anger can cause reactions which create far more stress and neurosis both in you and your children. Parental anger frightens children.

Parents should be firm — should "mean business" — when disciplining children, but differentiate between firmness and anger. If you wait until you are angry before you are firm, then your entire attitude toward the child will be colored with anger because children, reasonably, will often wait to see if the parent means what she says before deciding to obey. On the other hand, be aware that some children may equate firmness on your part with anger if, in the past, you have usually been angry when you were "firm." It may take some time and a softer (but firm) approach before the child believes that you can discipline without anger. Have patience. Try to avoid sounding angry when you want to sound firm. As a start, it helps to set your teaching goals well in advance and act when the child's behavior requires it, whether you are angry or not.

Pediatrician Byron Monroe heads a group devoted to peaceful discipline, a method for encouraging desirable behavior without the use of physical violence. They advise angry parents to yell, "I'm angry!" Then they call a time-out and employ peaceful discipline techniques. These center on the following methods of removing attention for unwanted behavior:

1. Ignore the child's behavior.
2. Distract the child from the behavior you want him to stop.
3. Isolate the child from the attention of others.

Some psychologists believe, however, that ignoring behavior signals a relative approval or acceptance of that behavior. Distracting the child rewards the child for the behavior that made the parent angry and offers the child an unwelcome tool to get center stage. Isolating the child seems to work best for many parents. The most effective method, however, starts before anger. After all, anger does not seem very peaceful. All agree that physical violence, which usually occurs during anger, must be avoided.

Frequent Anger

Some parents seem to be angry at their children most of the time. They chronically scold, "blow their top," complain, and verbally tongue-lash or physically punish their children. For some parents, this may simply be a power-trip. Others compulsively repeat the way they were raised by their parents, so the angry tone and feeling to them seems the only way to react to the child's behavior. As with any other emotional state, the child's response tends to subside over time. Routine anger becomes accepted and then ignored, especially when the child finds that the anger and love are balanced, so parental action rarely follows the anger. Still, anger has adverse effects. For one thing, the anger indicates criticism of the child and, thus, can constantly wear away the child's self-esteem. Also, anger usually signals frustration and inability — a clear sign of parental ineffectiveness. In any case, the anger of parents hardly contributes to the child's feeling of security.

Anger is not shown just by hollering, scolding or spanking. Some parents use the "Siberian approach" — freeze him with a look. Cold anger is very effective in radiating hostility and may be harder on a child than a spanking. Children do not tolerate coldness in parenting; they need warm loving parents. Alvin Rosenfeld and Dorothy Levine in discussing the outcome of different disciplinary styles state: "One factor has been frequently found to discriminate between children who do or do not develop behavioral symptoms: parental coldness."

If you find that you are angry at your child a lot, then it is best to seek some professional help. Start by asking your child's pediatrician or your own doctor for a source of counselling. Sometimes the physician will be able to give you advice after hearing you out — other times, he may refer you to a psychiatrist or psychologist for help. This does not imply that you should never be angry at your child. That would be like asking you to walk on water. But raising children should be fun and rewarding — not an ulcer-producing experience. So if you find yourself frequently hollering, spanking, and scolding in anger (or drinking a lot to recover), probably better methods of child-rearing exist for you to use.

Reactions to Anger

Children react to parental anger in many ways. First comes fear. Anger is powerful — it punishes by threatening the withdrawal of love and security as well as other possible actions. Watch a mother in a supermarket who angrily scolds her children. Then when the mom reaches for a can on the shelf the child ducks — blows often follow anger, and that hand which comforts, feeds and caresses becomes a punitive weapon. One would think that the child would avoid the angry parent when possible, and this does happen. However, even children who have been seriously physically abused will return to the abusing parent given a chance. Parental anger evidently makes many children feel terribly guilty. They return hoping that they are still loved, and apologetically and anxiously offer their love to the parent. Often, after an episode of the parent angrily berating, scolding or spanking, the child will say, "I love you Mommy!" He offers an olive branch in hopes of winning back the parent's assurance of love. It represents the child's insecurity and anxiety as much as love. It also represents guilt.

Not everyone agrees with the concept of "suppressing" parental feelings as you saw from Monroe's Peaceful Discipline recommendations. However, almost everyone urges parental self-control. If, for example, a mother wants to teach her son not to hit others when he is mad, she herself should refrain from hitting her son when she becomes livid about something he has done. Yet, pediatricians Rosenfeld and Levine do not recommend that a mother who is "livid" suppress her feelings.

> Her anger reflects her intense emotional involvement with her son, and the boy feels her disapproval. If their relationship is good, he will want to change so that he again finds favor in her eyes. After the situation calms down, the same mother can speak to her son and explain why she became so angry. Her good reasons will stimulate his natural guilt so that, in the future, he will be more likely to inhibit his own misbehavior.

That advice is reasonable if you are willing to accept guilt as a form of punishment for your child. Such strategy looks to me like a mechanism to excuse adult anger, the assumption being that many parents cannot control themselves. Guilt is not my preferred method of punishment or control, but it certainly does have a lasting effect on the child. And, realistically, some things that kids do probably should make us angry.

If you do not get angry often, even a mild display of parental anger can be very effective. At least save your anger for significant misbehavior. Do not waste your "heavy weapon" on trivia. Later, if you cannot think of a good reason or good explanation for your anger, you have probably overreacted. Keep in mind, if you use anger a lot, your child may not react with guilt. He may fight back instead. Children too have power. They soon figure out how to "push your button!"

The Button Pushers

Children will fight parents if they feel it necessary to retain self-respect. Although physically weaker than parents, they do have power. Some even fight because they want to dominate their parents. There are many ways to fight. Not uncommonly children deliberately misbehave to punish the parent by repeating the same immature action which angered the parent in the first place. This gives the child the power to strike back, to punish the parent for not minding the child or for having forced the child to do something he did not want to do. Thus the child can either deliberately or subconsciously decide to anger the parent to "get even." Once a parent and child are caught in the anger-punishment-getting-even trap, the family can become a battleground instead of a safe harbor. This type of warfare increases the sorrows of parenting and can be avoided.

The basic problem with anger is that it focuses all the attention and energy on a negative emotion. Logically, this makes it very difficult to use the other basic tools of teaching and control. I feel anger makes it harder to become a rational-authorititive parent. Oh, sure, rational-authoritative parents get angry. We all do. But we will be far more likely to be effective if we learn to use our power without anger.

Power Without Anger

You can usually exert enough power to control your children without anger. Some attitudes and techniques will help you control your child and, as a result, reduce the angry feelings and motives. To start, recognize that children are children and teenagers are teenagers. A lot of very immature, childish and adolescent behavior must be expected. Children are childish. Why get angry when the baby cries because of colic? He has no other way of expressing his discomfort or of calling for help. Why get angry when the toddler pulls the lamp cord and the lamp breaks? Toddlers have to push, pull, feel and chew anything they can grab. When your 4-year-old disobeys and defies you, keep in mind that children normally develop hostility and test their power capabilities at this age. Yours should be tested and under control by now. Later, in growth, many other types of tests occur. If your teenager comes home an hour late, remember your own teenage years. In all these cases, one can reasonably expect immature behavior.

There are far more effective methods of punishment than anger. So start by reducing your anger. First set your expectation thermostat down. Be realistic in what behavior you expect. If you want perfect behavior from your child, be prepared for disappointment. It is better to expect something less than perfection. This reduces the source of anger which follows disappointment. Adopt the sages philosophy, "Rather than curse fate because your glass is half empty, thank God that it is half full!" You will reduce stress when you learn to think positively rather than critically about life and about your child.

Discipline and Beyond

Go beyond discipline. Offer your child as much power over himself as you can. Let him be responsible for his own decisions even though you remain the judge. Share your power with him. When he makes wrong decisions, and he will for he is a child, then teach him that they are wrong for him. Concentrate on what the effect of the unwise decision can be on the child. This helps you cool off. Let it be his problem. But do not give up firmness and appropriate action in the process. Simply put the emphasis on the child and his feelings and behavior — not on yours. By establishing effective discipline and teaching him positive behavior, you will reduce the need to punish as well as your tendency to become angry. Set your discipline goals well in advance. Have a pre-existing plan to respond to the misbehaviors you can be sure will occur. Then act when the child misbehaves — do not wait until you are angry before you act. It is not easy for some. The first hurdle is for you to strive for maturity yourself. That is what parenting does for us — it forces us to grow up — whether we like it or not!

Johnny, like many of the third graders in his class, seemed to think that it was smart to act up, talk in class and test his powers by challenging the teacher. Mrs. Jones called Johnny's mother to report, "Johnny refused to stop talking in class today and was rude to me when I told him to stop. I had to get the principal to take him out of class. Unless he starts behaving and doing his work, he will have to be put back a grade. As you know, his grades were poor the first quarter. I think it is a time for us to have a conference. Can we set a time?" Johnny's mother's first reaction was defensive, and she was a bit angry at Mrs. Jones's criticism of her son. But she admitted that Johnny had been "smart-mouthing" her and probably was doing the same to Mrs. Jones. She was upset and angry at Johnny.

Let us look at some ways she can handle the problem:

1. Johnny's mother can "blow her top" and give Johnny a good tongue lashing or a spanking. If she does, then Johnny learns that he has enough power to make his mother very angry, and maybe even make Mrs. Jones angry. (She, who always "bugs" him to do his school work.) This concern about their anger distracts him from the main problem, that he may have to suffer the humiliation of going back to the second grade. Mother's anger and the teacher's anger become the focus rather than Johnny's actions.

2. Johnny's mother can get her anger under control, talk over a plan of action with her husband and Mrs. Jones and then calmly but firmly tell Johnny,

"Johnny, you don't pay attention in school and you talked out-of-turn in class and, on top of that, you were rude to Mrs. Jones. If you don't complete school work and if you don't obey Mrs. Jones, you are going to have to be put back into the second grade. Now Mrs. Jones, your father and I have decided you are too smart to have that happen to you. So Mrs. Jones will send a note home with you every day stating how well you did in school. If you don't bring home the note, if you haven't done well, then you won't be allowed to go out to play after school and you will have to go to bed at 8:00 p.m. instead of 9:00 p.m. If you have problems understanding your work, Dad or I will help you at home, although I think that you can get most of the work done yourself if you want to. But make no mistake, start shaping up young man or your play time will be very restricted."

Then, and this is important, Johnny's mother follows through. If Johnny does not bring home the note, then he is kept in the house with no friends and no telephone calls and forced to go to bed at 8:00 p.m.

But what if your Johnny refuses to go to bed? Should you get mad then? You can, but your anger will still not be too effective. Johnny rebels at the restrictions and wants to challenge you to see if he can win and stay up in spite of your rule. In that case, when he defies you to use your power, use it. You can grab his ear or arm and hold it tight, give him a warning swat on the rear and physically march him into his bedroom. Do not shout or scold. Just firmly (not angrily) say, "If you come out of bed, young man, I am going to ground you tomorrow — and swat you now!" Firmness and action carry the day. Act, don't talk. Act before anger. Be firm, not emotional and not angry. Let it be Johnny's problem, do not make it yours by "blowing your top."

You and your child can put up with a reasonable amount of anger anyway. After all, you are human. With enough parental love and care, some angry discipline can be tolerated. It is a good thing that we and our children can tolerate some anger. If not, we would be in bad straits because most of us have had our parents angry at us and occasionally get angry at our own children. But watch out for chronic anger or out-of-control anger. And keep in mind the trap which can occur when some children will get on a power trip and demonstrate it by "pressing your button" or "getting your goat." Separate the child's problem from your problem and teach him that there are no rewards for immature behavior. Neutral, non-angry discipline with love, like dispassionate law and judges, tends to work best. This puts you into the controlling role as teacher and judge. You judge your child's behavior and because you love him you teach him how to improve or correct it without an excessive show of power or passion. Above all, avoiding anger allows you to think more clearly and act more rationally. It also aids the digestion and enables sounder sleep with a clearer conscience.

Act Before Anger

You can avoid angry confrontations in other ways. Try not to anger your child and, in the process, teach him how to control his anger. First, be a good model by controlling your own anger. Second, allow your child to participate in deciding how he should act. Let him have a share in the power you must use to teach him how to behave in a positive and constructive manner. Discuss the reasons for your discipline, emphasizing the possible results of his actions or attitude. Encourage his views on your values and let him take part in deciding what and how much punishment he should receive or what reward he believes is due. This gives the child a sense of power over himself and is likely to lead to his adoption of your values and your standards of self-control as his own. For example, it has been found that children who are picked to monitor a class tend to identify with the values that they are told are laudable. They react to misbehavior more severely than children not given the opportunity to monitor others. They love that power! This tendency can be helpful in your day-to-day techniques of parenting.

Have Realistic Expectations

In summary, have realistic expectations based on your child's age and development. Concentrate more on his good behavior than on his bad behavior. Make certain that he (and you) recognize that "good" behavior is right for him, not just you. Do not wait for anger to trigger you to act. Use your powers reasonably, do not overreact. Again, act before anger. Decide in advance what sort of behavior you will reward or punish, and then act when the event occurs. Whatever you do, be warm and loving to your child. Teach him to act in a way that pleases you but make certain that he recognizes that such action mostly benefits him. Allow him the use of some power to help you decide what actions deserve which rewards and which punishments. Build his sense of personal responsibility for his own actions by letting him share the power of decisions. And learn enough about children to decide what behavior is appropriate for what age. Develop realistic guidelines to decide how much power you need to use and how much you can share at various stages of growth.

Each family can work out its problems and conflicting interests along lines of mutual respect. Such respect makes pathogenic attitudes unable to flourish. Having seen this work successfully in hundreds of families, I know that it is possible and practical.

W. Hugh Missildine, M.D.
Your Inner Child of the Past

X

Sharing the Power

Good parents do not enjoy punishing their children. If your child enjoys or defies punishment or seems to be satisfied after punishment, or continues the same unacceptable behavior, then you have a problem. If you find yourself punishing your child frequently, if you find yourself angry or disgusted with your child or yourself very often, then you need to change the way you use your power to teach and discipline. Even though a strong and practical case can be made that parents must punish their children, the less the punishment the better. In this chapter we will discuss the ways in which the child learns that he punishes himself by improper behavior, rather than that his parents punish him to prove their power, or to vent their anger. It helps the child recognize his responsibility for his own behavior. I call this technique Neutral Discipline. It fits in nicely with rational-authoritative parenting.

Rational Power Versus Emotional Punishment

Neutral discipline emphasizes rational power, not emotional punishment. Parents need to learn to use their power to control the child because they have to, not because they waited so long that they got mad and wanted to punish. Here, we will lay out ways of using power to efficiently control the child and convince him to behave well in the future. The plan is simple. Doing it is a bit harder. Basically, as your child grows, you expand his limits of freedom and self-direction. The limits, however, remain firm. This can best be understood with a metaphor. Assume that the limits of behavior are like the walls in your room. If the child runs into the wall, it hurts. So he soon learns not to run into the wall and instead starts looking for other ways to expand his limits — like the door, or even the window. The child rarely gets mad at the wall even though he may have hurt his head on it. And the wall does not get mad at the child — it is neutral yet powerfully unyielding. But just imagine what would happen if the child ran into the wall and then the wall jumped out and hit the child as he stood there rubbing his head. The child would be either afraid or mad or both. From then on he would regard the wall as an enemy and, depending on his personality, he would either lose self-esteem by withdrawing or attempt to retain a sense of personal power by trying to hurt the wall in return. An adversarial relationship would be established.

When the child runs into the limits established by the parent (instead of the wall) the same type of relationship can result. If the parent's punishment is fair and neutral then it becomes the child's problem. If the parent punishes in a bad mood, especially if she overreacts in anger, an adversarial relationship is created. The child and the parent become mad at each other and both overreact. The issue no longer revolves around the child bumping into the wall or breaking a rule; rather it becomes a power struggle between parent and child. The struggle obscures the underlying reason for the punishment and primarily teaches the child that the parent wants to punish him.

Natural Consequences

The consequences which exist for every action or inaction become the parent's most powerful disciplinary tool. Carefully explain why the child's behavior will not be tolerated and explain the consequences to the child. Often the consequences are natural. If the child cannot understand why his behavior may hurt him now or in the future, then immediate consequences may have to be implemented by the parent. The parent must act; so be it. The parent acts, hopefully not by rejecting the child by tone or punishing him by anger and scolding. The more rational action will be one of the other three basic methods of punishment: loss of privileges, isolation, or if really required, spanking. Or it may be that such punishments are not needed. Perhaps we can stimulate the child's conscience without much guilt.

Guilt and its results generally seem negative. Probably the air would be cleared if we called guilt bad and conscience good — and if all of the researchers adopted the same terminology and meaning. The dictionary describes conscience as "feelings within a person that tell him when he is doing right and warn him of what is wrong" and guilt as "a state of having done wrong." To a degree they are the different sides of the same coin. However, we want our children to develop a sense of conscience, not a sense of guilt. Our powers of teaching, of modeling, of rewards and punishment should all be aimed at convincing children to do the right thing now and in the future. This should be achieved without the side effects created by anger and scolding — without guilt, hopefully, even without punishment. This can often be accomplished by carefully using our parental powers to reason and act authoritatively.

Many effective parents find that if the child has accepted their good will and recognizes their power, occasional discussion of inappropriate behavior gives the child enough guidance to enable him to develop self-control. Rational and objective criticism coupled with a positive discussion of ideal behavior and its implied rewards, often pointing out a positive model, allows the child to make the choice. If she misbehaves then she loses some respect and possibly privileges because of her immaturity. She learns that she cannot earn respect or privileges or become center stage by unacceptable behavior. If she makes the wrong choice, in effect, she punishes herself. If she makes the right choice, she earns the reward. This method has the great advantage that it focuses upon the child's behavior and the consequences, and not so much on the parent's feelings. It becomes an excellent learning experience, helping implant a pattern, a habit of correct and successful behavior in the conscience to guide the future adult. Correct behavior does please the parent, and the child recognizes that the parent also receives a reward. So good behavior becomes part of the guiding conscience, a rewarding conscience, a fulfilling conscience. It avoids implanting crippling feelings of guilt and abandonment as a mechanism to assure correct behavior.

Freedom In Learning

Learning researchers compared two different ways mothers used to help their children assemble a construction toy. One group of mothers lectured their children on how to assemble the toy. The other group of mothers let the child try on his own, monitored his efforts and responded when he needed help. In essence, the first group of mothers approached teaching as a demonstration of their own power, offering little respect to the child. The second group of mothers respected the child's power to at least partly assemble the toy on his own. They also respected the child by responding when he needed help rather than forcing it on him. The child who received respect learned to assemble the toy more efficiently. In one method, the adult used power on the child. In the other method, the adult shared power with the child. The first group of children were powerless recipients of words. The second group of children were powerful explorers on their own who also had the power to get help from the mother.

The experiment on assembling a construction toy also offers a view of another significant reward — freedom. This goes beyond discipline. Children given the freedom to try on their own did better than those with a dictated format. Freedom allows children to expand to the limits of their talents, to the limits of their power and drive, to the limits of their environment.

As an example of this, learning researchers have found that children often learn better at home than at school. Young children learn what they want and when they want to. Parents and teachers who try to formalize and organize their teaching of young children often find that they are wasting their time. Children learn early that they have the power to use "parent deafness" or "teacher deafness" to escape demands and they exert their own power by not cooperating.

Burton White demonstrated an increase in the IQ of children whose power was respected. He has written of his investigations and findings in his interesting and informative book, *The First Three Years of Life*. He found that children of mothers who allowed them freedom to explore and responded to them when they needed help, had an IQ 15 points higher than other children. The other children were often kept in a playpen and read to on the mother's terms. The results were not as good when the child had to depend on the power of the mother to set the times she gave attention, rather than responding when the child wanted the attention.

Follow-up studies and experience confirm White's research. In Missouri, the public school system sent teachers to teach parents in the home to help their children learn in the first three years of life. They emphasized that the parents should be available to the child as a "consultant," responding promptly and enthusiastically to the child's overtures with appropriate language. Thus, they encouraged development of the child's use of power by offering parental respect for his efforts in exploration and developing skills.

The Missouri Project also encouraged parental use of power. Parents are controllers who set firm and consistent limits. Recognizing the parent as the final authority for her child, they noted that, in the second year of life, children attempt to assert their own power — usually by "negative" behavior, i.e., wanting things their own way. It was recommended that while the parent keeps overall control, "It is sometimes helpful to let your child win a minor struggle." This sounds very much like Baumrind's authoritative parent. The balancing of parental versus child power is at issue, and the child needs to learn how to use his power and that he has enough respect from his parents that he can, on occasion, lead and "make them mind."

> Mother was washing the dishes when 2-year-old Ted came running into the kitchen and breathlessly said, "Mommy, come and see! I did it! I did it!" pulling at her dress. Mommy smiles and dries her hands quickly and lets Ted pull her into the other room to proudly show her that he had managed to put his tricycle on the coffee table. While her first reaction was one of dismay at the mess and the scratch on the table, she controlled her need to rebuke Ted and said, "Well, aren't you strong! How did you get that tricycle on top of the table? But Ted, we don't put big things like that on tables because it can scratch the table. Here, I will help you take it down and tonight we will tell Daddy how strong you are. Don't put the tricycle up there again, though, because you don't want to scratch the table, do you?"

Mother managed to offer respect while educating Ted a bit about what not to do on coffee tables. If he did it again, she would take the trike away for a week. If Ted wants to put a purple sock on one foot and a white one on the other, let him. Soon enough he will act like all of us sheep and follow either our fashions or those of his peers. Respect his attempts to be "grown up," and his inventivenss and creativity, even if his color match seems awful. Many things insignificant to you can be very important to him. Compliment his efforts, admire his small accomplishments. Encourage his freedom to experiment and learn. Later suggest he tell his father about his minor victories. Not only can it make the child's day, but it may also help make yours and Dad's!

The importance of freedom in learning is underscored by complaints of a mother about her bright, eighth-grade boy:

> "He either gets A's or D's for grades. If he is interested in a subject, he gets so involved that he excludes everything else and gets top grades in that subject. But he forgets to turn in his homework in other courses and ends up with D grades!"

Pediatrician Berry Brazelton noted that when children get close to a major achievement, "everything else in their life goes to pot." Some educators complain that many students seem to "disconnect their intelligence from their schooling." Yet these students learn well informally. The implication is that students should mostly be able to take subjects that interest them up to a certain level in their life. Then they have to learn the discipline of doing what they do not necessarily want to do.

Formality is a manifestation of control and power. At home parents rarely set a curriculum — they delight in and appreciate whatever new skills their child develops. This open approach — respecting the child's power to choose to develop skills — allows the child to use his full powers on new projects. Teachers, on the other hand, are said to "select talent rather than develop it," because they have imperatives to teach certain subjects. Ultimately, the child must submit to the power of a formal curriculum, to the need for education in areas where he may have little initial interest. However, especially in the first three years of life, try to give a child the opportunity to learn what he wants, within the limits you can allow. This involves the rewards of freedom and respect and encourages the developing power of the child.

Permissiveness and Power

Freud's theory and the recognition that children have pride and need dignity may have resulted in the advice that children should be permitted to express themselves and their needs freely. Such advice opposes traditional folk wisdom that "children should be seen but not heard." The emphasis upon freedom of expression for children grew to include freedom from punishment, especially freedom from physical punishment. This resulted in a rather vague social movement called permissiveness. The pendulum reached the end of its momentum in the 1960's and has been swinging back since. Permissiveness has been blamed for as many social and personal ills as has child abuse. Let us look at a prototype permissiveness problem which occasionally faces parents, schools and society.

> Marilyn was a confident and somewhat brash 7-year-old. Her well-dressed mother was apologetic for asking the pediatrician about a problem Marilyn had in school. Considerably embarrassed, she said that she would have to take Marilyn out of her second grade class because she was disrupting the class. Silence. "How is she disrupting the class?" asked the doctor. "Well, she, ah — she masturbates in class when she gets bored," Mother replied in a subdued voice. Evidently Marilyn would pull up her dress and go at it in class when the mood struck her, just as she did at home. Her classmates and the teacher were distracted and embarrassed.

Would Freud have approved? Certainly it is a natural impulse, and research indicates that almost all people masturbate sometime or another. Nine-month-old babies find that it feels good and happily play with themselves. Not uncommonly parents ask pediatricians what to do about the child who masturbates with one hand while lying in front of television sucking the thumb of her other hand. The fact that parents tolerate such behavior in the home speaks to the degree that the theory of permissiveness has impacted parenting. It certainly would never have been permitted in the past. In fact, an elderly pro-sexual-expression pioneer recalled having been fitted with iron gloves as a child to keep her from masturbating! Certainly this experience was enough to make her a zealot for the cause of sexual freedom.

Quite possibly the current epidemic of AIDS added to the tragedy of sterility from venereal chlamydia and death from delta virus infections, which make syphilis and gonorrhea seem like kindergarten colds, will cause a pragmatic swing back toward more prudence in sexual matters. Regardless, over twenty-four sexually transmitted diseases exist, and parents must teach their children to protect themselves from them. Marilyn's mother did not want her child to become anxious or "hung up" about sexual expression, but she found sexual taboos necessary. Certainly masturbation can never be easily tolerated in schools because, if for no other reason, it takes the attention of students off of the multitude of other things which must be learned.

Children must be taught self-control, including control of the sex urge. While denial of basic urges may be unrealistic, control of impulses, childish or adult, is essential. Some advocate, "Let it all hang out!" All sorts of movements emphasize freedom for almost any sort of expression or childish behavior. However the real name of the game in growing up means learning to control impulses and behavior. Otherwise society would be in even more trouble than it already is.

Civilization does not tolerate unfettered expressions of emotional impulses very well. Many human urges must be controlled; for example, dishonesty, lack of consideration for other people and their feelings or possessions, and physical aggression. How does a parent control that which should not be permitted? Parents need to "socialize," really civilize, children so we can comfortably live with them in our democratic free society. Do permissive parents succeed in raising socially acceptable children? Possibly. However, the impression that Freud would have approved of Marilyn's behavior is wrong. He was unequivocal on one point: "Civilization is built on the renunciation of instinctual gratification."

Permissive parents come in several types. First, there are those whose children do all sorts of bad things even though the parent does not want to permit such behavior and thinks of himself or herself as a disciplinarian. (We will discuss this in the chapters on "When Discipline Fails.") Such parents permit children to behave badly in spite of attempts at discipline. These parents do not know how to use their power to control their children. The other type of permissive parents deliberately try not to use the power of punishment to control their children. It usually becomes apparent, however, that rewards and bribes do not always work; they may not be enough to teach children to become responsible and self-controlled individuals. So almost all parents punish to control their child's behavior. Although many permissive parents are strongly committed to not spanking their children, unfortunately their permissiveness often allows children to get so out of control that these same parents find themselves resorting to spanking — the very form of discipline they deplore. Their approach to discipline is not organized enough. Catherine Lewis feels this disorganization is the undoing of permissive parents. I feel that the source of the problem is parental reluctance to use power.

Contracts and Privileges

Most children's problems can be handled by the withdrawal of privileges or respect if the child knows that the parent has and will use the power to force him to accept the restrictions imposed. Of all the teaching methods, I favor this one most because it can teach the most if properly done. However, there are at least two situations where it does not work. Children below the age of 2 to 3 years often do not seem to realize the significance of withdrawal of privileges. Nor do withdrawal of privileges or respect work when they are used by the parent in an aggravating power-trip with hostility and scolding. Then the child may perceive the problem to be the parent's and not his. But overall, most of a child's discipline problems can be handled by withdrawal of privileges in a way which isn't harsh, isn't done to relieve parental feelings, and puts the choice clearly up to the child. The child's misbehavior remains the child's problem and correction is within the child's power. The parent simply acts, like the law of gravity, to enforce the consequences of the child's misbehavior, to withdraw rewards rather than scold and withdraw love. This can be accomplished smoothly by the Contracting Technique.

The contracting technique utilizes automatic withdrawal of rewards via a contract with the child. Parents contract with the child by spelling out the desired behavioral changes and establishing the child's responsibility for his own behavior. This offers the child his free choice of reward or no reward, making the behavior the child's problem, not the parent's. For example, take the case of 7-year-old "sloppy Joseph."

Sloppy Joseph had his 7-year-old birthday party. He was a normal, rambunctious child who gave his parents relatively little trouble. However, he dropped his clothes where he changed them and left his room and the family room in shambles. Mother decided that it was time to teach him to obey her often-repeated commands to pick up his room, and to stop doing the picking up herself. So at Joseph's party she gave him a contract along with the other gifts. The contract, printed in bold letters on a single piece of paper read as follows:

A CONTRACT FOR 7-YEAR-OLD JOSEPH

This, being Joseph's 7th birthday and demonstrating that Joseph is now a big boy and should have more privileges and responsibilities, allows us to make the following agreement with Joseph:

Joseph will be allowed to stay up until 9 p.m. instead of 8:30 p.m.

Joseph will pick up all his clothes, put the dirty ones in the laundry and hang up the others.

Joseph will be allowed to ride his bike on the sidewalk clear around the block.

Joseph must always tell Mother or Dad before riding his bike away from the front of the house.

Signed on his seventh birthday

Mon   Dad   Joseph

Joseph, of course, could not read but the contract was carefully explained to him and he was asked if he agreed and wanted to sign. He eagerly agreed and proudly signed. The contract was framed and put on his dresser. That day Joseph did pick up his clothes and was allowed to stay up an extra half an hour. A few days later, however, he forgot. That evening Mother had picked up all his clothes herself without saying a word, without a frown, and put them away. An hour before Joseph's regular bedtime she calmly said, "Joseph, get ready for bed now." "But Mom, it isn't even 9:00 o'clock!" Joseph scowled and said smugly and loudly, "And I am not tired!" Mother replied quietly, "Oh, but you are. You were so tired that you didn't pick up and put away your clothes today. So you obviously need more sleep. You didn't keep your part of the contract so you have to be in bed by 8:30 like you did when you were only five years old. Let's get started, now." The emphasis on the word now and the careful explanation of why Joseph was being "punished" — that is — losing the reward because he did not pick up his clothes was enough. Joseph started preparing for bed with a somewhat startled expression on his face. Point made.

Mother did not make Joseph go to bed earlier so much as a punishment, but as a condition of his contract. In reality, Joseph "punished" himself by failing to do his job. The above example of the mother's use of logic backed by her authority and power to force Joseph to obey his contract now is generally applicable beyond the age of three years.

Pushing the Consequences

However, you may protest, "My Joseph won't stay in bed or go to sleep." True, you can lead a horse to water but can't make him drink. While you can't force sleep, you can force compliance with your command to stay in bed. Sure, Joseph finds all sorts of excuses to get back up. From a drink of water, to going to the toilet, to kissing Mom good night again — the list can be inventive, exhausting and effective — if you let it. Some parents give up; some compromise by lying down beside Joseph until he goes to sleep. Some even let Joseph go to bed with them. In each case, Joseph has used his powers effectively to thwart his parents' will.

Mother must use her power to teach Joseph that she will force obedience. Allow Joseph, once, to briefly explain his needs to you, to get up once to make certain that he has no serious problem or that he really needs to "pee," and then tell him, "Joseph, you are not to get up again. If you don't settle down, if you keep calling me, if you get up again I will .... " Here you have several choices. The most important point is that you act and not talk. Spanking should be avoided at Joseph's age. It should be kept in reserve for open defiance. Scolding, as we saw, really takes away love — a rather heavy bedtime punishment; but forcing isolation represents one of the more effective methods of discipline.

Make Joseph stay in the bedroom by locking the door. A chain lock like those used on the inside of the front door can be put on the outside of the bedroom door so it can be left open a crack. Explain to him, "If you come out again I will have to lock the bedroom door. Then you will not be allowed to come out until morning. Now, which do you want? Are you going to stay in bed or do I lock your bedroom door?" If Joseph comes out again, gently put him back to bed without saying anything, go out, and lock the door. If he hollers or screams or knocks at the door or cries, ignore him and the noise. You have to prove that you mean business, that you are quietly exerting the power to make him obey. Once he accepts this fact, your Joseph will probably go back to bed and will obey better in the future. It has been reported to me that a couple of kids "went wild" when locked in. Even so, and even if the parents let them out, the act itself demonstrated power and the bedtime problem was reduced.

Restraints — Isolation

In a study done of children who were routinely forced to stay in auto safety restraints in the car, it was found that they finally accepted the restraint without fighting and, more importantly, became more obedient in general out of the car. This demonstrates that children do accept the parent's power. In my experience, children who do accept the fact that their parents are in charge and will use their power, generally are happier because they feel more content and secure. Certainly they are more secure and better protected while traveling by auto.

Restraint, isolation, and jail punish effectively. Obviously children should not be locked in closets nor kept in isolation for long periods. If the parent uses this form of punishment fairly and wisely, the child will require less punishment in the future. For the completely out-of-control child, the parent can physically but gently hold the child in her arms until the child ceases struggling and stays still. This demonstrates the parent's ability, and more importantly, the rational will and power to control, to force recognition of the parent's authority. It is a better method than losing one's temper and hitting the child. The parent need not say a word, or a simple explanation can be given, "Johnny, I am going to hold you tight until you quietly settle down and listen." Firmness and tightness should be in just the quantity needed to keep the child in the lap and discourage excess struggling.

Many parents use the valuable technique of "time-outs," forcing the child to sit in a chair or go to his room when he will not. If the child gets down from the chair before the time-out is over, simply stand in front of the child and tell her that she will not be allowed down until she has served her time. Do not scold, do not even explain. Just stand there with a neutral but determined expression on your face — you do mean business and you will act if she tries to get down too soon. The implied threat usually keeps most children in the chair. Generally, the next time-out will not require your physical presence. When the child accepts such restrictions, parental control is assured and a more harmonious family situation results. The kids can be much more fun for the parents and are usually happier and more secure. Less anger exists on both sides.

Confident parents can use their authority to rationally share power with their children. They demonstrate by action, the obvious, that the parent is in charge. Their discipline does control and their demands result in obedience and good behavior. As the child grows, rational-authoritative parents go beyond discipline. They give the child the reward and stimulation of freedom within limits. The limits remain intact regardless of the child's efforts to "break out."

A key to reducing the child's rebellion over limits is to utilize the contract technique. This gradually expands the limits while allowing the child the power to make choices and learn the consequences of his choices. It allows the parents control in a supporting, involved, yet neutral way. The child's reactions become the child's problems, not the parents'. The parents retain their power to limit the child's behavior without the punishment of guilt or the withdrawal of love implied by scolding. They allow and encourage the child to express himself and to argue and demonstrate why the limits should be enlarged. They demand good behavior and build the child's conscience while respecting the child and teaching him to stand up for himself.

Throughout the child's life, the balance of power is gradually shifted from the parent to the child as the child demonstrates his responsibility and ability to handle himself. This usually results in the development of the child's self-esteem, confidence, social responsibility and overall competence. It results in powerful children who can become powerful, effective, productive and content adults.

Experiences and scientific observations indicate the rational-authoritative parent as the most successful model for other parents. However, it helps to have a more detailed step-by-step method for raising children and dealing with the challenges of parenting. A close look at one such method is offered in the upcoming chapters.

PART III

Raising Powerful Children: The Steps

Few would deny the fact that children's formal education is strongly influenced by early learning experience in the home. During the years prior to kindergarten, all children will learn more and at a faster pace than at any other time of their lives.

Arthur L. Mallory
Commissioner of Education, State of Missouri
New Parents as Teachers Project

XI

Raising and Understanding Children

The First Three Years

There are at least one thousand and one ways of raising children. The power factor, a part of each of these 1,001 ways, generally has been ignored or dealt with very indirectly. As no single "right way" exists, I draw upon the successful experiences and feedback of many parents, as well as research about parenting, to offer a model which works well for most. But keep in mind that this is a model — not a sure-fire formula for the proper balance of power.

Instead of simply imitating the model, look for principles, guidelines and examples. Each reader will judge in the light of his or her own unique genetic instincts, childhood background, and adult experience. The techniques and attitudes you use, the amount of power you exert, will be modified according to your own personality and capabilities. The reactions of your particular child will also modify your approach. We are all different.

This synthesis of child-raising represents only one way to raise children. If everyone adopted it, I would be alarmed — and so would many others involved in the practice of pediatrics or research about the growth and development of children. Some disagree strongly with some of my advice, and certainly this model is not for everyone. However, in the context of a rational power balance, mutual respect and love between parent and child can lead to a harmonious and stimulating family. In this spirit, you are offered the following way to raise children.

Birth to Five Months

If you have a child now, you have already experienced the power of your baby's cry and smile. If not, look forward to the experience. It is not all roses though — for example, the labor and delivery can be hard. You have undoubtedly heard of the theory of instantaneous bonding at birth. It does occur — but not always. Sometimes either mother or baby or both are so exhausted that they would rather sleep than meet. You will fall in love with your baby somewhere along the line, so if bells do not ring right away do not be dismayed. You have a lot of intense time to get to know each other; a 24-hour-day every day of the week for the first two months is normal for most infants. They nurse every two to four hours around the clock. Obviously the rewards for parents outweigh the exhaustion or we would not have a human race. You will, probably sooner than later, enjoy your parenting job.

The Stress of Parenting

Meanwhile for those of you just starting, you should know that Mom and Dad do not always smell the roses together. Becoming parents puts new stresses on marriage. Researchers Carolyn and Philip Cowan point out,

> While becoming a parent is anticipated by many with celebration and joy, this dramatic change in adult life is increasingly being described as a time of stress and potential crisis . . . even if the events are anticipated and evaluated as positive. Estimates have been made that up to 83% of couples who had recently become parents reported experiencing a moderate to extreme crisis during the first year of parenthood.

Most of these parents recovered but few had seemed well-prepared for parenthood. We devote weeks of effort to getting ready for the day of labor and delivery. But there is little education about marital adjustment or child-rearing. Instead, "each prepared couple sets off to make the adjustments of the next twenty years virtually on their own." Part of the problem comes from our inner child of the past which accompanies us into parenthood. Often, if not usually, this inner child of the past exerts remarkably firm control. The Cowans lucidly explain:

> In our work with partners becoming parents it seems clear that men and women begin their journey toward parenthood as if they were on separate trains heading down different tracks, hoping somehow to reach the same destination — the formation of their family. Beginning with markedly different biological points of origin, spouses' different routes through childhood ensure their arrival at adulthood with different gender identities, role behavior, judgments, personality traits, and attitudes.

You will both be involved with raising your child, so try to become a team, try to understand each other's attitudes. One helpful method involves routinely spending ten or fifteen minutes each Sunday evening discussing what happened with the baby or children last week — and coming to a consensus on how you are both going to handle the problems which will probably occur in the coming week.

You Cannot Spoil Newborns

Your major task with an infant, aside from feeding, cleaning and protecting him, is teaching him to trust you. Hold him and play with him as much as you can. Try to meet all of his demands, and definitely meet all of his needs. Do not worry about spoiling him — he is born spoiled. You will not make this any worse by holding him all he wants in those first six months. After all, you have met all of his needs in the uterus during the first nine months of his existence — and being born was quite a shock! From the infant's standpoint, when you lay him on his back in the crib, no longer surrounded and cuddled with warm feelings and maternal noises, he feels abandoned — flat on his back at 20,000 feet with no parachute. The American Indians recognized this and their papoose baskets or some substitutes are still not a bad idea.

Maternal needs must be considered too. The baby wants to eat, sleep and be held 24 hours a day, and not much else. Mother, however, must also take care of herself. She has to eat, sleep when she can, and even still go to the toilet. Papoose baskets are not compatible with modern plumbing so you will have to lay the baby down at times when he still wants to be held. It does not hurt him to cry for 10 or 15 minutes while you perform certain necessary functions as long as he gets plenty of tender, loving care most of the time. And his cry, already powerful enough, does not need to be increased by his being picked up at the first whimper. Do not teach him to cry as the only way to deal with the world; do not create a crybaby. Anyway you will find it more fun and satisfying to go to your baby when he is not crying. Play and converse with him and pick him up. This teaches him to trust you while he develops the power of his smile to charm and control you.

Five to Nine Months

For the first few months infants mostly want to eat, sleep, and be held. Then he will increasingly examine both you and his own body closely, delighting in his growing knowledge. In the five to nine month period, however, he begins to develop a more calculating brain. If bored, he will experiment with techniques to try to get the world to mind. He, of course, considers himself the center of the universe and will use all the powers at his disposal to retain this position. One of his powers is the smile. Screaming his head off is another powerful and, in his experience, almost guaranteed method of getting attention. Do not fall into the trap of always letting him run you by the volume of his cry. Research psychologist Burton White feels that, whatever the technique: "If you find that you are picking up your baby and playing with her seven or eight times an hour for six or seven hours a day, you are moving into a pattern that will cause you some grief fairly soon."

Start Setting Limits

White sees this as the root of overindulgence. A wise pediatrician friend of mine said that a child should be left alone at times to learn to contemplate her navel. Start by putting the baby down for a nap at least twice a day and letting her cry it out if she insists. This also applies to night sleep problems which often occur around this age. If the baby has the power to get attention at bedtime by crying, she will keep it up. You will need to use your power of self-discipline to let her be when she cries. Naturally you do not let the baby cry when a possibility of illness exists. Sometimes the problem is the formula. Check with your pediatrician if you feel the crying is not simply for attention.

Sooner or later you must stop getting up five or six times a night, for if you keep that up, you will become exhausted and angry at the baby. Do not worry about his psyche if he cries a few hours the first few nights after you institute your "bedtime is bedtime program." Most get the message after three long nights and you need not feel guilty as long as you give him plenty of tender loving care during waking hours. Granted, it is really hard to let Baby cry it out, but it usually does pay off.

The Difficult Baby

Some children are much harder to handle than others. Psychiatrists Stella Chess and Alexander Thomas of the New York Medical Center wrote an article for pediatricians on "Temperament and the Parent-Child Interactions." About difficult children they note:

> Parents may be intimidated by the infant's frequent loud screaming and 'resistance' to training procedures . . . Such parents are more likely to pressure, appease, punish, or vacillate — all of the time communicating a host of negative feelings to the infant, such as hostility, impatience, or bewilderment.

This leads to an intensification of the infant's negative mood creating a vicious cycle because the parents, being human, become even more upset. But, they point out, the difficult child's innate temperament is not the parent's fault. (Isn't it great to see someone defending parents for a change!) Chess and Thomas recommend that parents not overreact to the child's power-trip. Have patience and give the child time to respond to your techniques. In other words, let it be the child's problem and react positively as much as possible. Perhaps it was experiences with such difficult children that led pediatrician Dick Russell, back in the 1920's, to offer the following advice to parents.

A most important element in providing proper discipline in the child is the establishment of regular habits. When they arrive home with a new baby, parents must remember that the cord is severed and the child has started on the long trip to becoming a separate and distinct individual. Whenever possible, the child should be established in his own room, in his own crib, with a regular schedule for eating, sleeping, and all body functions.

The long process of "civilizing" your child should begin by the eighth or ninth month. Generally this takes about 100 or so years, so do not look for instant results. Start by teaching your baby that he cannot always get immediate gratification. Use your power to ignore him at times; then nurture his powers by responding to him when he really needs you.

9 Months to 24 Months

To civilize your toddler, you must be able to control his actions, to make him mind whether he wants to or not. Many of the problems in child-rearing come from the parents' reluctance to use their power to make the child mind. But lack of limits leaves the child insecure. He finds he often "gets away" with not obeying, so he constantly tests the parent's words to see if any real limits exist. This can put the child in danger (for example, running out into the street) and becomes aggravating to the parent who may then punish the child. But such an inconsistent approach with a hostile tone, naturally angers the child. He may feel that his own worth has been challenged by a scolding, angry parent. The easiest way a child can get even is to repeat the behavior which angered the parent, thus making the family a battleground instead of a secure retreat from the pressures of the world. Parenting becomes a chore rather than a joy. And all because the parent has not exerted enough power to convince the child that she "means business" and that the child *must* obey, like it or not.

For example, if your child runs out into the street calmly pick him up, carry him inside, and put him in bed. Explain that he is too little and too tired to play outside. Leave him there for 15 to 20 minutes before you pick him up. Another solution is to use a harness. Tell the child that if he runs into the street he may get seriously hurt; therefore, you must put him in a harness because he is too little to mind, and you do not want him hurt. Do it and say it calmly. Do not get angry.

Convince the Child He Must Obey

There are many other ways of convincing the child that he must obey. Some toddlers never disobey and cheerfully quit whatever they are doing when told a gentle "No." Most kids are not that pliable. If yours is not, then start now to establish the ground rule that, under certain circumstances, you are the boss and have and will use your power to force obedience if you must. If you "bend the twig" early you can set the tone of parenting and encourage your child's productive growth. There will be fewer "fights" and more time for positive learning.

One way to establish that you mean business is to teach the child you will spank if you must. And for some children you probably must, or the child otherwise will not stop an unacceptable behavior. Start with several assumptions:

1. Practically every child ends up getting spanked even when the parents initially decide never to spank and even though many experts advise never to spank.

2. The less you have to spank the better.

3. If you do spank your child, do it because you love him. You must teach him to live with you and with the rest of the world. You do what it takes to control him, to protect him from himself, not because you are mad.

4. You can use other degrees of punishment instead, such as withdrawal of privileges (which is not very practical at this age), or isolation which often works.

Beyond that, other punishments include scolding or, later, you may find yourself using the punishment of guilt. Inevitably, you come back to facing the issue of spanking. Even advocates of spanking cringe at the idea of spanking babies. Psychologist Burton White believes that there is no need to spank before 14 or 15 months of age. Yet many parents have found that through spanking they can teach the child that the parent has the power to force obedience. If you discipline with love you can set the stage properly, as early as 9 to 12 months. Perhaps early imprinting leaves the child with the "instinctive" knowledge that he *must* mind the parent. Once accepted, this reaction makes for a far happier childhood. My experience with this technique has been consistently positive when parents do it in a non-hostile manner.

Making "Nos" Count

Crawling toddler-age babies have to explore and get into everything. Even after you baby-proof your home, they still can manage to get into trouble. As a result, mothers find themselves saying, "No, no, no!" repeatedly, all day long. By 15 months some little ones sing back, "No, no, no, no." The mother's "no's" have lost meaning and become a ritual rather than a control. Control is essential because the chief risks to your baby's life at this age are accidents and poisons in the home. Without control prevention is difficult.

To use your power efficiently to teach and control a toddler, you should not confront him with a whole world of "No's." Nor should you say "No" if you cannot or do not follow through. Instead, pick out two objects, such as the light cords and the stove, and use these to teach the basic lesson that when Mother says "No" she means "No" and that if the child does not obey, punishment follows, not because of Mother's anger but because he disobeyed. Thus, the child has the problem, not the mother.

When he heads for the light cords say "No" in a firm (not scolding) voice. Your toddler will probably smile in appreciation of the attention and continue toward the cords. Then say, "No, or Mother will spank," in a calm but firm voice. If he continues, keep repeating the key words, "No, Mother spank" as you go to the wall where you have hung up in plain sight a wooden spoon or paint mixing paddle. Keep repeating the "No, Mother spank" words while you go to him, pull up his pant leg and spank him on the calf. As soon as he cries, stop and go hang up the stick or spoon. Go back to him, pick him up and comfort him. You spanked him because you love him and did not want him to be electrocuted. You did not want to punish, and you are not mad. It is just like the law of gravity — if you fall, it hurts. Important, again, let him know by your action and attitude that it is his problem, not yours.

If you are consistent in your spanking about the two items first chosen to educate him about the rules, about your power and determination, you will find that he will start leaving them alone. Then you can add another item, such as your fireplace, to the list of "No's". Do not overwhelm him with a multitude of things which makes the world a forbidden place. Instead, gradually extend the list as he learns to leave forbidden items alone. This way, you can have him under control with only a rare spanking. Oh sure, he will occasionally have to test again to see if you still mean it; but, overall, there will be few spankings, each done on an effective, nonangry, nonfrustrated teaching basis which will convince him that he must obey you. You will have "bent the twig" and established a long-term attitude of discipline, of teaching. You will have wisely exerted your power and have control of your child. Teach him now to limit his own behavior so you will not have to be after him continually. Use your power rationally and authoritatively. This way you will be far more effective in helping him develop his own powers and competency.

Alternatives to Spanking

If you still do not want to spank, at least do not fall into the trap of distracting the baby each time he does something dangerous like pulling on a lamp cord. Smart little ones do not take long to figure out that pulling on the lamp cord effectively gets attention. So, if life has been a bit boring, he pulls on the cord! If you cannot bear to spank the baby for dangerous behavior, use the system of warnings described earlier and put him in "jail." The playpen serves rather well for this function. Keep the toys out of the playpen and primarily use it as a form of punishment. (I always thought that the bars of a playpen were quite similar to those in the county jail. One way or another you have to teach your child to stay out of harm's way.)

Avoid the trap of scolding and yelling to punish. I think that scolding is worse punishment than a nonangry slight spank. Others disagree. But most families who use the non-hostile wooden spoon discipline-with-love technique get good results such as clearer limits, fewer confrontations, less scolding and fewer spankings. This creates a happier environment with more freedom for the child.

Power as a Reward

You can teach even more by reward than you can by punishment. While teaching your toddler to respect your power, encourage the development of his own power. Start by letting him make you mind sometimes. Give him the freedom to explore and be ready and available to respond to his requests for help. When you stop what you are doing and help him explore a closet or read to him from his favorite book, you demonstrate his importance and power. If he wants to take you into the next room, go if you can. Remember Burton White's advice and do not overdo it, but praise his leadership and curiosity. Let him make choices.

A multitude of parenting roles come with raising children. You are a caretaker, servant, teacher, disciplinarian and consultant to your child. Burton White, reporting on three decades of investigations in his book, *Educating the Infant and Toddler*, writes:

> The Harvard Preschool Project recommendations for helping to develop intelligence ... emphasize the importance of learning conditions during the eight-to-thirty-six month period. Newly crawling infants should be allowed to practice their climbing and other emerging motor skills. *For most of their waking hours, they should have easy access to people who have a very special love for them.* These people should talk to them about what they are focusing on at the moment, using ordinary language to expand ideas and introduce new ideas. They should lavish affection, encouragement, and enthusiasm on their babies, thereby intensifying their interest and excitement in learning. They need not make use of elaborate educational toys or programs.

Dr. White has found that beautifully developed babies very commonly get no more than one and a quarter hours of direct interactional time with their parents in the 1 to 3-year range. So it does not take a huge amount of time to raise a toddler. What it does take is fairly consistent availability. Try to be present to respond, say five to ten times an hour. Such responses need not take much time.

Limiting the Toddler's Power

Around 12 months, many toddlers begin to realize their power-lessness. They are at the bottom of the totem pole — told when to sleep, what to eat, when not to cry! Everyone in their lives can do anything they can do, better. Depending on their innate nature, some may begin "serious" testing of their limits to try to expand their power. Others will become frustrated enough to have temper tantrums. They whine or cry, and if that does not work, they will lie on the floor and kick and scream — even bang their heads until they are black and blue. They are saying, "Stop the world, I want off!" Others get so upset, they will hold their breath until they pass out. Nature intervenes with the breath holder and even though he may turn blue, he will start breathing again. So how do you handle the tantrum problem? If you scold, spank or give attention, they find that, although the world does not stop, it does become focused on the child. Many children will continue to have tantrums because you spank — for many "hams," being center stage is worth it.

My favorite poet Ogden Nash wrote "But joy in heaping measure comes to children whose parents are under their thumbs." Unfortunately this joy may not be long lasting. Parents who are told that they must allow their children to assert themselves, to show initiative, often ask, "Do we let them run the family?" If you do let your child run you, then you are not functioning as a parent — you become a slave. You should, instead, be a consultant.

Allow your baby freedom to explore and respond enthusiastically and frequently to his achievements and requests. But you cannot always respond when he wants you to. When that happens do not let a difficult child get the upper hand with temper tantrums. Sooner or later he will find no joy in his control; first, because harrassed parents who give in ultimately become angry; and, second, because the rest of the world is not likely to obey him. You cannot always obey him either.

Dealing With Tantrums

If you and a friend are talking and your child has a tantrum because you are not paying full attention to him, ignore him. If he makes so much noise that you cannot hear, or if he comes up and slugs you demanding your attention, calmly pick him up like a sack of sugar while you continue talking with your friend. Take him to his crib and lay him down without a word. Walk out. Leave him until he quits crying and then go get him. Do not scold, do not give any more attention than you absolutely have to. When rewarded by being center stage for his tantrums, he will more likely continue them. That happened to Jimmy.

Jimmy's mother was alarmed because Jimmy's forehead was a mass of bruises, swollen, sore and black and blue. The bruises had accumulated over the past week as the 20-month-old boy would bang his head on the kitchen floor in the throes of temper tantrums. If Mother did not instantly stop what she was doing and respond to Jimmy, he would scream, throw himself on the floor and bang his head until she gave up and met his powerful demands, be it for a glass of juice or a toy. Heart in throat, Mother took Jimmy to the pediatrician. The advice given was simple. Ignore the tantrums completely; act as if he is not there while he has the tantrums.

Uncertain but desperate, Mother followed the advice. A week later she called the pediatrician to relate the following: For two days she ignored Jimmy's tantrums and head banging. On the third day, Jimmy came into the kitchen, while mother was stirring an omelet, and demanded juice. Mother could not stop at that moment so Jimmy threw himself down and began banging his sore head. Suddenly he stopped, got up and ran into his bedroom. Quickly he came back dragging a pillow behind him. He placed the pillow by Mother's feet and began banging his head on the pillow! Soon he quit the tantrums entirely. A power struggle settled.

Giving Over Power

As your child gets older, she will begin to try more sophisticated methods to be big. What she does depends on how she defines being "big." Her actions mirror the actions of the adults in her world, as she sees it. It can startle one to realize that that is how she sees us! She may scold you, try to boss you or do whatever else she perceives as being big and powerful. Burton White's research showed that at the 14 to 24-month stage the most striking qualities are the growth of individuality and the struggles with authority that normally occur. It can really be humorous to watch these power plays, these early attempts to be adult. However, take them seriously.

You must make your child mind, but turnabout is fair play. She needs to practice her version of power on you. So allow her to make as many choices as possible. Let her boss you on occasions — look on it as a form of play where she is the mommy and you are the baby. Also let her help you with your work. A turn at washing spoons or following you around the rug with a toy vacuum cleaner is a heady experience for a 20-month-old. Toys which mimic adult tools, for example a toy lawn mower, give the child the chance to play grown-up. She needs the chance to practice "being big," so she can develop her power and self-esteem.

If, by now, you have convinced your child that you have the power to make her mind, you will rarely have to spank. You will find that your best results in discipline come with a minimum of scolding. Instead, admire her efforts and applaud even the slightest accomplishment. This demonstrates your respect and encourages her efforts to develop. Emphasize the positive aspects of your child's behavior in such a way that she accepts "good" behavior as good for her — not necessarily just good for you. Rather than telling her she is Mommy's big girl, say, "You sure are a big girl now."

You need to begin the process of separating yourself from your baby. It is hard to let her grow up, but necessary. She may have her own separation fears when she finds that she can walk away and leave you. This can be pretty spooky, being able to leave mother. Help her overcome separation fears by playing peek-a-boo, a game in which you disappear but always reappear. Later extend it to playing peek-a-boo around the corner to condition her to the idea that she does not need to be with you all the time.

Interaction and Learning

Burton White observed the language teaching styles of parents whose children acquired language especially well during the first three years. Following is a list of characteristic behaviors of these parents by Burton White:

Table XI

**CHARACTERISTICS FOR
ENHANCED LANGUAGE LEARNING**

1. The child (between 9 and 24 months of age) usually initiated about ten interchanges an hour with her parents during typical daytime activities. The parents usually initiated a similar or smaller number of interchanges. (With first-born children, parents initiated more interchanges than were evident when later-born children were involved.)

2. The parents took the time to identify the interest of the child.

3. Words and appropriate actions, focused on the child's interest, usually followed.

4. The words used were at or slightly above the child's apparent level of comprehension.

5. Full sentences, rather than single words or brief phrases, were the norm.

6. Related ideas were introduced often.

7. Most interchanges lasted between twenty and thirty seconds. Lengthy teaching sessions were rare.

8. Stories were read often, but the child's attention did not become sustained until well into the second year. For a few months after the child's first birthday, picture books were used habitually for "labeling" sessions.

The Terrible Two's

The terrible two's need not be terrible if you recognize that the child acts in response to fears, lack of respect, a desire to run the world — or maybe all three! If you have a 2-year-old who gives you problems, go back to the beginning of this chapter and discover that it is not too late to start over. First make certain that your child trusts you by offering conversation, by touching and hugging, by being consistent in your discipline. Go beyond discipline by emphasizing the positive with praise and rewards, by being available and by being aware of the source of fears. One source of fears is the fear of separation from mother. As we noted before, when Johnny finds that he can crawl, walk and run away from mother, whom he regarded as almost part of himself, it can lead to confusion.

Fear of Separation

It is a big world and all of a sudden Mother is not in the room with him. So he cries and runs to find her. She is mopping the floor, and, not wanting him to track it up, she tells him to stay in the other room. That's too much! He feels rejected! Crying, Johnny rushes to Mother and grabs her legs. She has to pick him up to be able to do anything, so she does — crossly. Naturally Mother is a bit put out too! The floor must be mopped in spite of an unreasonable Johnny, but she sighs and tries to comfort him because she has little other choice except to put him in his room and listen to him cry. She briefly comforts him with an undertone of frustration — leaving Johnny with the fear: "Maybe she really does not want me!" So when he is put down, he immediately chases after Mother again. If he does leave her alone, Mother gives a sigh of relief and tries to get all her necessary housework done.

This is a trap. Johnny soon finds that, if he bugs Mother, he gets attention; and if he does not, he does not get attention. The more he chases Mother, the greater her practical need to get away from him. It becomes a vicious cycle, a parody of an anxious child pressuring a harassed mother in an attempt to assure himself of his security and her love.

You can help avoid this problem by looking for times when your Johnny is not doing anything particularly bad or particularly good and he is *not* demanding your attention. Stop what you are doing, put the mop or whatever down, and go give him a minute free. Not because he is good or bad, but because you want to, because you enjoy him. Tousle his hair, kiss him, pick him up and swing him around, throw a ball to him — you only need to spend a minute. You have other things to do and so does he. Let him do them. This often relieves the pressure and reassures him of your interest — of your love.

Some children have marked instinctive stranger fears, even to the point that they are afraid of grandparents or Father. This type of fear passes with time and conditioning. To handle the situation, have the rejected or feared grandparent sit on the floor and begin to play with some of the child's toys, pretty much ignoring the child. After a while, the child may join in the play. It takes time but it usually works. These stranger fears (or shyness) usually reduce anyway as the child's sense of personal power and competency build — as the child begins to feel respected.

Respecting Your Child

Respect, as comic Rodney Dangerfield complains, is hard to get. Many 2-year-olds resent being at the bottom of the social pecking order — some more than others. So they rebel, especially when they find their rebellion can be effective. Commonly they discover that they can thwart some parental power-trips, especially when the parent tries to force them to eat or go to the toilet. They find, in at least these arenas of cooperation, that they have the power of decision. So they fall back on the ego-satisfying action of ignoring requests by mother-deafness or by mute inaction, if not open rebellion. The most difficult of these forms of rebellion to deal with is the passive aggression of "not hearing" or the stubborn refusal to cooperate. Such behavior has caused more parental grey hairs and ineffective spankings than most of the other negatives put together.

Parents soon find it easier to keep a child from doing something than it is to force him to do something. The child protects his basic power of self-determination as much as possible. And in the areas of eating and toilet training, you will both be better off if you back off. Recognize that you are dealing with the child's basic ego. If he gives in and eats for you, he has lost a power struggle — lost the essential sense of self-esteem that the Mohandas Gandhi used to break the will of the powerful British Empire. In India's struggle for self-rule, the Indians lay on the train tracks by the thousands, giving the British the choice of running over them or stopping the trains. It worked. India's commerce ground to a halt and Britain ultimately gave up the struggle. India won back its self-respect.

Your 2-year-old must win some self-respect too, or his development will be blighted. You can help by looking for every opportunity to offer him praise, respect and other rewards. Remember that he tries hard to be adult, tries desperately to build some power. He needs a helping hand more than a hand on his bottom. He needs help exploring his world, finding stimulation such as new games and discovering he even has the power to say "no" to your help. He needs the attention of being read to and he especially needs a chance to practice his new-found powers of speech and socializing. All of these take the form of play — very serious business with a 2-year-old. Above all, his own desires should be respected as much as possible.

When 2-year-old Jane was brought to the doctor, she had not been eating. Her distraught parents had tried everything and could not even force her to take vitamins. She had not gained much weight and her parents were certain that something was terribly wrong with her. They had, at first, forced food into her mouth but she found she could spit it out faster than they could put it in. Then they begged, pleaded, cajoled, scolded, spanked — all for naught. A complete examination revealed that nothing was wrong with Jane. The pediatrician then did two things. At noon he had Jane eat at a table with three other 2-year-olds who were always hungry and put just a little food on all their plates. Soon the other children started taking Jane's food. After a few days, she decided that possession was a virtue and began eating to protect her food from her hungry tablemates.

The pediatrician asked the parents how they would react if they worked for a boss who took care of all their meals. The boss ordered the type and quantity of food they were offered and then became irritated if they did not eat every crumb off of their plates. "How long," the doctor asked, "would either of you put up with such denigrating pressure?"

The point was made. Children must have some essential powers over themselves and will go to almost any length to get them. The wise parent will recognize and respect these needs and allow the child as much of such power as he can handle.

Taming the Tyrannical Toddler

Some childen want more than just the power to make decisions about themselves. They also have the desire to run their parents. The techniques they use to achieve the role of boss are legion. Some use whining to get their way. Others resort to tantrums if the tantrums work. Some try to charm their parents into submission to their desires or sulk if that does not work. But one way or another, some little would-be tyrants get their parents under their thumb. Those parents literally jump when the child commands. They become slaves rather than parents and indulge the child's every whim.

Overindulgence may start from parental love, but that kind of love does the child no good. Once out of the parent's sphere of influence, the child will have to face a social structure unlikely to overindulge him. Such children often become bitter at a society which they do not think recognizes their innate worth, their requirement to be number one at all costs. What it takes for parents to redress such a power imbalance is a firm hand, occasionally applied to the child's buttocks. It requires the parent to take over and make the child submit to the parent's will and authority.

Another method of rebelling is running away. Some children have no fear and delight in taking off on excursions of their own. Taking such a 2-year-old shopping in a crowded store becomes an anxiety-producing, ulcer-making adventure for Mother or Dad. You look at an item on the shelf and you have lost a child! It can be dangerous, and in this age of overemphasis on child snatching, it can be a harrowing experience. Handle your fearless explorer by either not taking him shopping with you or, if you have to, using a harness and a leash. Better that than the possibility of having him run out into the street and getting hit by a car.

Over a period of time, you will be able to educate your "excessively mobile child" to stay with you when you are out in public. First make shopping with you a privilege rather than a duty. Get a sitter because Johnny is too little to go shopping and has to stay home. Later, as a reward for some sort of "grownup" behavior, ask him if he wants to go to the store with you. Perhaps you can offer to let him pick out a toy. Tell him, however, that if he does not stay right with you as big boys do, that he will not get the toy and will not be able to go shopping again until he grows up some more. If he runs away, put him immediately back in the harness and calmly say, "That's too bad, Johnny. You did not stay with me as you should so you have to have the harness. And you act too little to be able to pick out a toy."

Unfortunately, some Johnny's and Betsy's rather quickly figure out that you will be embarrassed if they have a tantrum or cry in public. They correctly perceive that this puts them into a position of power. So they cry or scream to punish you for not minding them or not buying the toy. Do not give in. Many parents are so mortified that they give in to avoid a scene. Instead, skip the rest of your shopping, swallow your embarrassment, and pick the child up and calmly leave. Take him home and get a neighbor to watch him while you go back and finish your shopping. Do not scold. Do not get angry. Do not let him manipulate you or "force" you into buying him something you do not want for him. Act. If you give in, you set the stage for future problems and power fights. Win now, and then you can hold your peace. If you do not win now, it will be worse in your child's 4th year.

XII

Raising and Understanding Children

Ages Three to Nine

The 3-year-old, one of my favorite ages, is an interesting creature
with an active, blooming personality, growing intellectual capacity and an
increased awareness of the people in his world. He can be a lot of fun.

> Little Jenny's father was ordering their dinner at
> McDonald's. He turned to Jenny and asked, "Do you want an
> ice cream sundae?" "No!" said an indignant Jenny, "I want it
> today."

Often 3-year-olds tend to be very literal and misunderstand our
confusing English language. They also have an open mind which can accept magic as reality. When facts do not suit them, they will turn their back
on them by entering their own personal imaginary world which they
structure to suit themselves.

At this age, they develop an acute sense of possession and want to
know what belongs to whom. Among other things, they note the differences in plumbing between the sexes and become concerned about their
own anatomy and role. Little girls who have an admired older brother in

school may announce, "When I grow up and go to school, I am going to be a boy!" Who knows, perhaps it can be issued along with the equipment for school?

Some little boys may decide that it is better to be a girl and start trying out dresses. While downtown shopping, one enterprising 3-year-old boy, put his father into shock when he said, "Let's go in the store and buy Mommy a penis." In their magic world, things can change easily. They would not be surprised if they levitate; and, for them, Superman is as real as policemen. Boys especially have a need to experience power, even if vicariously — thus the obsession with toys such as He-Man, the Hulk, and a host of other muscle-bound, ferocious dolls. Some 3-year-olds develop imaginary friends they can command. All of this offers a cushion against the realities of their world.

Building A Positive Self-Image

Parents have a major impact on the self-image of 3-year-olds. Tell a 3-year-old "You are bright," and she will usually nod her head in agreement. She may also believe you if you say, "You are dumb." Likewise, if you tell Jane "You are a nice girl who doesn't hit other people," she may accept this as fact even though she may have recently belted her little brother. Thus, it becomes important to offer a positive picture to a 3-year-old who will more often than not try to live up to that image. Still, children are not really "blank slates" which parents fill in. Each child has a partially predetermined personality, and physical and intellectual capacity; but parents can have an effect upon the thoroughness of the use and development of those capacities. So think positively about your child and try to stimulate her to full development as best you can. A positive attitude may override a lack of talent. The coach of the world champion Celtics basketball team was asked what was more important in a player, talent or attitude? He replied:

> "Attitude takes you farther — as a person and as a player. If a player doesn't have talent, he can show some scrap; he can show some hustle. He can be the best loose-ball getter."

Reasoning With Your 3-Year-Old

The 3-year-old enters a new era of intellectual awareness. You can reason with him on a more abstract plane than you could in the first three years of life. But to reason effectively, you must look at the world as he sees it — usually from a more honest, openly selfish viewpoint than most adults admit to. So to reason with him, you need to point out what the consequences of his actions are for him — and play down the parent's response. It is better to say, "If you don't stop that, you will have to go to your room because you must be tired or you wouldn't act this way," than to say, "I have told you before, if you don't stop that, I will be mad at you!" In the first case, the child has a problem and a choice allowing him to learn to exert the power of self-control. In the second case, the issue centers on the parent's feelings and, if the child obeys, he loses "face" or self-esteem by giving into the parent's power.

Modeling Self-Control

While we divide the discussion of power and discipline by age, problems do not necessarily respect such boundaries. Most 2-year-old's feelings and actions carry over into age three. The power-trip surfaces as the omnipotence complex (and hopefully peaks at the age of three). At this time most children want to be God and run the world. You, the parent, are the world. So they do what they can to get you under control. However, limits are essential both to protect the child and to teach him to live congenially with other people. You need to retain control as you grant him the freedom to experiment with some portions of life. Growing means expanding the limits. The expansion may seem slow to the child, but slowness usually pays because of the child's undeveloped self-control. He will learn some self-control from watching you use your power of self-control. He also learns by observing other adults and children who handle increased freedom and responsibility. In the process, the young god should experience the power of self-control and its role in self-determination and freedom. But if he is unable to control himself, then the old narrower limits of discipline will have to be invoked. These limits remind him to control himself so he can get along with other people.

Teaching Respect

In the past, folk wisdom was that a child should be seen but not heard. The concept still rings true for two reasons. First, children who never outgrow their selfish demands to be center-stage and first in line become very difficult to live with. Probably those are the ones who gravitate to politics and acting for a living. Second, if a child succeeds in getting everything he wants while still a child, then why should he want to become adult? Children should not be given adult privileges until they earn them, until they assume adult responsibilities. So do not allow your child to rudely interrupt adult conversations. Force him to grant some respect to the adults in his world. A "yes, sir" or "no thank you, ma'm" never hurts anybody. If your child does not respect adults, why would he ever want to become one? A very firm hand is still needed at this age.

Mary was a bright-eyed, precocious, 3-year-old chatter-box. Whenever Mother tried to talk on the telephone or to guests, Mary would interrupt with a constant line of chatter, even pulling on the guest's dress to get attention. Mother would constantly have to stop her conversations with others and answer Mary's insistent demands for attention. While Mary was cute and precocious, if occasionally irritating to adults, she didn't have many friends her age because she tried to dominate their play. Later she had problems in school because she could not be quiet during lessons. To correct the problem, Mary had to learn to share center-stage. Mother realized that children should be seen but not always heard.

Before the next guest came Mother told Mary that it was very childish and impolite for her to interrupt adult conversations and that she would have to be quiet if she stayed in the room with the adults. If she wanted, she could go to the family room and play, but she was not to interrupt adult conversations. When the guest came, Mary started her usual line of prattle. Mother and her pre-warned guest ignored Mary completely. So Mary marched over to the guest and pulled her dress, loudly saying, "Mrs. Smith, did you see my new doll that Mommy got me?" Mrs. Smith ignored Mary. Mother, keeping up the prior conversation with Mrs. Smith, took Mary's hand and led her to the door, saying briefly, "Go into the family room and stay there until I come for you." She then went back to Mrs. Smith. Mary shrewdly looked back at Mother and burst into tears. Mother calmly got up and closed the door into the family room so she and Mrs. Smith would not have to compete with Mary's sobbing.

A persistent Mary might have to be put into her room and even locked in if she refused to stay. But after a few times, she will learn that she cannot gain center stage by her verbal assault or tears. Meanwhile, at other times, she can be invited to participate in certain adult conversations and learn that one of the prices for being included is to wait one's turn and another is to respectfully address guests as, "Ma'm or Sir." However, be sure to give her a turn and occasionally include her in the conversation. Such behavior by the parent increases the virtue and prestige of being adult and gives Mary more reason and stimulus to act grown-up rather than childish.

The 4-Year-Old

As children reach the age of four, they usually find that many other people in the world also have a God complex and, therefore, do not respect the child's omnipotence. As a result, many 4-year-olds become angry and hostile toward a world which will not mind them. Depending upon their personality, they may openly fight city hall, sassing and harassing parents and others, or they may retreat into the stubbornness of passive-aggression and refuse almost all cooperation. Although some 4-year-olds do not seem to have a hostile bone in their body, most of them become very annoyed when parents will not mind them. In retaliation, many rebel. This is less likely to happen if you have convinced your child early on that he or she cannot be God.

Correcting Disrespectful Children

Do not respond to the rebellion or hostility from your child with counter-hostility. Your scolding, icy tone, body language, hollering or spanking, simply court more hostility. Your child learns adult behavior by modeling and mimicking you. If your hostile child sees you acting hostile, then his actions become more acceptable. On the other hand, do not ignore his hostility. Some children of this age assume that a behavior left uncorrected is acceptable behavior. Children should not be allowed to sass or bad-mouth their parents or other adults. So teach by example or, failing that, by directly controlling their actions.

Respond to disrespectful children with firm discipline. Usually you can use withdrawal of privileges, "time-outs," or isolation. The very hostile child should receive very few spankings. Spank only if the child openly defies withdrawal of privileges or refuses to accept isolation. Always give the reason you have to spank. Do not spank when you are angry or to relieve your feelings. Afterwards remark, "It's too bad I had to spank you." Do not apologize. The spanking was the result of the child's misbehavior, not your desire to spank. Therefore, let it be known that the spanking was the child's problem, not yours. Later, after things have settled down, follow through with a hug and brief explanation of why such behavior will not be tolerated and offer a positive outlook for the future saying, "You learned from that spanking. People will like you better when you act more grown up. Big boys have more fun than little boys."

Fears of the 4-Year-Old

After bad behavior and hostility, whether punished for it or not, the children may feel quite insecure. Then it becomes olive branch time. They offer love to the parent they temporarily hated. Children usually feel that they hurt you when they get mad at you. They also assume that you are probably equally mad at them. After all, children are primitive. Like the voodoo witch doctor who believes he can harm an enemy by putting a needle through a doll made in the image of that enemy, children believe that their feelings have power. Actually, so do we. We stand and roar at the players on the football field, urging them to win. When they do win after such a demonstration, we often feel quite smug. We succeeded!

Children do believe that their own feelings have an effect, especially on the parents. There have been cases when a child became panic stricken after shouting at mother, "I hate you, I wish you were dead!" The child then fears that she may have caused real harm, that mother might indeed die and it would be her fault. Occasionally a child will not let the parent out of sight because she fears that if she does, the parent may die or leave.

Fears of all sorts usually peak at age four. Children go through the band-aid stage and the monster stage to the biggest fear of all — that of being separated from home and parents. They begin to realize that they live in a big world and they could get lost or kidnapped. So they worry.

The Separation Trauma

Children also discover that one ultimately grows up and, when one grows up enough, one leaves home. Of course, they are not ready to leave and find the concept frightening. Many think it over and come up with a smashing solution — they will marry Mother or Father and thus never have to leave. This creates a sort of warm feeling in parents even if they have to convince the child that he cannot marry them. These worries are exacerbated when the child discovers the concept of the final separation, death — when you leave and never come back. It bothers them greatly, so they ask all sorts of questions trying to find a way around the finality of death.

Even if convinced that they will go to heaven in a golden Mercedes with angels playing harps all the way, children are not about to leave just to go to heaven. Most adults share the same feelings. In the child's feelings, death just does not compute. Gradually, they stop the persistent questioning — it is easier to bury the subject. Often they will then have nightmares or odd fears which represent suppressed death fears. Later on children will find ways to protect themselves from death. Some announce that they are not going to grow up, explaining that, "If you grow up you get old and die!" — the Peter Pan in us all — a comforting myth that gives us some protection against harsh reality. Generally try to keep children away from the concept of death, certainly away from funerals (unless of the parent of a 9-year-old or older). Overexposure can create lifelong anxieties and other psychological disorders. A child young enough to believe in Santa Claus is young enough to be spared much exposure to death.

The 5-Year-Old

Fears do get under control when the child gets older. By age five, children want to be big and important, a status incompatible with being little and afraid. So they try to conquer their fears; but underneath it all, fears still exist. First, there is the fear of leaving home for kindergarten. Many kids, when told that they are going to school say, "Thank you but I would just as soon stay home with Mother."

> Sitting on the examination table waiting for her preschool physical, 5-year-old Jane asked if she would need any shots. When told yes, she picked up her dress and calmly informed her mother, "I don't think I want to go to school! Let's go home now."
>
> Later, after the shots had been given, she thought it over and changed her mind. "I guess I will go to school now," she informed her mother.

Separating for School

Even the child who goes to school happily and willingly finds that he shares a jungle with 30 other wild animals. Other kids may get in line in front of him or even dislike him. Then there are teachers who make him sit down and be still! So a good amount of homesickness occurs in school and when school is out, Johnny heads straight home wanting more love, more attention and more security.

> Johnny says to himself, "You could pour love over me by the bucketful and I still wouldn't have enough." When he gets home, he notices that Mother and Father "waste" a lot of time on each other, when he wants it. So he tries to increase his share. Underneath it all, he has not given up the idea of marrying Mother. So when he sees Mom and Dad together, he butts in, elbows between them, attempts to become the center of attention. Over a period of time, he finally decides that he cannot have the same relationship with Mother that Dad has, and gradually he accepts the idea that, sometime in the dim distant future, he may leave home. With this concept well in mind, and stirred by

a few adolescent hormones, he begins the process of looking for a substitute. This is the genesis of the song, "I want a gal, just like the gal, that married dear old Dad." If I can't have Mom, I am going to get one just like her! But right now, he is faced with the jungle of school, the uncertainties of the future and the dawning realization that sooner or later he will probably have to leave home — rejected!

Many children around the age of four to six years really worry about the possibility of having to leave home in the future. Some of them, as a result of this worry, decide not to give up the idea of marrying Mom or Dad. So they court one parent, directly or indirectly, competing with the other. Often Johnny will feel that he has truly replaced Dad as number one in Mother's eyes. This relieves some of his anxieties about the future at the expense of Father, but one cannot hurt a parent he loves without some sense of guilt. And guilt hurts. So childlike, he tends to blame the one who made him feel guilty. This makes him angry at Dad, and he gets even by doing those little things which drive Dad up the wall.

Warring With the Same Sex Parent

The stage is set for a fight that, underneath it all, can last a lifetime. Neither participant recognizes how it started. They do know that they do not really like each other. This leads to the classic triangle situation of two against one; for, as Mother sees the anger in her husband toward her Johnny, her maternal instincts cause her to protect Johnny. This makes Dad even more angry, and the family can be split into warring camps with Mother and Johnny on one side against Dad on the other.

To avoid the problems which ensue from this situation, there are several points to keep in mind. First, a child may be undergoing his own private form of hell over leaving to go to school. He may not feel powerful enough to handle that! Children sometimes need more TLC than we think they do. Second, Mother and Father must be a team. It is almost better for both parents to do "wrong" things in child-rearing as a team than to do "right" things separately, in conflict, and be played apart. Third, when a child does act hostile or immature, do not react in the same way. If you do, you have made the child's behavior your problem by getting emotionally involved. That lessens the reason for the child to change his behavior in spite of the power you use to punish. Instead of getting mad, let it be the child's problem, one which requires you to act, to discipline and control, but not one that makes you upset.

Dealing With Regression

Let the child be upset by the consequences of his actions. Recognize the natural childishness of his actions and emotions. You need to help him mature. So do not mimic his hostility. Instead, point out to him in a factual, non-angry tone, "Johnny, you are six years old now, but you are acting like a 3-year-old. How come? Come over here and sit with me and tell me about it." In other words, you will accept him as a 3-year-old.

Avoid saying, "Johnny, when are you going to act your age?" or "Why don't you grow up?" This approach essentially tells Johnny that you want him to grow up and also implies by tone that you will be happy to have him off of your hands — happy to have him separate from you. But underneath it all, he fears separation most of all. Children frequently react to that threat by regressing and acting babyish; as babies they were safe and accepted and not threatened with being pushed to grow up and leave. So, instead, point out factually the immature way the child is acting and accept him anyway.

Accepting immature behavior does not end the problem. You help your child mature by treating him as he acts. If he acts like a 3-year-old, treat him like a 3-year-old. If he wants to go out and ride his bike, you say "no" and point out that 3-year-olds do not ride bikes, or perhaps cannot go out to play in front of the house. If this justified limiting of privileges angers him and he storms around or refuses to obey, then calmly but firmly say, "I guess I was wrong. Now you are acting more like a 2-year-old having a tantrum. You must be tired! Go in to bed now and take a nap." If he refuses to obey and go to bed, say, "Now you are acting so little that I may even have to spank you if you don't go into bed right now."

Side-Stepping Anger

When you do have to punish, including spanking, do it because you have to. If you spank because you are angry, then the child may feel that he wins by getting spanked — he forced a confrontation and got you into a fight — showing that he is on closer to equal terms with you and is got enough of his own licks in the squabble to anger you. So when you tell your child you will have to spank if he does not obey, do not say it through clenched teeth. If you do, the same words take on an entirely different meaning, such as, "I can hardly wait to get my hands on you because you have made me mad!" In that case, the lesson of the spanking is lost: it proves only that you are more angry, more physically powerful, and can punish. The child's actions which initiated the problem become less important.

If you can discipline calmly, then the issue remains focused on the child's immature actions and less on the parental reaction. Many parents who have never spanked their child until they were angry or who easily anger, say, "I don't know if I can stay calm." Granted, it is easier said than done. However, self-control enables you to use your power effectively. Become a good role model by demonstrating mature behavior so your child will at least be motivated to start acting a little grown-up. Control yourself. Don't let your own inner child of the past run you — don't expect your child to act maturely unless you can.

Keep Your Sense of Humor

When children do not respond well to your attempts to discipline, humor can be lifesaving! It really is humorous to see, say, a small third grade girl keeping a family on the ceiling.

Jeanie was temperamental. Outside the home and in school she was an angel. Everyone liked her. But Mother, who had a boy whom she got along well with, clenched her jaw as she told of Jeanie's problems. Jeanie had tantrums, hit brother, argued with Mom and Dad, and defied their orders to go to her room. She continued this behavior even though the parents were strict. They took away privileges, they scolded, they followed through and made her go to her room. But she persisted and Mother realized that she and Father were in a chronic fight with Jeanie. Mother hollered and became more and more irritated as Jeanie became older and the problem escalated.

Mother was taken aback when she was told by her pediatrician that she was permissive. "I am not," she said, "I do follow through!" However, it was pointed out, "Jeanie still misbehaves — and you permit it even though you punish. The difficulty is that you have made her behavior your problem. You have given her the power to be center-stage, to manipulate you and press your button — to get you angry. So, although you do punish her by all the techniques you mentioned, she is punishing you back. And you permit that to happen! You take her whole problem on yourself and you take it all too seriously. When you talked about your other child, you were relaxed and content. When you talk about Jeanie, you look uptight, angry, and unhappy. Yet, she is only an 8-year-old. The reasons you don't control her, the reasons you still permit her to behave this way are two. First, you have let it become your problem. Second, you are taking it all too hard. It is sort of humorous to see an 8-year-old running you — and that is what she is doing.

"Learn to laugh at yourself a little — and when she does some of these outrageous things — laugh at her instead of getting mad. Oh, you still act. Send her to her room or what have you, but really let it be without malice. Much of her silly behavior should be treated as such. That way, she won't get the impression that she is acting very powerfully, and she may learn to laugh at herself more. If all of you can laugh, you have made an important step toward better relations. It isn't all that serious, so stop clenching your teeth. I'll still give you a gold star on your Mother's badge!"

If the child decides that there is not much to gain by wielding her powers of misbehavior, she will more likely behave. The child needs to realize that her actions are silly and that people do not respect them. If she recognizes that her actions do not gain much respect for her or do not increase her power, she will probably quit. Then she will look for better ways to become center-stage. Humor can be healing for us all. A good laugh may be better than a good spank.

Starting Fresh

If you do have to spank, give a couple of stinging whacks to the child's rump and steer her into bed without much scolding. Just quietly say, "Stay here and nap until you can come out and act a little nicer." After ten or twenty minutes check on her. Sometimes she will actually be asleep. If she is not acting up, hollering, crying or fussing, say, "Come on out now. Would you like to play, to have a snack, or maybe go to the store with Mother?" In other words, the episode is over. Things are back to normal. You both start again. Don't dwell on her misdeeds. It might be reasonable to say, "You're a neat girl and you're too smart to do that again, aren't you?" Do not make a "federal case" out of it, but do try to plant the seed of the idea that *she* wins by doing the right thing — do not make her think that she must do the right things just to please *you*. You have to prepare her to make the right decisions when you are not around. When the punishment period, the nap, the time out, the spank or the withdrawal of privileges or whatever is over, start fresh and look forward. Do not heckle the child about what she did wrong yesterday or this morning. She gets a chance at a fresh start each time. Go beyond discipline and control by giving her the freedom to try again.

If you find yourself facing the same problem with your child repeatedly, in spite of following all this good advice, then be sure to read the chapter "When Discipline Doesn't Work." If you have a preteen or teenager, read on.

Risk-taking behavior, which from an adult perspective may be troublesome and deviant, is characteristic of competent adolescents.

R. Jessor
Longitudinal Research on Drug Use
Washington, D.C.
Hemisphere Publishing Corp.

XIII

Raising and Understanding Preteens and Teens

The teen years have long been looked on by most adults with alarm. Other adults, however, apparently seeking the Fountain of Youth, embrace the concept and try to act like teenagers themselves. They chase the concept of perpetual youth in fashions and actions. But teenagers inadvertently thwart the efforts of the over-the-hill population. Teen fashions and fads change too rapidly. Thoughtful adults must wonder about the worth of arguing over long hair or punk styles. By the time those children have grown up and stepped into business suits, their hair is of reasonable length. Meanwhile, the new teenagers sport butch hair cuts. Yet underneath this kaleidoscope of fads and change, some stability still exists.

Despite multitudinous rebellions and risk taking, most of those young people turn out to be good solid citizens — turn out to be you and me. So you need not wring your hands when you think about your children becoming teenagers. Even though many a cynic proclaims that the age of adolescence and the seventh and eighth grades of school should be abolished, most harbor a grudging admiration for each new generation. Oh, the problems are real. Teenage sex, pregnancy, drugs and values deserve concern, but these problems largely spring from a vacillating and frequently permissive society. We often seem uncertain about how to deal with our own values and rules. Uncertain parents also contribute, again a form of permissiveness. So for answers on how to deal with teenagers, we first have to turn to society and to ourselves.

Our Uncertain Environment

Children have relatively few teenage crises when raised in a stable small town environment with cohesive values and a common religious orientation. However, suburban and city children have far less stability — they stand on the shifting sands of conflicting social values. When uncertainties occur, humans tend to group together for safety, mutual support and reassurance. Teenagers naturally group together, for they will live together for the rest of their lives. Also they have not had as much opportunity to fail, collectively or individually, as has the adult population. Thus, they may look with unwarranted optimism at their own rationalizations and current values. Much of this response comes from the unstable environment they inherit.

Fear of nuclear war and overpopulation dilute the heritage of freedom and progress we bequeath to our young. This often leads to a rejection of social values which apparently do not offer security. Rebellion occurs against the older generation which fails to protect its children or guarantee a sound future. The rebellion mixes protests about the uncertainties of life with the normal teenage declaration of independence. It takes many forms including poking fun at adult society and standards, often via musical lyrics or comedy. Rebellion involves sex, dress and attitudes, as well as escape through drugs and rock music. Desiring security, answers and fun, teenagers flock lemming-like to new fads, fashions and movements. Many parents throw up their hands in response to such rebellion. Relations can become polarized with both parent and teenager angrily refusing to give in and lose face.

Facing Our Teens/Facing Ourselves

Often parents who have the best educations in the world do not know how to deal with their own teenagers. Part of this uncertainty represents the residual of each of our rebellions against our own parents. Or we may have mixed feelings about the real worth of social values, current and past. Some of us fear that our teenagers will make the same mistakes we did as teenagers. We can easily overreact to our own fears and our teens' restless probing of current values. Some of us remain uncertain about the value of our own compromises with the world. Others handle uncertainties by rigidly denying them and establishing an unyielding attitude toward all but a narrow way of life. Perhaps what we fear most about facing our teenagers is that we have to face ourselves again in the process. And many of us are crippled in our presentation of values because we recognize that we, as people in glass houses, should not throw stones.

In spite of our unpreparedness, perhaps unwillingness and frequent uncertainties, most of us do a fair to middling job of raising our teenagers. Still, many can improve their parenting effectiveness by education. They can reasonably hope to become better parents than their parents were. Of course perfection still escapes us. But a teenager probably cannot stand perfect parents anyway. So relax and let us look at some of the basic needs of the preteen and teenager which do not vacillate as much as styles of hair and dress.

Meeting Basic Needs

The problems of teenagers start well before the teenage years. Burton White's investigations into the first three years show that the IQ is affected by the type of parenting. Learning attitudes gel early. The IQ is stimulated best by rational-authoritative parenting. However, you can still improve your child's attitudes and capabilities between the age of three and the preteen years by providing a secure sense of family, by placing reasonable demands upon him, and by giving him respect and the opportunity to develop his own powers. Your demand for high goals stimulates competency. A positive parental attitude gives the child confidence and a sense of self-worth. This enables him, in return, to understand and respect the people around him.

Some of you may decide that you have not quite succeeded in getting your child to that state of perfection. One wonders if those children who do enter the preteen years as perfect specimens are not the result of their own unique genetic predisposition rather than the parent's efforts. Regardless, it is never too late for you to have a significant effect on your child and his future. Whether you started when he was three or are starting fresh, the same basics apply: demand, control, understand, respect, support, and love. Then free him and enjoy it all.

Our world of mixed values magnifies the negative via the press and television; so, naturally children come to question life, parents and society far sooner than they did in other times. A pediatrician friend of mine once called and asked if I saw 9-year-olds acting, rebelling, and questioning like teenagers. The answer was yes. Children develop faster both physically and "socially" than they did two or three generations ago. So the questioning, the rebellion, and the withdrawal typical of teenagers may surface as early as their eighth or ninth year. Their social development can be distorted easily by the press, peers and performers. In any of these arenas, our values may occasionally be threatened. This presents you with a greater task as a parent. You have to use all of your powers to encourage a feeling of security and confidence. Your child needs to find a place in life for himself or herself. While he tries, it helps if you respect his efforts and worth in the face of many challenges.

Balancing Security and Challenge

Children need security as well as challenge. As much as possible, the family, whether traditional or single parent, should offer security. Avoid dumping your own worries about finances or toxic wastes on a growing preteen or teenager. It is better to offer a calm and confident acceptance of your own socio-economic and ethnic status as was perhaps best elucidated in the play, *I Remember Mama.* In this true story, Mama always told the children not to worry as they struggled along economically, saying that if things really got bad she would go to their bank savings account for funds. But she always insisted that they could get along without that help. Meanwhile, she made them stay in school and develop their talents rather than go to work and quit school. Later it turned out that the bank account was mythical, used by Mama to prevent the children from suffering serious worry. She knew they needed security to develop and meet the challenges of education without being distracted. However, that does not mean that children should not work to help support the family.

Sometimes a practical need exists for whatever income the teenager generates. The experience of producing, of holding a paying job, builds confidence and helps children and adolescents prepare for adult life. It also demonstrates that the child is needed and important to the family and society, that he has the power to earn his way. Every child needs the opportunity to earn money, pay his own way when possible, and therefore, respect himself. This should start early in life at home with unpaid chores as his share of family life. Later they can be paid for defined home jobs when they are completed. Neighborhoods and society should facilitate the ability of the child and preteenager to earn money by doing useful tasks outside the house. Teenagers should always have job opportunities, but they should not be allowed to spend the money selfishly, only on themselves. They should be forced to contribute to the family larder. If you do not need the money then put it away for their later education, but do not give them a free ride. Life will not, and your job is to prepare them for life.

One of the limitations in current American society is that often teenagers do not seem to be wanted in the job market. Of all of the conditions which will threaten their self-confidence and security, rejection by adult society may be one of the more damaging. Local communities and government should back up parents by establishing mechanisms enabling every teenager to be gainfully employed. At the very least, parents at home should emphasize the practical value of a child or teenager helping with ordinary chores, with or without an allowance. Rather than dwelling upon the family's relatively low financial status, parents should emphasize the positive aspects while they plan and work toward a higher status. Remember Mama.

Setting Limits for Working Teenagers

The idea of encouraging teenagers to find jobs as a way of preparing them for the responsibilities of the world may have a down side. Ellen Greenberger, Ph.D., investigated the phenomena of working teenagers and found that some may be more harmed than helped. Frequently, their work interferes with their study and schooling, which should take priority. She found that working youngsters use alcohol and marijuana and drop out of school more than those who devote full-time to school. One could argue as to which came first, but certainly schooling should have a priority.

Dr. Greenberger feels that teenagers do not really learn about money but instead develop "premature affluence: a taste for a luxurious but false life style that doesn't take food and housing costs into account." I must agree. She recommends that parents:

1. Discourage freshmen and sophomores from working more than 20 hours per week.

2. Question them about fellow teenage workers to see if there is exposure to drug abuse.

3. Make certain that the adolescent spends enough time in extracurricular activities which can help his overall social and intellectual development.

4. Refrain from abdicating their authority; but instead insist that their teenagers save and spend responsibly.

Here again, we find that most professionals studying child-rearing advise rational-authoritative parenting. Some of the most effective parents I have observed spend a lot of time guiding their teenagers. They go to the school, check the homework, and often intercede to make certain that they get the best teachers for their children. They involve themselves in their children's lives. Recognizing that adolescents do not always have the experience and knowledge to make wise decisions, the parents intercede when they can be of help. At the same time, they respect the children, listen to them, support their high goals, and when reasonable, let them make as many of their own decisions as they can. They know that excess freedom can be dangerous. They also know that they have to earn the respect of their adolescents by the way they themselves live and by the way they treat their children.

Teaching Values

Values are as important as security, guidance, demanding, and involvement in the child's life. Every teenager needs to adopt solid values so he will be able to live with us as a responsible, acceptable citizen both now and as an adult. Most values are absorbed from the parents. Ideally, parents have and try to live up to high values. Parents may not always succeed in living up to their values, but it is vital that they make the effort. Because we are human and imperfect, it helps to belong to and get feedback from some sort of social or religious organization that has redeeming values.

From the Girl Scouts to Kiwanis, from town councils to church or synagogue, outside encouragement and models of good values help. Every child should be, at the very least, exposed to religion as part of an overall education. For those who can join a church and become part of the church community, one's reward does not have to wait for the hereafter. Children who embrace church life receive some security and values even in our current insecure urban and suburban areas. If nothing else, it puts them in the right ballpark.

The extended family should also be preserved. At times conflicts with relatives occur, but usually there are far more positives than negatives. Having an extended family gives one a sense of roots, of belonging. Investigate the ancestry of your family and trace them back as far as possible. A family's successes, failures, strengths, weaknesses and personalities offer lessons for ourselves and for our children. This can be especially helpful for single parents. With a bit of planning and occasionally a bit of sacrifice, you may be able to move close enough to your child's grandparents to be able to share each other's lives a bit — and to offer the heart warming mutual support we all need.

Building A Support System

If you do not have family, at least try to form one. Gather a circle of friends and acquaintances from work, church, of clubs and give enough to them that they will regard you as a friend and take some interest in you and your children. For your sake and that of your children, try not to go it alone. If you are in a busy area where most people do not have much spare time, it may be difficult to make friends, so you will have to be a bit aggressive. Use your powers of discernment and positive thinking. It sometimes takes 100 contacts to find the right friend for you and your children. Do not be deterred by initial turndowns. There are people out there who will fit with your personality and values. Your child also will have to socialize with many people to find the ones he will group with.

Skirting Rebellion

Your preteen or teenager's friends will become more and more important to them as they grow. Still, you certainly do not have to accept all of his friends. If there are some bad apples who are immoral, liars, in trouble with drugs or the law — put your foot down. This shows that you really mean what you say, that you will not accept as a friend of your child another adolescent whose values and actions repulse you. At the same time, you had better make certain that you accept *some* of your children's friends and even go out of your way to have them over on weekends or even vacations. Get to know them before you judge them. If your child will not bring a friend home, you may need some counselling to be able to find out why. That situation is a set up for rebellion or depression.

No matter how good a parent you are, expect some adolescent rebellion. Adolescents want to be adult, big and important, yet they are almost completely dependent on you. You have awesome powers: you offer security, you accept or reject your child's actions, friends, efforts in school and his manners. If you overbalance your attempt to control, it puts your adolescent in a powerless situation and robs him of the ability to make enough decisions for himself. He is not free to succeed or fail and learn from the experience. While using your powers to control, remember that when your child reaches the age of 18 he will be a legal adult, free to make up his own mind. So encourage enough freedom to teach self-reliance while reining your child in if he strays into dangerous territory. In using the power to rein him in, it pays to be tactful. If you control in anger, you may set the stage for instant or ultimate rebellion against you — often best demonstrated by rejecting your values.

Contracting

Discipline your adolescent with love. Be warm, concerned and business-like, but go beyond discipline. Be his consultant. Make a contract with him and spell out the rewards and punishment which occur contingent upon how well he carries out his part of the contract. Discuss his expectations for his life and establish limits for him. How he lives with these should become his decision, within broader and broader limits as he grows and matures. If things do not go well, do not play the powerful, angry or hurt mother or father. Instead, recall the rules and then carry out your part of the bargain.

If you have to punish, grounding or reduction of privileges should suffice. You should not have to punish an adolescent physically. If you do find this necessary, you need some outside help. Generally if you act more than talk, a youngster will respect and obey you more. Take away the keys to the car, have the telephone taken out, send undesirable "friends" away. Do not do this capriciously or without warning. First talk over the rules with your child and ask him what privileges he thinks he should be entitled to and what restrictions should be applied if he doesn't carry out his part of his contract with you. It might be best to establish some overall ground rules when your child is between 10 and 12 years old rather than at the more rebellious age of 14 or 15.

Your child needs to know and understand the ground rules, for they represent his path to the future. You should both consciously recognize that your power diminishes as he grows, as he demonstrates that he has the power to handle himself. Such recognition removes a considerable source of frustration. Using Illustration 1 (page 11), you can diagram the growth of his power and capabilities while yours diminish. When he was born, he had 20% self-determination — when he leaves, he will have 80%. If nothing else, this shows him the light at the end of the tunnel. It puts the two of you on common ground when it comes to asking for and granting freedom with responsibility. It allows him to see that you respect him and his opinions and will listen to them and weigh them carefully, whether or not you agree.

Respecting Your Child

Children and adolescents seek out and value adult respect. Your ability to offer respect gives you a powerful mechanism of motivation, reward and guidance. Granted you cannot respect immature behavior, but excess criticism does not help either. There are always many traits you can find that you like about your adolescent and some things which you can respect. If you have been fighting with your child so much that you are unable to like or respect her, then you do need outside help — and so does she.

You will need less help in handling your children if you look at things from their perspective and try to understand each child's personality and actions. It is not too difficult if you remember that you, too, were a teenager not so terribly long ago. Your adolescent needs your understanding now even when you do not agree with his actions. Perhaps he needs to know that you went through many of the same trials and dilemmas that face him. He needs your mature opinion, guidance and, occasionally, your rules. He will be more likely to accept your advice and control if he recognizes that you care enough about him to really listen. Perhaps one of the most common complaints of teenagers is that "My parents don't understand." Note that it is not that "My parents don't agree with me." Actually they are often relieved that you do not agree and that you are trying to protect them from some wrong decisions, but they do not want to be made out to be fools — they need your understanding of the forces that drove or led them to their position, tenable or not. Above all, aside from your understanding and innate respect, they need your faith in them and in their future.

Think Positive

Your adolescent respects you and your opinions even while he currently denies that you have any modicum of sense. Even in the 15-year-old stage, usually the peak of selfish introspection and challenge of parental authority, he carefully watches how you act. He listens to what you say and how you say it. If you express the feeling that your Johnny is "going to be a bum" or your Jenny "is going to be a whore," then Johnny and Jenny may believe that you are right and accept the prediction as their future — sometimes acting the way you claim they will. Occasionally such actions are done out of spite because they know you are angry and disgruntled with them; therefore, they strike back by doing what they know will make you even angrier.

Always express your faith that a positive future exists for your teenager — it gives her something to aim for, something to live up to, a good purpose in life. It can help to tell a child that Mr. Jones said, "You are a winner!" or that "You are very much like your great Aunt Jane, who was really admired and liked by everyone. She worked hard and played hard and accomplished a lot." When a child does poorly in school, another way of giving hope for the future is to reminisce:

> "You know when I was your age I almost blew it in school, too. But your Grandpa convinced me that it was my problem and that just because I didn't like my teacher, I shouldn't let this stop me from learning. And by gosh, it worked. I did buckle down although it wasn't easy and I gradually got my grades up. I wonder where we would be now if I hadn't finished school?"

Earning Privileges

Most teenagers do not really want you to spoil them or do everything for them. Oh sure, gifts are nice and it is great having a chauffeur to drive them places; but underneath, they have a greater need and desire for independence — for freedom even from your love (or anger) and the guilt it may engender. Their development requires freedom. They need practice in using freedom now. They should be able to look forward to increasing freedom and self-reliance in the near future. Keep in mind that your 14-year-old's four short years of total dependence on you seems like forever from his perspective. You may convince him about the light at the end of the tunnel but he needs considerable encouragement on the way. For example, when you let him experience earning his own way, you demonstrate your respect for him.

Whether it be a desire for clothes or a car or a VCR, let your adolescent earn it. It is not your duty to give him all he wants or to sacrifice for what, in the long run, will be trivia. Concentrate on a proper home, education and environment. Let his consumer desires be his problem. That does not mean you do not help now and then — but he should learn early how to hold a job, how to complete a task, how to earn and handle and save money while continuing his education. He needs the opportunity to do these things and not be crippled developmentally by overindulgent parents. Likewise, he should earn his privileges. Life is not a welfare state.

To encourage maturation, use the privileges/responsibility contract. For birthdays or promotion to the next grade of school have a small party and, as well as congratulations and gifts, give him a new contract for the year. On a sheet of paper write down three new privileges or freedoms he will be allowed. Opposite each reward write down the responsibilities he must assume to retain the reward. Perhaps your 15-year-old will now be allowed to go out with her boyfriend in a group. In turn, she must be home by a certain hour or she will forfeit that privilege. Your 12-year-old may be allowed to go to Saturday afternoon movies if he helps with the dishes every night. If he "forgets" then on Saturday when he announces that he is going to the movie, calmly point out that he cannot because he did not do his share of the work at home. If a child refuses, openly or passively, to help around the house, do not put a plate on the table for him. Make him get his own food. Do not be a slave to your children. Generally the more work they do, the more satisfied they will be with themselves even if they are not likely to admit it.

Becoming Friends

Treat your teenager as you treat adults and friends. Expect from them increasingly adult, responsible, friendly behavior. Keep in mind that you rarely lecture your friends: you rarely criticize; you do not pontificate. If you do, your friends are not likely to be friends for long. So why act that way with your teenager? Every person desires some respect. Your children are too important for you to drive them away from you, to reduce their friendship toward you by your negative behavior. When you must criticize, criticize the action or the issue, not the child. Do not nag or harangue — politely act. If your son wants to play football in high school, point out that if his grades are not up to standard, he will not be allowed to play. Then let it be his problem. Politely and calmly refuse to give him permission to join the team if he does not succeed in getting adequate grades. Use your power over yourself to keep cool. Do not scold or say, "I told you so." Keep him as a friend even while you refuse some of his   requests.

There are often times during the teens when you may worry that you can never be friends with your introspective, opinionated, self-indulgent, selfish child. But after all, most of us were that way once and grew up to be quite superior people. Don't give up on yourself or your teenager. Hang in there; look for the humor in situations instead of dwelling on the bad aspects.

Forgive and forget just as your parents probably did with you, even though you may not remember. And even if you were a perfect teenager and your child is not, do not despair. A few years down the road you will find that your young adult offspring no longer thinks you are as dumb as you were when he was 15 years old. Demand good productive behavior. Meanwhile, help him build his values by the way you act; help him build his self-confidence by giving him the feedom to make his own judgments. Do not give up on your demands for responsible behavior.

Help him become courageous and competent by encouraging him to try his wings; encourage him to try new things. If he falls and fails, do not criticize. Do not "make a federal case" out of his shortcomings. Give him a helping hand with some explanation and guidance so that he can start over and try again. It is a great way to make a friend and it will be nice to have your child as a friend. Recognize that raising teenagers need not be difficult if you let them do a lot of the growing up themselves.

Parents already have the power, they just don't realize it. Problem kids are born different. They begin to control parents at four months gestation — they're difficult long before they ever see the light of day.

Paul Wood, M.D.
The California Physician

XIV

When Discipline Doesn't Work
The First Half of Childhood

Not all children are easy to raise. In fact, some can be downright difficult. You have already read many reasons why discipline does not work. Still more reasons exist. However, overuse or underuse of power by the parent creates most of the problems. Psychiatrist Missildine calls overuse (authoritarian parenting) overcoercion or perfectionism and underuse (permissive parenting) oversubmissiveness and overindulgence. As we have seen, a rational balance of power as used by rational-authoritative parents usually produces the best statistical results. And the experience of many parents I have known bears out these statistics. Yet the rough guidelines for rational-authoritative parenting do not always lead to the right power balance or the right results.

The lack of really effective simple guidelines can be explained in many ways. First, we just do not know enough. Parenting deserves far more research and attention than it receives. Second, the complexity of the subject defies simple solutions. Simplicity attracts, but humans are not simple. Even if one assumes individual simplicity, we vary so much from person to person that simple solutions still do not work for everyone. Yet simplicity attracts because it implies the ability and the power to control.

The history of mankind bulges with attempts to simplify our world. The history of parenting bulges with attempts to simplify the profession of parenting. We still try. Some, individually, seem to succeed. We study those fortunate families and attempt to distill their wisdom so we can all use their formulas. In a sense that is what this book is about. Some very valuable insights, lessons, and guidelines have been discovered. You will probably find many of these very useful to you — whether you succeed up to your expectations as a parent or not. But do not feel that you necessarily misread our map of how to be the "perfect" parent if you find that you seem to have lost your way.

Each Family is Unique

Maps for parents do not always work because a lot of parents and their children do not conform well enough to our models. We differ in too many ways, and so do our children. So we should not always expect statistical wisdom and long-term experience to help. Whether you get help or not from statistics depends upon which side of them you land on. That they work for the majority does not help if you are the minority. So the careful measurements from the long-term studies by the Institute of Human Development do not apply to everybody. If they do apply to you, they will be very helpful. However, when they do not, and when discipline does not work, you probably need individual help. Some examples of problems which may fit your situation are included in this and the following chapters. If they seem like your problems, they may offer a start toward a solution.

Regardless of the cause of problems with your child, keep the faith. Avoid labels as much as you can because labeling a child often makes people feel that they need not try to help. When teachers were told that certain children had high IQs, they demanded more of them and the children responded by doing better in class. Yet the children were actually of normal intelligence. The psychologists had tricked the teachers to demonstrate the significance of the attitude of the teachers. The same thing applies to parents. Keep the faith and maximize the potential of your child. Demand the best. History is full of examples of famous people like Churchill and Einstein who had serious problems as children yet outgrew them. So do not overreact to your child's problems. Remain optimistic, emphasize the positive, and give the child the feeling that he can succeed.

Examine Yourself First

Subconscious, irrational, emotional reactions frequently create our decisions about discipline. The parent's inner child of the past does the directing instead of the parent's rational assessment of the needs of the child. Or parents may consciously rationalize their permissiveness by pledging to not raise their children the way they themselves were raised by their authoritarian parents. Measurements demonstrate that usually, but not always, permissiveness leads to the poorest results for the child. Granted, we do not want to repeat the mistakes of the past; on the other hand we do not want to make the mistakes of the future.

When discipline does not work you might first ask, "Am I using too much or too little power as a parent?" Many children respond easily with practically no need for an open show of power. Stubborn or aggressive children may require more power than their parents feel comfortable using. And power is not always easily used. What counts is what the child can tolerate. Learn to be flexible and adjust your power, your demands and control. Different children, like each of us adults, have different tolerance levels, abilities, problems and needs.

The single most common failure of discipline I witness comes from parental uncertainty. This results in either powerlessness from inaction or confusion from constant changes in technique. Children can be successfully raised in all sorts of ways by parents who are convinced that what they do is right. Uncertainty usually results in vacillation, in "trying everything," and in constantly changing limits. The result is a lack of real limits or security for the child. Permissive parents have problems in child-rearing because they do not want to use their power or do not know how. Yet consciously or subconsciously all parents use power and punishment.

Another cause of problems springs from parental anxiety. Over-anxiety may come from past traumas. If you once thought your child might die, if you were profoundly affected by the death of a close brother or sister, if you suffered a miscarriage, then you may be vulnerable to excessive anxiety. Some parents are unable to be away from their children because of their fears. Others are unable to discipline. Some try to keep the child a baby. Others are excessively worried about illness. These parental problems can lead to difficulties with the child who may react with fear, or take advantage of the parent's indecision and get completely out-of-control. If your child is fine around everyone but you, then obviously you have a problem.

Burton White believes a lot of children become spoiled from underuse of parental power. He points out that many children "begin to whine skillfully to overcome resistance."

> Many parents routinely make allowances for the fact that the child is "only a baby" and then allow unpleasant behaviors such as throwing objects, kicking or hitting people ... They seem to make allowances partly because the baby is the most wonderful thing they have ever experienced, partly because they are afraid that the baby might not love them so much if they are firm, and partly because of the difficulty of coping with a child who repeatedly seeks out situations in which she can challenge the authority of the parents.

Authoritarian, over-controlling parents can also improve. Missildine points to overcoercion as the most common pathogenic parental attitude in our culture. Lack of respect for the child underlies authoritarian parenting. The power of control alone is not enough. Authoritarian parenting does not work well for a lot of children.

Many parents consider themselves traditional or rational parents when, in fact, they are permissive or authoritarian — or even rejecting. Such self-delusion usually results from the belief that hollering and scolding, or "reasoning" without action disciplines the child. But the child soon learns about empty threats or implorements. They see little reason to change their behavior. A parental tirade mostly represents a parental temper tantrum. Yet many such parents truly believe that they discipline the child by such actions. Scolding and anger do punish the child, but they do not necessarily force the child to change behavior. Even spanking does not change the behavior of some tough children. It doesn't teach "a good lesson."

Some problem children don't follow the rules and seem to resist all logic and all parental love and child-rearing techniques. Humans are not always predictable, and a parent can raise three children without problems only to find that a fourth just doesn't respond the same way. Sometimes the parent's personality and the particular child's personality and temperament clash. Once in awhile the parent sees in the child traits which she does not like in herself. Other times the child has traits which seem foreign and unacceptable to the parent. So a standard method can hardly be expected to work effectively on everyone. We are too different from one another. But we still share a lot in common.

Overuse of Parental Power

One of the most commonly unrecognized discipline problems in the first three years of life is overuse of parental power rather than permissiveness. Many people do not attach enough importance to the small child's need for respect and self-determination. Without realizing it, some parents are ego robbers — they over-control and overpower the child. The results differ with the child. Some rebel openly by defying the parent. Others rebel subtly by retreating to the quieter passive aggressive stubbornness of "You can't make me do it!" If you find that your child disobeys excessively, sasses or bad mouths you, or has excessive temper tantrums and you find yourself spanking or hitting or shouting a lot, then obviously what you are doing is not working.

The trap of angry punishment creates many problems. When you punish in anger, it shows the child only that you are powerful enough to hurt him. If your child is a fighter, this can result in a chronic fight. Avoid this trap by learning to control your inner child of the past; learn to laugh at your own child-like emotional reactions and grow up a little. Control yourself and your anger by recognizing that you are bigger than your child and more experienced. Humor really helps here. When you find yourself having tantrums in response to your child's tantrums, learn to laugh instead.

In a group session discussing problems of child-rearing, the mother of 2-year-old Josie said, "My child has temper tantrums and when she does, I get so mad I don't know what to do! I have spanked and scolded her and nothing works! Then I get so mad I hit her!" Her face reddened and she began pounding the table with her fist as her complaint unfolded. The pediatrician suggested that she learn to ignore the tantrums and that before she attempted to "discipline" that she should get herself under control. "Go into the next room and count to 100 before you decide to do anything," he suggested. "Then it would be best to ignore the tantrums, to act as if she isn't there." The next day the mother called the pediatrician and said, "Well, she had another tantrum so I counted to 100. Then I counted to 1000. Then I spanked her!" The pediatrician laughed and soon she joined in.

This signified a real attitude change. Mother learned not to take her own emotions so seriously and realized that things were not all that bad. Then she was able to begin the process of looking at the problem logically rather than emotionally. Working with her pediatrician, she found first that she bossed her child too much; in fact, she admitted she would not put up with anyone who treated her like she treated her child. So she allowed Josie more freedom to choose some of the things she wanted to do, and began helping her when she wanted help — not guiltily pushing herself on her. She realized that she had been scolding too much, so she stopped the critical tone she customarily used on the child. It came out that Mother had been raised by a hostile, critical mother and she now vowed not to raise her child the same way.

So she changed her ways of discipline. She began to let it be the child's problem and not make it her problem. She learned to say calmly yet firmly, "Honey, if you climb up on the cupboard again, you will have to sit in the chair in the corner for three minutes." When Josie did it again after that "time-out" she said, "Now, you knew you were not to do that so I am going to have to put you in your room for a rest. Don't come out until I come for you or I will have to spank you." When Josie came right back out of the bedroom, Mother calmly turned her over her knee and gave her a few significant swats on the bottom until the child cried and then put her back in her room. Later she took her out of bed, gave her a loving hug and said, "Would you like to go out in the yard with me?"

The punishment was over. Mother could be fun and a friend as well as a pain and bossy. Once Mother learned to control her own tantrums it did not take long for Josie to learn her childish tantrums did not pay off either and that when she obeyed she and Mother could have fun together.

To change, the parent must go beyond authoritarian discipline. One "simple" technique or attitude change will help improve authoritarian parenting. Learn to respond to your child rather than just impose your will on the child. Responding implies respect and acknowledges the child's power and importance. Most children will then, in turn, be more likely to respect and accept your advice.

The Passive-Aggressive Child

It is harder to handle the child who does not rebel openly.

Jim was a 2-year-old who had refused to go to the toilet and then started going into the closet to have bowel movements. When spanked for that, he became constipated and was brought to the doctor with some fifteen pounds of hard stool in his colon, cramped and miserable. The doctor helped Mother clean out the colon and put Jim on medicines and a diet so constipation would not occur again. He then told Mother to put Jim back in diapers and leave him in diapers for a month without any further attempt at toilet training. Mother arranged for Jim to play with a toilet-trained 3-year-old and after a couple of months Jim announced that he wanted to go to the toilet like Ben. He did.

Some problems will not respond to parental power — they are too basically tied to the child's ego development and are really under his power. After all, ask yourself, "Who do you go to the toilet for?"

When the Child has too Much Power

Discipline also doesn't work well when the child has too much power. Sometimes it doesn't work because the parents refuse to use physical punishment and their other punishments are ineffective.

The parents of 4-year-old Tanya were concerned because she hollered at her parents when they wouldn't do what she wanted. They brought her to the pediatrician when she told them that she hated them. "We both do everything we can to make her happy," said the distraught father, "but she wanted a new dress again and when we said no, she got really angry at us!" It turned out that they had bought her a new dress of her choosing the week before but she then decided she didn't like it and the store would not take it back. Mom felt they could not afford another one so soon. This incident was just the tip of the iceberg. Tanya really ran her parents. They did just about everything she wanted and she had become more and more demanding. It also turned out that Tanya did not keep friends long. The other children would soon find someone else to play with because she was so bossy. Her brashness finally got to Mother and, in spite of the fact that Mother had decided never to spank her children, she got mad and slapped Tanya when she called Mother a bitch. Then Mother cried and her husband scolded her for abusing Tanya. It was really this that moved them to go to the pediatrician.

It was not an easy case. The father was, at first, adamant about not spanking his daughter or allowing Mother to spank her, but he finally agreed that what they were doing was not working or they would not have come for help. He also agreed that Mother may have had reason to get mad. Still Mother felt guilty about hitting Tanya. Both clung to the idea that they would not spank. The methods of control, of reward and punishment were explained and they saw that rewards alone would not help them control Tanya. The issue logically resolved down to how they were going to convince Tanya that they had and would use their power to control her. A plan was devised with a step-by-step mechanism of rewards and punishments. They tried indirect praise when Tanya was acting, as she did at times, the sweet, charming and loving girl that she could be underneath it all. Rather than complimenting her directly, they called their relatives and friends and bragged on the telephone a bit about her, telling how much other people like her. And they naturally gave her smiles and hugs anyway for the loved her dearly. Almost too dearly!

When Tanya became bossy, they offered her a choice, telling her that she was acting so little that she would have to go to bed earlier and take an extra nap at the time of her misbehavior unless she apologized. When she acted like a 4-year-old should, she could stay up. If Tanya threw a tantrum, argued, or made faces at them as she sometimes did, they quietly put her to bed at once telling her not to come out until they came for her. If she came out sooner, Mother or Father said, "Tanya, go back to bed and stay there. I will spank you with this wooden spoon if you come out again." When she came back out, they pulled down her stockings and gave her a few quick, stinging swats on the back of the leg until she cried and then put her calmly to bed with a hug. Later they got her up (she usually cried herself to sleep and did take a nap) and went about the rest of the day as if nothing happened.

Father, at first, wasn't comfortable about this but agreed to back off and give it a try. He and Mother established a routine weekly ten-minute conference about Tanya on Sunday evenings to discuss her behavior and response to discipline and the happenings over the past week. They anticipated what problems she might present over the next week and agreed about how they would handle misbehavior with punishment and good behavior with rewards. The pediatrician, recognizing Tanya's ability to manipulate her parents by attitude, emphasized that they look as much at her attitude as at her actions. If she pouted, scowled or scolded them, that was reason enough for isolation. Over a month, Tanya began to improve. She acted happier and didn't try to boss her parents as much. She was naturally rewarded in another way — friends started to play with her more as she reduced her excessive bossiness.

Disciplining Together

Competition between Mother, Father and child leading to what some call an Oedipus complex, (even if it has nothing to do with sex at this stage) has been considered earlier in this book. Though not statistically proved, it is probably more common than many realize. Yet parents seldom recognize the symptoms of a conflicting triangle in themselves. The case of Billy, which follows, is rather severe but it makes the point. Mother and Father really need to become a team if they hope to raise their child with the least possible strife. The problems which result from marked parental differences in raising a child can come back to haunt them. If you find yourself upset or angered because you believe that your spouse is too easy or too hard on your child, keep the problems of 5-year-old Billy in mind. Start communicating and compromising with your husband or your wife so you can resolve your differences before your own "Billy" plays you for suckers.

> Young Billy looked angry when his parents brought him in to the pediatrician for a routine check up. Both parents were present, something a bit unusual for such examinations — and neither looked content. Billy insisted on sitting in his Mother's lap and all three had somber expressions. After the examination, Billy was sent to the playroom and the parents unfolded a story of constant strife in the home. Basically, it was Mother and Billy against Father. Billy was usually good for his Mother but was a hellion with his Father. He seemed to go out of his way to do things that Father did not like. As a result, Father really did not like Billy. Mother said it was Father's fault, that he was too hard on Billy. Father said it was Mother's fault, that she was too easy on Billy.

The child's manipulative power has created this conflict. To get the extra attention he wants, he will do what it takes. If he has to, he will be a bad boy, or a clown, or even a good boy. He still has not given up the idea of marrying Mom. It does not matter whether he manages to wrap Mother around his finger or not. If he wants to badly enough, he will think that he has succeeded and base his feelings on that assumption.

If he decides that Mother is his best bet, he goes all out to impress her, to be her "good boy." And he may succeed, or think that he has succeeded. Whew! Now he feels more reassured, relieved, safe. But then he looks at Dad. He has displaced Dad as number one. He believes this hurts Dad. And if you hurt someone you love, you feel guilty. None of us likes feeling guilty. So we try to blame it on someone else. If we have to, we will spend three years with a psychiatrist so we can blame the whole thing on Dad! A child, like an adult, resents feeling guilty and, in his mind, Father makes him feel guilty. So whose fault is it? Father's, of course!

What usually happens in the guilt/anger cycle is that Billy does some silly kid thing that makes Dad mad. Dad goes up the wall — and Billy looks at this emotional phenomenon with keen interest. He managed to hurt Father, to get his goat, to drive him up the wall! This gives Billy a feeling of satisfaction. It offers an excellent way of getting even with Dad, and he recognizes that he has found a significant source of power in this particular misbehavior. So he continues to use that power, he continues to misbehave because he finds it rewarding to "get even."

It does not take long for Dad to recognize that Billy's hostility is aimed at Dad. An already upset Dad gets even more upset and angrily clamps down on Billy. This creates war. The sad part about it is that such a fight can last a lifetime. I am sure you have seen the not uncommon event where a 50-year-old mother gets together with her 20-year-old daughter who lives across the country from her. They embrace happily but shortly after that one says something that the other takes exception to and they start fighting again. They both have such emotional sore toes that they really cannot enjoy each other. It's a sad way to live.

If the situation where Mother is the good one and Dad the bad one persists, other problems will arise. When Billy becomes an adolescent, he will begin to develop sexually and experience sexual feelings. By that time, his true love is Mother and his true hate is Father. But children, like almost all mammals, have an anti-incest feeling. Mother cats will chase away their kittens when they grow up. A mother bear will kill her cubs if they don't leave her territory once they have matured. Adolescents don't really understand why, but their feelings sometimes force them to reject the parent whom they love too much. Now we adults know that you can separate sex from love even if it isn't always easy. But an adolescent knows only that he has an aversion toward the mother he loves. So he finds reason to explain his instinctive need to get away from her — to separate.

The adolescent is almost forced to find fault with Mother to explain his need to reject her. This, of course, really adds to the problem because he has already rejected Father and now must reject Mother. Most of these children attach to their peers for the support and love they can no longer accept from parents. Often they run away or become sexually active in an attempt to expunge their anti-incest feelings about the loved parent. The parents must get out of this good guy/bad guy trap as soon as possible.

They should start by having Mother do more of the disciplining, forcing the child to obey, punishing if necessary. Dad should begin to treat the boy as a friend, to take him to ball games or shopping with him and later help in his little league team or his scout troop. This will begin to reverse the good guy/bad guy roles a bit.

There are several basic points that should be recognized in this situation. First, a child may be undergoing his own personal form of hell without a lot showing on the surface. Sometimes he needs more tender loving care than he gets. Second, Mother and Father must be a team. It's often better to make mistakes as a team than to each do right things separately and be played apart. The third point is that when the child does react in a hostile and aggressive manner the parent must not react back in the same way.

We have to learn to control our own inner child of the past if we are to be able to control our own child now. The best way is to make your child's behavior his problem and not yours. The principle is that when the child does the right thing, he wins — not Mom or Dad. And when he does the wrong thing he loses — not the parents. This is the best way to teach him that he is responsible for his own actions. It also fulfills your unwritten contract to prepare him to do right things when he leaves you and goes off on his own.

Attention Deficit Kids

Not all cases of trouble with discipline occur because the parents didn't do a good job. A good number of children have innate problems with hyperactivity, find it difficult to concentrate or have learning disabilities. All have to do with brain function; most are probably genetic. We know far too little about brain function and brain neurochemistry — although it represents an expanding frontier in medical science. We do have a variety of things which can be done to help most of these children. Pediatricians have medications which will improve the concentration and self-control of many children with Attention Deficit Syndrome or hyperactivity. Educational psychologists can identify areas of learning weakness and special education teachers have techniques to help children overcome many of their difficulties. The first step is to recognize that the problem is not simply one of discipline.

Mother knew that Frank was different when she carried him in the uterus. He was always moving and kicking. After birth he had colic. Frank started walking when he was 1 year old and shortly made a shambles of the house. By the time he was 2, he would run away whenever the opportunity presented itself. His parents "tried everything" without success and gradually came to resent Frank because he simply wouldn't listen to reason. He did talk well and seemed to understand but would repeatedly get into trouble.

By the time Frank was 4 and had outgrown the harness he had suffered many accidents, and was always "getting into trouble." He responded to his parent's frustrations, worry and anger about his behavior with counter-anger. In the park, he would laugh when his mother told him to stay near her. He ran away and was repeatedly lost.

When Frank started school, the problems increased. He would roam around the classroom and talk. Often, even in the first grade, he would run away from school. The parents had become hostile toward Frank most of the time and the school psychologist could see enough counter-hostility that he tried to counsel them about discipline but was unsuccessful. The pediatrician also failed to get the parents to control Frank without hostility. He then suggested a trial of medication called Ritalin which helps some children concentrate.

The parents refused to try Ritalin. They fought the idea of "drugging" their child for another year until the school threatened to expel Frank because they could not cope with him. The parents then agreed to try Ritalin and on the first day Frank's behavior improved markedly. He was able to sit still in class and seemed to be learning. He stopped his aimless running away. The parents were astounded and could then stop feeling hostile towards Frank. They gradually began treating him more like a wanted, normal child. As time went on, Frank's learning ability seemed to increase and he caught up in school. When he was off the Ritalin, he again had trouble concentrating but because he had accepted parental control and had better relations with them since he began treatment, he ran away less. While still hyperactive, he had better self-control even off the medication.

Most children like Frank get into deep problems because they are perceived by their parents as bad. They are bad — for themselves and for their parents. They ignore commands, cannot remember instructions and usually, but not always, appear hyperactive and nervous. The parents' attempts to use their power to control and teach seem for naught. Worry, frustration, and anger follow. The child then grows up with disappointed parents, and social and school failure — creating low self-esteem in the child and chaos in a family.

A good number of these children can be helped with medication. Ritalin, Cylert, Dexadrine and some other medications seem to allow their brains to function better. It is like giving a vitamin to a vitamin-deficient person. The results are prompt but the medication is out of the system in six to eight hours and needs to be given every day. While on medication, normal discipline seems to work better, allowing an improved parent-child relationship.

These children need extremely firm limits to teach them how to control themselves. As they get into the early teen years and puberty, the brain function seems to mature and the medication can usually be stopped. No adverse effects or drug dependencies have resulted from the use of such treatment. If you find that none of your attempts to control your child work, you may find it helpful to discuss the problem with his pediatrician. Many of these children have underlying learning or psychological disabilities and also need an educational work up and counseling.

A whole host of conditions can interfere with a child's concentration, or even attention to people and things in his everyday life. Some of the problems show up as an inability to make friends. Others create "discipline" problems of apparently uncontrollable misbehavior, like the child who roams around in school or just looks out the window ignoring the teacher. Often these brain problems create emotional problems and make the child a thorough loser. I suggest that you read about a new approach to these problems by Dr. Melvin Levine, Professor of Pediatrics, University of North Carolina School of Medicine in the next chapter, "When Discipline Doesn't Work — The Second Half of Childhood." Dr. Levine is Director of the Clinical Center for the Study of Development and Learning at the Child Development Research Institute. He has recognized what many people have not — that adolescents can develop new learning problems in junior high and high school. But Dr. Levine's findings also apply to younger children, so if your discipline and your power and love do not work for your child, read on.

Diet and Behavior

A very small group of children may have problems with self-control when they eat certain chemicals. Allergist Benjamin Feingold called attention to these children and developed the Feingold Diet which eliminates all food colorings and preservatives. There has been great debate in skeptical medical and educational circles as to whether these children improved because the parents expected that they would, and thus treated them differently, or whether a few actually had a reaction to the various coloring agents. Probably some children do react to food dyes which are derived from crude petroleum and which, in any case, are hardly essential. Others have pointed the finger at refined sugar as a cause of misbehavior in children who seem to lose all control after a sugar binge. It is certainly possible that a few children do indeed become "drunk" on sugar. Stranger things have happened (like the poor man who was always drunk because yeast in his intestines converted sugar to alcohol). The best way to determine if chemical reactions explain your child's misbehavior is to completely eliminate the suspected substance for a week and then load the child with the substance for the next week and compare his behavior. It may take more than one elimination trial and challenge to achieve a reasonable test. And all such tests are a bit suspect because the parents usually change their approach to the child once they decide that the chemical causes the bad behavior, not the parents or the child. This reduces the frustrations. It lowers the urge to force "good" behavior by various punishment techniques, and the expectations for good behavior are increased. But who cares? If it works, it works.

Dr. William Crook fervently believes that he has found the cause of many problems, including difficult-to-manage children. His theories are explained in his books *The Yeast Connection* and *Solving the Puzzle of Your Hard-To-Raise Child*. He believes that the growth of yeast in the bowel causes all sorts of pathology. There is no scientific data or acceptable proof that yeast causes such problems, but it is conceivable, although unlikely, that a few discipline problems are indirectly related to allergy or reaction to yeast growing in the intestine. Another possible cause of problems has been pushed by Dr. Crook. This one many of us in pediatrics occasionally see, the milk-allergy-tension-fatigue syndrome. These children are irritable and often lethargic and pale because they react adversely to milk. However, these chemical or allergic reactions are not the cause of most difficult-to-manage children.

Difficult Temperaments

Medication and diet help a small percent of children. The personalities of many others make them difficult to raise. It may be the child's temperament or other poorly understood anomalies. The onset may be very early. For example, if you have an infant who by 4 months seems unhappy when you hold him, resists your efforts to feed him, and is awake most of the time, talk the problem over with your pediatrician. The baby could be hypersensitive to touch or to any stimulation and may seem to somehow block out the world. You might need considerable professional help to learn how to deal with him.

If your 4-year-old will not talk, will not get dressed, has tantrums and all your efforts and those of good day-care personnel have not helped, the child needs a thorough work up. Your pediatrician can help and you should start there. There may be a neurological or chemical problem. Some pediatricians have a special interest in brain function and weaknesses. Others may refer you to specialists for more intense investigations. A small percentage of children have brain, nerve or chromosomal difficulties which demand an entirely different disciplinary approach, a different use of parental power. Various temperaments create various problems. Professor of Child Psychiatry Stella Chase from New York concludes from her long-term studies that some children in the infant and toddler stages present special difficulties for parents. She comments,

> [These children] were irregular in . . . sleep, wake cycles, hunger schedules, tended to have negative reactions to new situations . . . with loud crying, shrieking and struggling. . . . Once they adapted to a new situation, they responded with . . . intense ebullience and laughter.

Neither we nor anyone else has found any significant direct correlations between the characteristics of parents and the presence or absence of difficult temperament.

Dr. Chase suggests that these children can be helped by approaching new situations one at a time with quiet, patient, consistent parental handling. However, she cautions that parental pressure for quick adaptation stresses the child and creates other behavior problems. University of Pennsylvania Pediatrician William Carey notes,

> The temperamental child is different and difficult; often negative, slow to warm up, easily distracted or excessively persistent, and adapts poorly. Key to handling is the parental response. If your temperamental child screams and you scream back, more problems are created. If your baby was colicky, excessively fussy, slept poorly — it may be that you have a temperamental child. If he stresses you and you react, if you have unrealistic expectations, then you may make the situation worse. Negative inflexible children are difficult to parent and difficult to teach. Parents need to recognize that the problem may not be food allergy or inept parenting but really comes from the child's innate personality. As a start, do not blame yourself, do not feel guilty or angry. You will need to learn to look at the real needs of the child and not overreact to the child's peculiar actions.

Calming Methods

The child with a short attention-span is harder to discipline and teach than the child with a normal attention-span. It requires a careful look at the child to decide if he is "bad" or mischievous or if he really cannot help himself. In the latter case the parent must learn to manage the child in a way which will calm him rather than criticize him. In the case of a child with a short attention-span, parental directives must be short, easily understood and promptly enforced. Do not give more than one instruction at a time and make certain that when you do give the child an instruction, you have his full attention. Do not be disappointed or aggravated if he forgets and repeats the same "bad" behavior soon after. Patience, consistency, firmness and an accepting, neutral attitude gradually help get the child under control.

For the hyperactive child, try to avoid those things which set him off and exacerbate his hyperactivity. Steer him into an activity which calms him, be it soccer or television. For the impulsive child try to avoid situations which trigger out-of-control impulses. Such children may need special diagnostic workups, special consideration and special methods of handling.

If your baby demonstrates angry colicy behavior, and has excessive temper tantrums, above all do not react by shaking, shouting or spanking. Learn to control your own anger, colic (yes, it can lead to ulcers!) and temper. Let the tantrums run out without rewarding them with attention. These children generally find that the world does not reward their bad temper or peculiar temperamental behavior and gradually learn to control themselves. You may well have had similar problems as a child and you learned how to control yourself, didn't you? If you did, you can see hope for your child. If you did not, you can see that the problem will not be solved by a power struggle with your child. So try to understand your child and this may allow you to make life easier for both of you. If nothing else, let it be the child's problem and do not make it yours. For even the hard-to-handle child, the answer is to ultimately help him learn responsibility for himself.

Keep A Positive Attitude

To teach your child responsibility use your power firmly on him and on yourself. Keep in mind that "bad" behavior is usually childish and immature and naturally can be expected from children. The key is to treat the child pretty much like he acts. If your 6-year-old acts more like a 4-year-old call her over to you and say, "Sit down with me a minute, honey, and tell me all about it. You are sulking like a 4-year-old. How come?" Do not use the common scolding negative approach that, "You are 7 years old now! When are you going to act your age?" Do not say, "When are you going to grow up!" These may come through to her as threats — Mom wants me to grow up and leave. The fear of separation is still paramount, and to be pushed to grow up can be really scarey. In response, many children regress even more, act babyish again in hopes that they will be accepted as little, with less threat of having to leave home. So accept her as a 4-year-old in this case, even give her a hug as you discuss the immaturity of her actions, so she does not feel that you are pushing her to grow up.

While you do what you must to gain control of the situation, remain positive about your child. First, let him know indirectly that you and others feel that he will turn out all right. Avoid saying, "You are going to amount to nothing!" Instead keep the faith. When things calm down, casually turn the conversation to the child's future. Tell him that Uncle Ned said he would probably become an engineer, or a big-league baseball player or what-have-you. Ask him what he wants to be — and whatever he wants, accept his dream. Look for things about your child that you appreciate and respect and let him know that you like him — and why. Get other people to help him build his self-confidence and help improve his image. Try to have some good times with the family having fun together. Do not always concentrate on the bad things. Do not always try to improve things. Enjoy life! Make being with the family an attraction — not a chore.

One important thread through all of this teaching is that you have the will to use your power, to act. Another important thread is that you are fair, that you realistically judge the child's actions. Do not respond to your youngster's childish actions by acting childish yourself. In other words, you have to grow up. That's what being a parent does for you. The feeling of pride in knowing that your actions are mature and wise helps make it all worthwhile. You are also rewarded by your success in helping your child develop and grow in a positive and productive manner. All of this plus your parental love and pride makes up for the natural down times which occur in parenting when discipline does not work.

The life histories of thousands of famous and ordinary people demonstrate that the ball game of child development is never over, that even youngsters who seem to be careening toward maladjusted lives can ultimately emerge as wholesome and productive adults.

Julius Segal and Herbert Yahrais
"How to Cope with Your Problem Child"
Family Health/Today's Health

XV

When Discipline Doesn't Work
The Second Half of Childhood

When your child enters the pre-teen years, she has spent half of her minor life with you. When she becomes nine years of age, there are only nine years left until she is legally an adult. During the first nine years, hold her very close. During the second nine years (while holding her close), you must start letting her go. Ultimately, you give your child the gift of freedom. She becomes more fully responsible for her own life and will have learned from you enough redeeming social values to be an asset to society — often even when discipline seems not to have worked. She will probably straighten up when she has the power to make her own decisions. The outcome depends partially on how you achieve a workable balance of power — how you hand over power and self-determination to your child. It can usually be done without the necessity of those "terrible teen" years. Even if you feel that you have not done a good job in the first half of her childhood, you have an excellent chance to do a good job in the second 9 years, during the full bloom of adolescence.

Adolescence means "period of change." The child changes into the young adult. Actually, this is the second adolescence. The first adolescence occurred during the change from the uninhibited toddler into a youngster disciplined enough to sit down and be quiet in the classroom. During this first adolescence the child learned to control his various urges — his ego, love, anger, fears, omnipotence drive and ambitions — a big job. In the second adolescence, all of these same urges and emotions are subconsciously examined again, polished, and integrated into the personality which will soon become the adult. During this time the parent has a second chance to help the child mold into a self-sufficient, confident and worthy person. What a blessing!

Many of us feel we need a second chance. Our kids do not always grow up the way we want them to. But they can change — thanks to the adolescent's need for parental acceptance. Parental acceptance is the key that makes a second try workable. You may feel that you accomplished only half of what you desire during the first half of your child's life. Forget that and instead concentrate on the fact that the glass is half full and "thank the Lord." Do not dwell on the fact that the glass is half empty. Even the "bad" child has a lot of good in him. Accept your adolescent warmly. Respect him, and emphasize the positive.

Cliff was a good looking 12-year-old, albeit somewhat messy and lazy. He had barely made it through the 6th grade and his parents were concerned that he would get into real trouble now that he was starting junior high school. He was arguing more and more with them, slamming doors and often was late coming home from school. Mother found cigarettes in his jeans and had received a warning notice from Cliff's teacher about skipping class in this first quarter of school. On the other hand, he was bright and occasionally went to a Boy Scout troop with his friends, although he was still a tenderfoot after a year.

Using Power Productively

How would you go about "straightening him out?" Many parents use an unabashed power-trip. "Cliff, either you get better grades and stop being so nasty or I am going to ground you!" Often this results in a power-struggle in which if Cliff "straightens up" he has lost face, lost to the parent's power. If he refuses to obey and continues to get bad grades, he achieves a perverse sort of power victory over his parents. "You can't make me!" Other parents use their power more productively.

Dad can decide that Cliff is worth, at least, some of his time. So he talks with Cliff's scoutmaster and volunteers to go with the boys on a weekend camp-out. Mother talks over Cliff's academic problem with Cliff's teacher and with Cliff they set up a program where Cliff can ask for a half-hour's help from Mom or Dad each evening in math and social studies. Cliff wants to go out for baseball in the spring, so some goals are set by the coach and principal at the quiet instigation of the parents. If he gets a 2.5 grade point average and no grade less than a C, he can go out for baseball. If not, no baseball team participation. Mom and Dad tell Cliff that while they cannot stop him from sneaking smokes, they will neither allow him to possess cigarettes, nor let him smoke at home or around them.

Rational-authoritative parents demand better behavior and confront Cliff. They give him his limits and his options. However, they do not heckle or criticize but treat him as politely as they would any of their friends. They really do emphasize the positive.

Mother makes certain that Cliff can overhear her telling Aunt Sara on the telephone that Cliff's scoutmaster said Cliff was one of the brightest boys he knew. Father reminisced one afternoon coming home from a family outing to the beach how he had almost blown it in junior high and one of his teachers helped him by forcing him to work harder. As the school year came to a close and the family vacation was planned, Cliff was asked if he would like to bring a friend camping with them by the lake.

Most importantly, while the parents projected the image of a positive future for Cliff and obviously had faith in him, they did not criticize him when he did not finish his homework on time. That was Cliff's problem. They demanded responsibility on his part and laid out the requirements for better behavior and grades. But they made it Cliff's problem, not theirs. If he wanted to go out for the baseball team, he had to keep his grades up.

Cliff did not really get around to studying very hard so he could not go out for the team. Dad, rather than criticize, took him to the city to see the Dodgers play and they both enjoyed the outing. In substance, the parents were determined to use their power to teach Cliff that he was responsible for his own efforts. They demanded better behavior but demonstrated that they were willing to help. Whether he learned a lot in school that year was of less importance.

Many adolescents do not really realize the significance of working for good grades in school. And parental demanding does not always help. The real dedication to study begins when one realizes the boundless possibilities offered in this world of ours. An eagerness to explore one's potential generates excitement and an appetite for unknowns. Each unique student possesses talents and, by becoming aware of them, realizes his own hidden gifts. The satisfaction of working hard generates a process of exploring the ultimate potential of each individual. So how do you convince them to try? Can you use power?

Depression in Junior High Students

One of the more difficult discipline problems occurs when some students enter junior high school and their prior good grades become bad. They begin rebelling and often seem depressed. There are, of course, many possible reasons. Some of these we have discussed. Others have been largely unsuspected. We can recognize when teenagers become depressed. They often withdraw to their rooms, become angry at their parents, or simply look unhappy. Considering the frequency of teen-age suicide, depression should be taken seriously. Sometimes it stems from social problems with friends. In that case, listening to the child — offering some love — may help. If it does not help, then look further.

One cause has been recognized only recently — late onset of learning disability. Although many children have obvious learning problems in elementary school, another group of children, usually conscientious and hard working, get through elementary school intact. When they enter the middle school, they and their learning abilities meet new challenges. Many cannot handle the increased rate, volume and complexity of learning tasks they face.

Children do not all develop at the same rate. The physical differences so obvious in junior high are on the surface. More important differences exist in learning, or in coordination. Some children have no athletic ability and, while they need physical education, they do not need to be pushed into sports where they are certain to fail and suffer humiliation. Problems may also exist in language development, memory or attention. In school, children are publically chastised for their weaknesses. This would not be tolerated by adults. The response is usually depression or rebellion — at the least a loss of self-esteem. Too little attention or respect is given to variations in brain development during adolescence.

Some youngsters do not really start learning well in some areas until several years after their peers. This reminds me of one of the brightest and most productive people I know. He did so poorly in high school that they graduated him because, as he says, "It was their patriotic duty to get me out so I could be drafted!" Later he studied law, became a doctor, a researcher and a teacher. It is unlikely that Churchill, Napoleon or Einstein would have survived our rigid school systems. Brains are different, and differences bother teachers — and many parents.

The number of things which can go "wrong" are legion. Some children have trouble with the present and concentrate only on the future. Others have problems with social control when more than one or two other people are involved. Some have a mental inability to predict the consequences of their behavior. A good number can only think and concentrate if they are physically active and moving. Hyperactivity does not all go away with puberty. Some have trouble organizing their lives; some do not know how to memorize. Lots of verbally capable adolescents may have their working memories exceeded. Some children have problems keeping awake and concentrating for over 15 minutes at a time unless they have a break and some physical activity. Yet they are stuck with 50-minute classes!

Some of these children even seem well adjusted, but underneath it they feel that something is wrong with them. People, especially adolescents, rarely trumpet their problems and shortcomings. So most of these adolescents keep these feelings a secret. They live in the totalitarian government of education, often with parents who constantly urge them to "do better." Stimulated by parents, some do well for spells and then lapse back into a pattern of failure. They have problems processing some varieties of information and find that what the teacher tells them frequently does not stick. Their "software program" does not function well enough for the traditional junior high school learning environment. Embarrassed, knowing that something is wrong with their abilities, they frequently attempt to compensate by macho activities or by becoming the class clown.

They receive love and pressure at home but no respect and little help. When their grades do not improve they become totally dependent on their peers to bolster the little self-esteem they have left. Often they find solace by associating with peers who also have problems. It becomes "the outcasts" against the "establishment" of home and school. Parental and school power do little to help and may only create an adversarial environment.

Chronic Success Deprivation

Many of these adolescents can be helped. Dr. Melvin Levine of the Clinical Center for the Study of Development and Learning at the University of North Carolina calls this "Chronic Success Deprivation." He and others have developed techniques to aid in diagnosis of such problems which include:

1. Auditory distractibility where background noises make it difficult for some students to listen to the teacher.

2. Day dreaming where associative thinking sets off a chain of thoughts which reduce attention to the teacher.

3. Uncontrolled impulsivenesses and many other problems of brain functions which interfere with learning.

We really know very little about the complex human brain. Yet progress has been made and many of these children can be helped. Strict discipline and power use by parents or schools do not always work. If you have an adolescent whose problems could stem from educational weaknesses, consider getting help. Go to your pediatrician to find out about special sophisticated testing and teaching programs. Sometimes psychiatric rather than educational help is needed.

Dr. Melvin Levine has developed the art and science of diagnosis and treatment of attention deficits more deeply than anyone to date. To help children, parents and teachers understand the various factors which can interfere with productive attention, he has developed the concept of the child as the pilot of an airplane. The various control functions required for the plane (the child) to "fly" smoothly appear on Illustration 3. Called the "Concentration Cockpit," this ingenious illustration allows children to

THE CONCENTRATION COCKPIT:
EXPLAINING ATTENTION DEFICITS TO CHILDREN

Melvin D. Levine, M.D.,
Professor of Pediatrics, University of North Carolina School of Medicine
Chapel Hill, North Carolina

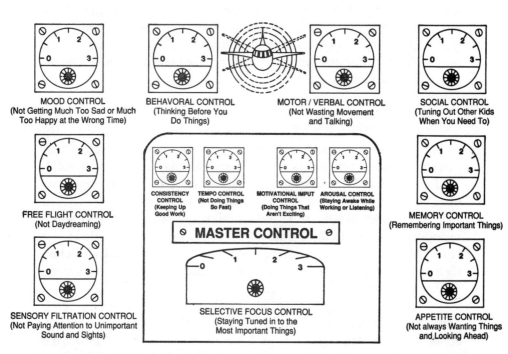

MOOD CONTROL
(Not Getting Much Too Sad or Much Too Happy at the Wrong Time)

BEHAVORAL CONTROL
(Thinking Before You Do Things)

MOTOR / VERBAL CONTROL
(Not Wasting Movement and Talking)

SOCIAL CONTROL
(Tuning Out Other Kids When You Need To)

FREE FLIGHT CONTROL
(Not Daydreaming)

CONSISTENCY CONTROL
(Keeping Up Good Work)

TEMPO CONTROL
(Not Doing Things So Fast)

MOTIVATIONAL IMPUT CONTROL
(Doing Things That Aren't Exciting)

AROUSAL CONTROL
(Staying Awake While Working or Listening)

MEMORY CONTROL
(Remembering Important Things)

⊙ **MASTER CONTROL** ⊖

SENSORY FILTRATION CONTROL
(Not Paying Attention to Unimportant Sound and Sights)

SELECTIVE FOCUS CONTROL
(Staying Tuned in to the Most Important Things)

APPETITE CONTROL
(Not always Wanting Things and Looking Ahead)

The Concentration Cockpit is designed as an aid in the management of children with attention deficits. It is intended to serve as a means of clarifying the various symptoms of this deficit so that they can be more fully understood by the children, their parents, and their teachers.

©1988, 1987 by M.D. Levine. Distributed by Educators Publishing Service, Inc., Cambridge, MA 02238

0-8388-2059-X

see what is required for them to fly, to function smoothly. It gives the child a sense of power over himself and draws his attention to what he must do to function well. Dr. Levine is teaching practicing pediatricians throughout the country the art and science of understanding attention deficits. Many children who do reasonably well in school but who have discipline or social problems have some of the various difficulties that Dr. Levine has mapped out. Parents and teachers can use their power to help these children by first, trying to understand the child's problems; second, getting the professional help needed; and third, helping the child learn what he or she needs to do in order to surmount the social, discipline or school problems which make the child a loser.

Signs of Serious Problems

If you notice a sudden change in behavior in your teenage child, you should give it serious attention. Sleeping longer than before, irritability, depression, or increasing mood swings can all spell trouble. Sometimes drug use creates the problem. Often this starts with marijuana, perceived by many as being mild and harmless. But pot suppresses short-term memory and abstract thinking as well as motivation and mood. Because it has an affinity for fatty tissue and no enzymes exist there to quickly detoxify it, it can stay in the brain for many weeks and cause chronic irritability. But drugs may not be the problem.

An increasing number of teenagers are depressed — often depressed enough to commit suicide. Be alert to the teenager's need to talk about his or her feelings. Learn to listen more than to talk. Respect the teenager's moods and, without prying, ask if he is feeling sad. From there you may be able to steer him into counseling. If your child will not talk, ask the school counselor to intercede. Luckily most teenage problems are not so serious. Many stem from just rebelliousness or laziness. But when these symptoms occur, you have cause to suspect drug use. Some adolescents can take drugs for awhile without overt signs or symptoms. Most, however, do change some — yet if you accuse them of using drugs when they haven't, the lack of trust creates its own problems. You might casually say you understand that drug users are often hard to spot for some time, and say with a smile, "I don't have to worry about you — you have better sense!"

Table XII

SIGNS AND SYMPTOMS OF DRUG USE*

1. **Behavioral signs**
   - Chronic lying about whereabouts
   - Sudden disappearance of money or valuables from home
   - Marked dysphoric mood changes that occur without good reason and that cause pain to the family and patient
   - Abusive behavior toward self or others
   - Frequent outbursts of poorly controlled hostility with lack of insight or remorse for this behavior

2. **Social signs**
   - Driving while impaired, auto accidents
   - Frequent truancy
   - Underachievement over past 6-12 months with definite deterioration of academic performance

3. **Circumstantial evidence**
   - Drugs or drug paraphernalia in room, clothes, or automobile
   - Drug terminology in school notebooks or in school yearbook
   - Definitive change in peer group preference to those peers who lack purpose, are unmotivated, and may be known to use marijuana

4. **Physical symptoms**
   - Chronic fatigue and lethargy
   - Chronic dry irritating cough, chronic sore throat
   - Chronic conjunctivitis (red eyes), otherwise unexplained

*From Schwartz, R.H. M.D. and Hawks, R.L., Ph.D., "Laboratory Detection of Marijuana Use" *Journal of the American Medical Association*, Chicago Vol. 254 No. 6 (August 9, 1985) pp 788-792. Copyright.

Helping the Self-Destructive Teen

Adolescents should not allow their possibilities to be wasted by being late for class, talking in class, not completing assignments, and so on. They should be receptive. Teachers love to teach receptive students. But what if the teenager does not respond? John Lazares, a high school principal in Hamilton, Ohio invites parents of such kids to spend a day in school with the pupil. For example, Susie was not excited about school and was skipping classes so her mother, invited by the principal, quietly accompanied her from class to class as a silent observer. Susie, mortified and ashamed, responded like most other adolescents saying, "Do anything you want but do not have my mother come in!" When the parent accompanies the child to school, it demonstrates the parent's power of involvement, of affection and caring. You can invite yourself if the principal has not yet set up such a program. It uses the motivational need of adolescents to save face. Susie's problem was mild, however, compared to Cynthia's.

Fourteen-year-old Cynthia's problem was severe. She was skipping school, smoking pot and sneaking out of the house at night after her parents were asleep. She went to the local planned parenthood clinic and got birth control pills which Mother found along with some marijuana while straightening up Cynthia's room. So the family went to a psychologist who advised a firm hand. When Cynthia defied them all and kept leaving home at night, Mother finally put her foot down. She took a leave-of-absence from her job and drove Cynthia to school, picked her up after school, and stayed with her all the time at home. She put a cot in Cynthia's room and slept there. Cynthia was not allowed telephone privileges or visitors.

The school was put on notice to call if she did not show up for class. Cynthia rebelled and skipped school so the school suspended her for a week. Mother then stayed with her 24 hours a day, not saying much except that she loved Cynthia and was not going to let her get into any more trouble. They visited the local library so both could have some books to read and Mother took Cynthia to the nearby university book store to shop for a gift book for her favorite uncle. That weekend the family went to San Francisco Bay and picnicked while watching the windsurfers. Cynthia sat sulkily away from the rest of the family. Father went over and sat a bit closer to her, not saying a word, acting relaxed and available. When the week's suspension was over, Mother asked Cynthia if she were ready for school and got a fervent "Yes!"

Mom said Cynthia could arrange for a tutor if she needed help to catch up in math, which she found difficult. And Mom calmly but firmly said, "Cynthia, it's up to you. I am going to go back to work now. But if you start missing class or sneaking out again, I will quit work and you and I will stay home together. Really, I do not mind it." And with a smile said, "You are not bad company. But I will not allow you to use drugs and you are not going to be allowed to go out with anyone until your grades are passing. You are not going to go out with boys at all until you finish your freshman year. We are going on a trip back East this summer; and, if you want, you can invite Mary or Joyce to go with you — but Janet, that girl who got busted for drugs, is off-limits to you. You are to have nothing to do with her outside of school and I would prefer that you not see much of her in school. She is not welcome here. She is bad company for you."

Sometimes this approach works. It demonstrates that the parents care and will use their power to keep the adolescent from making really serious mistakes. For it to work, the parents should not scold or talk down to the child by attitude or words. A positive future must be subtly projected and academic help offered but not forced. However, Cynthia's problems were mild compared to Janet's.

Good Guy/Bad Guy Parents

Janet's parents had a really severe problem. Janet would run away from home repeatedly and for longer and longer times. She was on pot and cocaine and had to have an abortion. Her situation at home had long been bad. She had been Dad's favorite, and he could not stand to see her punished and refused to let his wife spank Janet. Janet and Mom seemed to hate each other. When Janet went through puberty, she began withdrawing from Father and would not allow him to hug her. She flared up at him over almost anything. Finally she began to stay away from home longer and longer. Father would telephone her friends and walk the streets looking for her. On two occasions he found her and brought her home. But she "split" again.

By now Janet was 16 years old. Father was offered a job in another state and did not know what to do about accepting it. The parents had occasionally taken Janet to a pediatrician whom she liked, so they finally turned to him for advice. He had been somewhat aware of the problem and several years before had advised counseling but had been ignored. Now a crisis existed and the parents came for help.

After a few sessions with the parents, he advised a complete reversal of roles, asking Father to stop chasing after Janet and putting Mother in a more supportive role when they saw Janet again. The pediatrician advised that Father take the job and that the family move to the other state. He had them leave word with a neighbor that the pediatrician knew where the family had moved.

After a month or so Janet turned up at the pediatrician's office with gonorrhea. He treated her, and when she asked where her family was, he told her that yes, Mother had left their new address hoping that Janet might get in touch with them. Janet's whole attitude gradually changed. She seemed relieved that Dad was not trying to track her down. She ultimately stopped her drug use and promiscuous sex, got a job and some funds from Mother to help her go to junior college and get her high school equivalency diploma. Later she married a college instructor and settled down.

Janet's basic problem started back when she was four years old. She decided to marry Dad and this meant she needed to displace Mother. By five years old, she had found that she could be "Daddy's girl" and she was somewhat contemptuous of her competition, Mother. Mother's discipline was undercut by Janet's guilt/hostility reaction which resulted from her knowledge that she had Father wrapped around her finger. If Mother tried to punish her, Father would intercede. As noted before, this basic complex is not uncommon. Still, what happens later on when the child enters puberty often makes the problem of the earlier years look minor. By puberty, Janet hated Mother and loved Father. But as she began to develop from a girl into a woman, she also experienced an increasing normal anti-incest instinct.

The anti-incest instinct is fairly deep-rooted in most mammals including human children, especially when they develop a sex urge. They instinctively reject the parent who is too close without really understanding why. They simply feel that they can no longer tolerate the "loved" parent. Thus, Janet was no longer "Daddy's girl." In fact, she ran away from home to avoid him. Unfortunately, Daddy did not recognize why Janet left and went after her. This increased Janet's need to "split" and to develop some sort of relationship with other men. She did. It was not until Dad left her alone that she began to feel comfortable about approaching the family again. To one degree or another, these feelings bedevil many teenagers, especially if an uncomfortable good guy/bad guy triangle exists. This situation develops during earlier years and cripples the relationship of one of the parents with the child. Later, when puberty and sexual feelings develop in the adolescent, this leads to rejection of the favored parent.

Confusing Love and Sexual Feeling

A more serious problem can occur when the parent allows his love for a child to slip over into sexual feelings. The issue of child sexual molestation by a parent unfortunately is real and evidently more common than most of us had imagined. Part of the problem has to do with some fathers' sense of power over their children. Power has long been known as an aphrodisiac, and some men have a hard time separating their sexual urge from the love of the child in spite of the anti-incest instinct. This form of immaturity and lack of common sense, as well as moral values, can create severe problems. The child loves Father, wants to please, and often gets "turned on" by sexual advances. Such unfortunate molestation may go on for years, a secret between Father and daughter. However, the anti-incest instinct, plus the guilt the girl feels about cheating on Mother, sets up lifelong problems for the child. Some react by becoming promiscuous, others by becoming frigid. All react with guilt. Fathers or mothers who find themselves tempted sexually with their children had better get a hold of themselves and go for help.

Federal Judge Sol Gothard said, "The average sexual abuser of children is gainfully employed, has a better than average income and is church-going." Sexual molestation leads to increased teenage promiscuity and drug use. He claimed that it is "generally accepted" that 10% of boys and 23% of girls are sexually abused. I believe those figures are grossly exaggerated; I have run across very few cases in my practice. Still, one case is one too many.

People should be aware that pre-adolescents and adolescents often fantasize about sex when their hormones begin to stir. They do not yet know how to separate sex from love and they do love their parents. There have been incidents where an innocent caress was interpreted as a sexual advance by a girl. Occasionally around this age, a boy will become threatened by a mother who embraces enthusiastically just as she did when he was little. The boy — or girl embraced by Dad — may back off and want to be left alone. Some can become very uncomfortable having to hold their sexual feelings under control around loving parents. Confusion and anger toward the parent may result, leading to a desire to run away.

Growing up and adjusting is hard enough for adolescents without having to fight to control their sexual urges in this manner, or even to deal with innocent parental seductiveness. The time comes when parents have to go from the close hug to a squeeze on the shoulder. This surprises parents who see and feel nothing at all sexual in their honest love for the child. It is one of those traps in parenting that can catch you unaware. Sure, you hold them very close, but you must remember to let them go.

When All Else Fails

Regardless of the cause of the problem, the time may come when you have to use your right and your power to turn your teenager out of the house. It is never an easy decision or an easy action. However, if done with tact, it can help some adolescents learn and mature in spite of the dangers inherent in turning them loose. Boyd's case represents an ultimate good outcome from such a forced separation.

Boyd was 17 and turned off on school. His problem seemed to start when he was doing poorly in the 8th grade. While he was not openly rebellious and occasionally appeared to try to study, he did not get very good grades in spite of tutors, special schools, or the boarding school into which his college-educated, professional parents put him. He smoked pot for a year or two in junior high, but his parents did not think that was too bad.

Boyd's grades went down further, and his attitude became surly. Finally, at the start of his senior year in high school, he announced that he was not going to finish school. This led to a confrontation with his busy father who had little time to spend with him. Father finally ceased arguing and said, "Boyd, either you finish school or, if you think you are big enough to refuse, then you are big enough to go out and earn your own living. So go back to school and try, or get your things and be out of the house by this weekend. I will sign to release the $300. in savings you have so you can put money down for rent. You can keep your car. I will pay the liability insurance on it until you are eighteen. So you had better go out and get yourself a job and earn your way. Mom and I are always available. Come by and see us when you can — but you live in your own apartment. When you decide that you want to go back to school, we will help you. Good luck, son."

Boyd was a bit taken aback but he rose to the challenge, rented a cheap room and a took a job as a laborer in a lumber yard. His folks gave him no money but dropped by and checked on him once or twice a month. He began routinely showing up at home once a week. Mother gave him some food to take "home" with him. They treated him as a friend. No criticism was offered, and they showed some respect that he was able to earn his own way so quickly.

After a year or two, Boyd had ceased pot because, as he said, "I saw some of my friends burn-out and I don't want that to happen to me." When he was 20 years old, he enrolled in junior college and finished his high school work. He explained to Dad, "You know, it really is hard to get a good job without a high school diploma." Later he became a good carpenter and builder while accumulating enough junior college experience to convince himself that he did not want an academic education. Instead he took only special courses in carpentry and practical math. At one time he moved back home for a year so he could afford to take a full-time training course in carpentry. He and his folks built on their relationship of mutual respect and friendship, as well as love, and refused to try to overpower each other to get their way.

For some teenagers true freedom can only come when they accept the responsibility for themselves and support themselves. Although partly a matter of pride and dignity, it is partly a matter of the need to have the power to decide one's own destiny. Sometimes the parents' career goals for the child and the teenager's personality, abilities and needs are incompatible. When that happens, the world need not come to an end. Many paths exist which can lead to contentment and self-worth. Some parents of teenagers mistakenly feel that they must use all of their power to force their young adults to live up to their parental expectations and goals. If they truly respect their offspring, they will grant them the gift of freedom. Let them decide their own destiny and, while still loving and helping them, force them out of the nest if necessary. The time comes when they must fly on their own.

Above all, do not give up. Keep trying to help your child, but do it with respect. Whatever your child's potential, do your best to establish the conditions which enable him to best develop his talents. Stay optimistic, regardless of what people label him. Help him feel that he has the ability to improve himself, that he has some control over himself and his future. Demand his best efforts and applaud his progress, however little it may be. Support him and praise him — always look for and emphasize the good. This way you will both have happier lives.

I can handle anything — I have children!

(Bumper sticker)

XVI

Rational-Authoritative Parenting

To Control Your Child, First Control Yourself

Power, of course, should be used carefully. In making decisions about handling children, we need to look at the long-term. Snap decisions come easily, but logic and solid principles demand actions which will stand up in the long run. Credible and involved parents can use their power with honest diplomacy to help their children prepare for a socially responsible future. Credible parents use their power, their rational authority, to push their children toward competency by strong demanding actions. Credible parents nurture their children's self-esteem and power by respecting the child and demonstrating a willingness to listen to the child. They discipline, punish, and control. But they go beyond that.

The successful rational-authoritative parents in Baumrind's studies were perfectly willing to confront their children about behavior, ideals and principles. Yet they modified their actions when the child could convince them of the validity and justice of the child's views. Actually, parents do not give up power in such situations — instead they nurture the child's power by respectful attention whether they agree or not. They then make their decisions, partially influenced by the child's presentation. The actions taken often indicate that the child has a positive and frequently powerful effect in the exchange. Thus, parents use their power of reason and self-control to go beyond discipline. They demonstrate that the child can have an effect on his world.

Building Autonomy

Rational-authoritative parents allow the child a gradually increasing amount of power as he demonstrates more self-control and responsibility. When the child is unable or unready to accept power, even though he may want it, the rational parent listens and then explains what the child must do to obtain more power. This encourages the child to develop self-control and builds his self-esteem by offering a vision of the future when the child can assume more power.

Rational-authoritative parents encourage the child to stand up for himself. This allows the child autonomy, building the self-direction and independence that characterizes and motivates most successful adults. At the same time, the parent remains in charge. That is not always easy. It takes a lot of judgment to establish a successful balance of demanding control and adequate freedom. It takes the power of rewards and punishment. Power and punitive discipline may seem to conflict with the child's autonomy and interfere with parental love, but this is not necessarily so.

Discipline, power, love, and the child's autonomy are compatible, even inseparable. Without power, the force and determination that make love productive and discipline effective, little can be accomplished. Your basic power starts with your knowledge, energy, optimism and dedication — the love you have as a parent. Rational-authoritative parenting requires mature, thoughtful adult behavior. First, and most importantly, you use your power to discipline and control yourself. For all of us, the hardest part to control is our inner child of the past. That part of our make-up directs most of our emotional behavior. It controls the way we parent, either directly, by modeling after the images we have of our own parents, or by reacting and doing just the opposite.

Our inner child of the past often leads us to child-like parenting, creating many problems which could be avoided. Immature parents do not help their children mature as well as reasonably mature parents do. While maturing is not easy, the pleasure and pride we take in ourselves as we do mature make it worthwhile. Nothing makes us grow up as much as being a parent. We learn to control and better appreciate our inner child of the past when we have our own child in the present. The recognition of our increased power and effectiveness contribute to the satisfaction of parenting. The accomplishment of caring for, of raising a child and helping him develop his skills, talents and personality, rewards parents well.

Be Optimistic

Emotions certainly represent a major part of parenting. The philosophy just expressed stresses joy, pleasure, pride, satisfaction, and love. There are also the emotions of sorrow, frustration, depression and anger. You have the power to control such negative feelings-in several ways. First, keep in mind that raising children is rarely all smooth. Do not let the temporary downs get to you and do not exaggerate the problems. Be optimistic. Children need your sense of optimism. Your optimism says to your children, "You are going to turn out just fine!" A child generally feels that the parent knows best. So even if things have not been too smooth, this optimism says things are not all that bad and they will be far better tomorrow. This supplies the essential ingredient of hope, which helps overcome the anger and the feelings of powerlessness and failure.

Optimism also represents faith in the child's future and confirms your reasonable high expectations. It helps build a child's confidence and self-esteem. So, as you can see, optimism represents a powerful force. Even if things are "so bad" that you have to seek professional counseling, keep in mind that such a step, such a commitment, represents an optimistic viewpoint. Something good *can* be done! You and the child are worth the cost and effort.

Controlling Emotions

Controlling emotions in a positive way increases your own sense of well-being. This also helps control the feelings of anger, frustration or depression which can hurt you and hinder your child's emotional growth. In the chapter on anger, we discussed several methods to help you avoid getting angry.

Of all the advice I give parents, the most valuable is not to discipline in anger. Such a powerful emotion can do all sorts of harm — physical harm, as well as emotional harm through instigating rebellion, causing depression, or creating guilt in children. Yet many parents react by saying, "I don't think I can control my anger!"

There is a widespread belief that, if a person can be convinced, allowed, or helped to express his feelings, he will benefit from it. This is not necessarily so. Anger is used for retaliation, vengeance, or restoring one's rights. Parents have the power and the right to control their children to a degree, but they really should be above retaliation against their children. Children, like people of any age, react to anger with counter-anger whether they flee or fight. Parents discipline to teach their children how to behave. Anger emphasizes the parent's discomfort more than the child's misbehavior. It pays to keep your eye on the ball — on your job as a parent — to teach your child how to behave properly rather than to respond to the child's improper behavior by behaving improperly yourself.

> *"Letting off steam" is a wonderful metaphor and seems to capture exactly how angry outbursts work, but people are not teapots."*
>
> Carol Tarvis, *Anger, the Misunderstood Emotion.*

Control of anger, becomes part of mature parenting. Even if you do get angry, your demonstration of self-control, of refusing to act in anger, represents a clear lesson in control to your child. You will be respected for such power of self-control. Ultimately, you will be imitated.

Of course, it is easier not to get angry in the first place. Anger can be avoided in several ways. First, act *before* you become angry. Have a pre-set plan of rational-authoritative discipline and do not wait until you are frustrated to use your power. As you begin to reduce your anger and get it under control, you will take a giant step toward maturity, toward rational-authoritative parenting, toward rational discipline with love. You will benefit personally, aside from having happier, better adjusted and more competent children. The other benefit will be your realization of how powerful you have become — and the satisfaction of knowing that you have self-control and can use it while developing a more effective method of parenting.

For those who still feel that it is healthy to express anger, I recommend that you read Carol Tavris's book, *Anger, The Misunderstood Emotion.* This well-reasoned presentation of the consequences of anger offers sound motives to avoid and control the immaturity of adult temper. After reading *Anger,* if you find it difficult to develop self-control, I suggest that you read psychiatrist Hugh Missildine's fascinating book, *Your Inner Child of the Past.* In this book you may find a description of your own inner child of the past and valuable suggestions on how to deal with the feelings your past evokes.

Once you experience the power and satisfaction of self-control, you will be better able to use your powers wisely to control your child. This enables you to learn how to gracefully, gratefully, and proudly give up that control as the child matures. It will help your child become an independent, competent socially adjusted adult.

Good Parenting Begins at Birth

Self-control should start when you bring Baby home. Newborns are so small, so vulnerable that any negative feelings create a sense of guilt in parents. Luckily your powerful instinctive, maternal and paternal feelings of love, pride and possession will help you overcome many problems: the lack of sleep, the hard work, long hours, the distasteful tasks of cleaning the baby's rear end and wiping his wet burps off your dress or suit. Generally this positive balance allows you to enjoy your infant, play with him, hold and handle him, comfort him. A good balance of power also allows you to put him down and let him alone occasionally when he is too fussy, rather than holding him in a panic or becoming angry because you cannot stop the crying.

Keep in mind that both you and your spouse have needs too, and do not forget to "baby" each other. Work as a team and look to each other's needs. The responsibility of having a new baby can create lots of stress in a marriage. Try to give to each other as well as to the baby.

Although you cannot spoil newborns, at about eight months your baby's instinctive brain and observant eyes become more tuned up. And Baby figures out that "If I cry, if I press the button, Mother hops." Remember, if you permit your baby to overpower you with demands, you create problems, now and in the future, for both of you. Baby must begin to learn that he cannot always run you. You have to exert enough power to control the baby, because without that control, you cannot later protect the baby from himself or teach him how to get along with other people in the world.

Reward and Punishment

Parents control and teach because they want to; they punish because they have to. You use your power by rewarding and punishing. For the crawler and toddler, you reward positive behavior mostly with freedom to explore, as well as your attention, praise and enthusiasm. But the toddler's exploratory behavior, his feelings of omnipotence and his desire to dominate can frequently lead to trouble. For punishment, you may be so lucky that a simple verbal "no" will induce good behavior. If not, jail can be the next step — the playpen or the crib. However, the great majority of parents will, sooner or later, be forced to spank because their toddlers must be controlled.

Whatever method you use, you have the opportunity to set the stage properly — to convince the child that you have the power to make him obey by punishing as well as rewarding. If you convince the 9 to 15-month-old child that when you say no, you mean it; and, that if he does not obey, he gets punished, you will have to punish far less in the future.

At any age, the rules must be clear and the choice of behavior left up to the child. If refusing to obey brings on punishment and obeying brings rewards, then the child has the opportunity to make a choice. Problems occur, however, if the parents attempt to coerce, to force the child always to act exactly like the parent desires. Children should be allowed to choose, even to make the wrong choice sometimes, as long as they take the consequences. Without the ability to choose, it becomes difficult to learn how to act properly or take responsibility for one's self. If the child has no ability to choose, then whatever the issue, the parent has made it his problem. If you teach the young child the consequences of obedience or disobedience, he will respect your opinion more than if you allow him to disobey without consequences.

A pervasive problem which causes much confusion for parents comes from the issue of who receives the reward or the punishment, parent or child. Parents may, without realizing it, make the child's behavior more important to themselves than to the child. This doesn't teach the vital lesson that parents usually *want* to teach — that the *child* will benefit most from a particular behavior. Such confusion can apply to both rewards and punishment. If the child feels manipulated by an overpowering parent, she has less motivation to obey. Children need to be taught self-motivation so they will behave properly in the parent's absence and later when they grow up. It should be clearly understood that rewards and punishments were earned *by* the child and *for* the child.

Attitude is Important

You will get better long-term results if you take your emotions out of your discipline. It is not so much which reward or punishment you use as the attitude with which you use it. Set up the rules so that a child's behavior brings expected consequences and let the child reward or punish himself. In this way parents can teach their children to behave well without a lot of anger and rebellion. If the child does develop guilt, it is because he did not act wisely, not that he did not please his parents and fears abandonment. After all, it was the child's behavior that resulted in the punishment. Parents must let the child's behavior be the child's problem, not the parent's.

If the parent disciplines in anger instead of love, the child instinctively becomes afraid and angry in return. Then the issue becomes the attitude of the parent rather than what the child did. The stubborn or determined child soon learns that the parent is not powerful enough to force him to always obey. And the child learns to use his power of misbehavior to strike back and punish the disciplinarian by making her or him angry. In the long run, this rebounds on the child making him feel guilty and unworthy. If the child does not strike back because of fear, the overpowering, overcoercive parent reduces the child's self-esteem and often creates depression and passive behavior.

If the attitude of the disciplining parent is that she does not want to use her power to control the child, to enforce obedience, the child still develops problems. First, the lack of clear limits creates anxiety and insecurity. Second, the child has more power than he can handle, and many such children will get into extra trouble. Third, the child's perception of his own power and importance suffers when he grows up and associates with others in society who feel that they are at least equally important. This can be a major shock to the child and may warp his social views and philosophies. The permissive parents' refusal or inability to use power puts the power equation out of balance — the child gets more than he needs or can handle.

Parents can also love their children too much. If the parents protect too much, give too many gifts, or show excessive concern, both the parent and the child can be hurt. The child may be smothered, may feel that the rest of the world should pamper him like Mother or Father, and may become disenchanted when the world does not pay homage. Some mothers may feel overly hurt when the child goes to school, shows interest in others, develops other loves, or does not seem to care enough for her. Above all, excessive or selfish love does not help the child prepare for the outside world. It can rob him of freedom.

Balancing Parental Power

Dr. Missildine pointed out all sorts of problems from overcoercion (or overpowering) a child and called it "the most pathogenic parental attitude in our culture." Interestingly, fatigue is prominent in adults who were raised by parents who overused their powers of command. Overuse of power by parents is a symptom in itself, an acting out of parental anxiety about the child. It may demonstrate underlying questions that the parent has about his own adequacy as a parent. Such parents "prune" too much, seem to fear giving the child the freedom to make up his own mind. The child receives a constant barrage of anxious, irritated, threatening commands, "Start your homework. Turn off the radio! No wonder your grades aren't better!"

Next to overcoercion, Missildine feels that underpowered parents, or permissiveness, is the next most common pathogenic parental attitude in America. He also noted that a child can suffer from both — one parent being oversubmissive and the other overpowering. I have noted this problem frequently, especially when the parents react against each other's attitude toward child-rearing. Permissively-raised children may become adults who are often attractive and personable but are impulsive, fickle, and inclined to overeat, overdrink, waste money and ignore important matters. They are often startled to find that their impulsive behavior has hurt other people. They have problems setting and keeping to realistic goals, even though they can be creative and confident. They win love easily yet can abandon the loved one without a thought. Often they use temper tantrums to try and get their way.

The prototypical authoritarian parent on a power-trip with the child and the prototypical permissive parent who overindulges the child are extremes. But many of us can recognize some of these problems — some of these feelings — when thinking about our own parents, ourselves and about our own children. As a parent learn to look at yourself and try to decide logically what part of your parenting is good and what part can be improved upon.

Privileges, Respect, and Freedom

You will probably get better results if you offer your child privileges, respect and freedom rather than material bribes or even your feeling of "love." Respect is perhaps the most powerful reward. Love is the most treacherous; for, if you are willing to offer it as a reward, you may have to take it away as a punishment. Such deprivation can be very heavy punishment and can threaten security and reduce self-esteem. Whatever reward you offer, it should be appropriate, fair and consistent. Praise, as we have seen can be tricky, but it can be useful — especially if it is not used to manipulate, used as a bribe. When the child does behave well, there should be prompt reinforcement. Give some credit for trying. In their book, *Changing Children's Behavior*, the Krumboltz's offered the example of Polly noting that

> Six-year-old Polly had never before attempted to make her own bed. One day she pulled up the blanket on the bed. Her mother told her that her bed looked nice. The next day Polly pulled up the blanket and also straightened her pillow. Again her mother noticed her improvement. On successive days, Polly began pulling up the sheet along with the blanket and finally the bedspread. Although the bed would not pass military inspection, it represented a substantial improvement for Polly and her mother expressed appreciation.

Look for natural and spontaneous actions to reward. Good behavior becomes its own reward. Correct behavior entitles the child to self-satisfaction and pride. By behaving correctly, he earns the respect of those around him who demonstrate this by attitude and praise.

Respect can also be shown by offering trust, which at times means freedom. Let Sue, age 16, go on her first date without a lot of last minute do's and don'ts — ask her when she will be home, letting her make the agreed-upon decision with her parents, along with the agreed-upon contract if she fails to make it home by the time she said she would.

Go Beyond Discipline

In the process of using your parental power to discipline your child, whether by reward or punishment, gradually turn over more and more of the power of decisions to the child. Go beyond discipline. This demonstrates that you have confidence in him and believe that he will do his best to succeed. It gives the child the vital and heady experience of using and developing his own power and practicing self-control. You do not really give the child your power, you help him develop his own. You gradually reduce your control and increase his freedom. The smooth transition of power to the younger generation creates satisfaction and pride. It makes parenting even more worthwhile. It makes growing up fun and exciting, stimulating and challenging. Rational power transfer can bring out the best in you and your children. Parenting, helping your child build his powers so he will have good self-esteem and confidence, is challenging and exciting. At times it can be frustrating and aggravating. But no one ever told you that being a parent was easy, did they? What it takes to use your power wisely, to discipline rationally with love and to go beyond discipline, is faith, hope, and charity:

> **Faith** — that the child will eventually mature and develop his potential to become a welcome, responsible citizen.

> **Hope** — that we as parents can use our powers to wisely discipline with love and an attitude which makes our rewards and punishment effective, allowing the child enough autonomy and self-esteem to develop his values, talents, powers and happiness.

> **Charity** — for both us parents and our children because few, if any, ever come very close to perfection.

Sources

Aldrich, Robert M.D., *Children and Youth in Cities: The Story of Seattle's Kids' Place*. In press.

Austin, Glenn M.D., Richards, John M.D., and Oliver, Julie, *The Parent's Guide to Child Raising*, Rolling Hills, CA: Robert Erdmann Publishing, 1978.

Austin, Glenn M.D., Richards, John M.D., and Oliver, Julie, *The Parent's Medical Manual*, Rolling Hills, CA: Robert Erdmann Publishing, 1978.

Baker, James, *Elementary Psychology*, New York: Effingham Maynard and Company Publishers, 1891.

Baumrind, Diana, Ph.D., "Authoritative Parenting in Adolescent Transition." Family Research Consortium Second Annual Summer Institute, June 2-6, 1987, Santa Fe, NM. University of California, Berkeley, Institute of Human Development, Family Socialization Project.

Baumrind, Diana, Ph.D., "Familial Antecedents of Adolescent Drug Use: A Perspective," (In C.L. Jones and R.J. Batties' *Etology of Drug Abuse: Implications for Prevention*. N.I.D.A. Research Monograph No 56 D.H.H.S. Publication No. (A.D.M.) 85-1335.

Baumrind, Diana, Ph.D., *Familial Antecedents of Social Competence in Middle Childhood*. In review.

Baumrind, Diana, Ph.D., "Rejoinder to Lewis' Re-interpretation of Parental Firm Control Effects," *Psychological Bulletin*, 1983 Vol 94 No 1.

Behrman and Vaughn, Nelson, *Textbook of Pediatrics,* 13th Edition, Philadelphia: W.B. Sanders Company, 1987.

Brazelton, T. Berry, M.D., *What Every Baby Knows,* Reading, MA: Addison-Wesley Publishing Company, 1987.

Brazelton, T. Berry, M.D., *Working and Caring,* Reading, MA: Addison-Wesley Publishing Company, 1985.

Carey, William M.D., "The Difficult Child," *Pediatrics in Review,* Elk Grove Village, IL: American Academy of Pediatrics, August, 1986.

Chamberlain, R.W., "Parenting Style, Child Behavior and The Pediatrician," *Pediatric Annals,* Slack Inc., Thorofare, NJ: September, 1977.

Chess, Stella M.D., "Commentary on the Difficult Child," *Pediatrics in Review,* Elk Grove Village, IL: American Academy of Pediatrics, August, 1986.

Chess, Stella M.D., and Alexander, Thomas M.D., "Temperament and The Parent Child Interaction," *Pediatric Annals,* Slack Inc., Thorofare, N.J.: Vol 6, September, 1977.

Cline, Victor Ph.D., *How to Make Your Child a Winner,* New York: Walker and Company, 1980.

Coolsen, Seligson and Gabardino, "When School is Out and Nobody's Home," National Committee for Prevention of Child Abuse, 332 South Michigan Avenue Suite 950, Chicago, IL 60604-4357: 1985.

Coopersmith, Stanley, *The Antecedents of Self-Esteem,* New York, W.H. Freeman and Company, 1967.

Cowan, Philip A., and Cowan, Carolyn P., "Couple Relationships, Parenting Styles, and the Child's Development at Three," Paper presented to Society for Research in Child Development, April 1987. (The Cowan's are in the Department of Psychology, University of California, Berkeley).

Cowan, P. A. and Cowan, C. P., *Research on Support for Parents and Infants in the Postnatal Period,* N.J.: Ablex Publishing Company. In press.

Cowan, C.P., et al, "Transitions to Parenthood," *Journal of Family Issues,* December, 1985, Vol 6 No 4.

Crook, William G., M.D., and Stevens, Laura, *Solving The Puzzle of Your Hard-to-Raise Child,* New York: Random House, Inc. 1987.

Cupoli, Michael, M.D. (University of South Florida), Presentation given to the Spring meeting of the American Academy of Pediatrics, Orlando, Florida, 1986.

Dornbusch, Sandy, "Helping Your Kid Make The Grade," *The Stanford Magazine,* Vol 14 No 2 (1986).

Dornbusch et al, Stanford Center for the Study of Youth Development, *The Relation of Parenting Style to Adolescent School Performance,* December 1986. Accepted for Publication.

Fenichel, Otto M.D., *The Psychological Theory of Neurosis,* New York, W.W. Norton and Company, 1945.

Friedman, Alma S., and Friedman, David B., "Parenting: A Developmental Process," *Pediatric Annals,* Thorofare, N.J., Slack Inc., October 1977.

Freud, Sigmund, *Civilization and Its Discontents,* London: The Hogarth Press, 1930.

Goleman, Daniel, "Feeling of Control Viewed as Central in Mental Health," *New York Times, 7 October, 1986, page C1.*

Gordon, Thomas, *Parent Effectiveness Training,* New York: Peter H. Wyden, Inc., 1970.

Green, Morris M.D., "Vulnerable Child Syndrome and Its Variants," *Pediatrics In Review,* Elk Grove Village, IL: American Academy of Pediatrics, September 1986.

Greenberger, Ellen, Ph.D. (U.C. Irvine). Presentation given to the Spring meeting of the American Academy pf Pediatrics, San Francisco, 1987.

Guidubaldi, John Ph.D., "Latch Key to Success," *Parenting,* March 17, 1987.

Guidubaldi, John Ph.D. and Nastasi, Bonnie K., "Home Environment Factors as Predictors of Child Adjustment in Mother-employed Households: Results of a Nationwide Study," paper presented to the Society for Research in Child Development, Washington, DC, 1987.

Hoffman, Martin L., "Altruistic Behavior and the Parent-Child Relationship," *Journal of Personality and Social Psychology*, (1975) Vol 31 No 5.

Hoffman, Martin L., "Moral Internalization, Parental Power, and the Nature of Parent-Child Interaction," *Developmental Psychology*, (1975) Vol 11 No 2.

Jessor, R., *Longitudinal Research on Drug Use*, Hemisphere Publishing Corp., 1978.

Kanner, Leo, M.D., *Child Psychiatry*, Springfield, C. Thomas, publisher, 1960.

Kaufman, Marc, *The Littlest Lama*, Reprinted with permission from The Philadelphia Inquirer, March 8, 1987.

Koestler, Arthur, *The Ghost in the Machine*, New York: The Macmillan Company, 1967.

Krumboltz, John D. and Helen B., *Changing Children's Behavior*, Englewood Cliffs, N.J.: Prentice-Hall, 1972.

Lepper, Mark R., et al, "Consequences of Superfluous Social Constraints: Effects on Young Children's Social Inferences and Subsequent Intrinsic Interest," *Journal of Personality and Social Psychology*, 1982 Vol 42 No 1.

Levine, Melvin D., M.D., "Attention Deficits: The Diverse Effects of Weak Control Systems in Childhood," *Pediatric Annals*, Thorofare, N.J. Slack Inc.: February 1987 Vol 16 No 2.

Levine, Melvin D., M.D., Concentration Cockpit, Educational Publishing Service, Inc. 75 Mouiton St, Cambridge MA 12238.

Levine, Melvin D., M.D., *Developmental Variation and Learning Disorders*, Cambridge, MA: Education Publishing Service Inc., 1987.

Lewis, Catherine, Ph.D. "The Effects of Firm Parental Control," *Psychological Bulletin,* 1981 Vol 90 No 3.

Lieman, Alan H. Ph.D. and Strasburger, Victor M.D., "Sex, Drugs, Rock 'N Roll — Understanding Common Teenage Behavior," *Pediatrics, Supplement,* Elk Grove Village, IL: American Academy of Pediatrics, October 1985 Vol 76 No 4.

Macdonald, Donald Ian, M.D., "How You Can Help Prevent Teenage Alcoholism," *Contemporary Pediatrics,* November, 1986.

Mallory, Arthur L., "Parents as Teachers Program Planning and Implementation Guide," Jefferson City, MO: Missouri Development of Elementary and Secondary Education, 1986.

Missildine, W. Hugh, M.D., *Your Inner Child of the Past,* New York: Simon and Schuster, 1963.

Norwood, Robin, *Women Who Love Too Much,* New York: Jeremy P. Tarcher, Inc., 1985.

Perry, D.G. and Perry L.C., "Social Learning, Causal Attribution and Moral Internalization," from J. Bisanz, Bizanz and Kail *Learning In Children,* New York: Springes-Verlog, 1983.

Robertiello, Richard, M.D., *Hold Them Very Close, Then Let Them Go,* New York: Dial Press, 1975.

Rosenfeld, Alvin, M.D. and Levine, Dorothy, M.D., "Discipline and Permissiveness," *Pediatrics in Review,* Elk Grove Village, IL: American Academy of Pediatrics, January, 1987.

Russell, Dick M.D., (See Austin, G., *The Parent's Guide to Child Raising).*

Schwartz, Richard H., M.D., and Hawks, Richard L., Ph.D., "Laboratory Detection of Marijuana Use," *Journal of the American Medical Association,* Chicago: Vol 254 No 6, (August 9, 1985)pp 788-792, Copyright, A.M.A.

Segal, Julius, Ph.D., and Yahrais, Herbert, "How to Cope With Your Problem Child," *Family Health/Today's Health,* May, 1981.

Steinbeck, John, *The Log From the Sea of Cortez*, New York: Viking Penguin Inc. 1985. Copyright E. Steinbeck, T. Steinbeck and J. Steinbeck, IV, 1979. Reprinted by permission of Viking Penguin Inc.

Tavris, Carol, Anger, *The Misunderstood Emotion*, New York: Simon and Schuster, 1982.

Thomas, Billie and Novak, Tom, *Who Stole Mrs. Wick's Self-Esteem?* The National Committee for the Prevention of Child Abuse, 1986 (Write for free catalog, N.C.P.C.A. Publicity Department, 332 S. Michigan Avenue, Suite 950, Chicago, IL 60604-4357).

Turtle, W.J., M.D., *Dr. Turtle's Babies*, New York: W.B. Saunders Company, 1973.

Walters, Gary. C. and Grusec, Joan E., *Punishment*, San Francisco: W.H. Freeman and Company, 1977.

White, Burton, Ph.D., *Educating the Infant and Toddler*, Lexington, MA: Lexington Books, D.C. Heath and Company, 1988.

White, Burton, Ph.D., Newsletter of The Center for Parent Education, 55 Chapel Street, Newton, MA 02160.

White, Burton, Ph.D., *The First Three Years of Life*, New York: Prentice-Hall Press, 1985.

Wiesel, Elie, *What Really Makes Us Free*. Reprinted with permission from Parade, copyright 1987 and Georges Borchardt, Inc., New York, N.Y.

Woolston, Joseph L., M.D., "A Child's Reactions to Parent's Problems," *Pediatrics In Review*, Elk Grove Village, IL: American Academy of Pediatrics, (December, 1986) Vol 8 No 6.

Index

RATIONAL-AUTHORITATIVE PARENTS PRODUCE COMPETENT CHILDREN

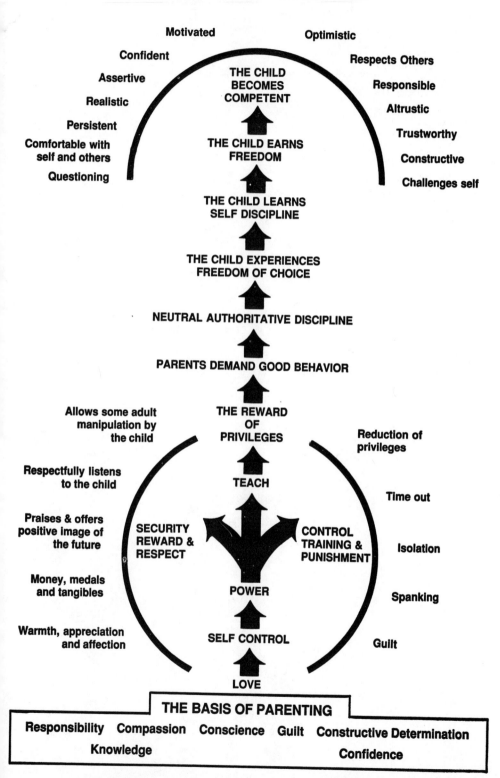